D1796734

Visions of *Sharīʿa*

Studies in Islamic Law and Society

Founding Editor

Bernard Weiss

Editorial Board

Ruud Peters
A. Kevin Reinhart
Nadjma Yassari

VOLUME 50

The titles published in this series are listed at *brill.com/sils*

Visions of *Sharīʿa*

Contemporary Discussions in Shīʿī Legal Theory

Edited by

Ali-Reza Bhojani
Laurens de Rooij
Michael Bohlander

BRILL

LEIDEN | BOSTON

Library of Congress Cataloging-in-Publication Data

Names: Bhojani, Ali Reza, editor. | De Rooij, Laurens, editor. | Bohlander, Michael, 1962– | Al-Mahdi Institute, organizer. | University of Durham, host institution, organizer.
Title: Visions of sharīʿa : contemporary discussions in Shiʾi legal theory / edited by Ali-reza Bhojani, Laurens de Rooij, Michael Bohlander.
Description: Leiden ; Boston : Brill, 2020. | Series: Studies in Islamic law and society, 1384-1130 ; vol.50 | Includes index.
Identifiers: LCCN 2019032181 (print) | LCCN 2019032182 (ebook) | ISBN 9789004378384 (hardback) | ISBN 9789004413948 (ebook)
Subjects: LCSH: Islamic law—Congresses. | Shīʿah—Doctrines—Congresses.
Classification: LCC KBP350 .V57 2019 (print) | LCC KBP350 (ebook) | DDC 340.5/90182—dc23
LC record available at https://lccn.loc.gov/2019032181
LC ebook record available at https://lccn.loc.gov/2019032182

Typeface for the Latin, Greek, and Cyrillic scripts: "Brill". See and download: brill.com/brill-typeface.

ISSN 1384-1130
ISBN 978-90-04-37838-4 (hardback)
ISBN 978-90-04-41394-8 (e-book)

Copyright 2020 by Koninklijke Brill NV, Leiden, The Netherlands.
Koninklijke Brill NV incorporates the imprints Brill, Brill Hes & De Graaf, Brill Nijhoff, Brill Rodopi, Brill Sense, Hotei Publishing, mentis Verlag, Verlag Ferdinand Schöningh and Wilhelm Fink Verlag.
All rights reserved. No part of this publication may be reproduced, translated, stored in a retrieval system, or transmitted in any form or by any means, electronic, mechanical, photocopying, recording or otherwise, without prior written permission from the publisher.
Authorization to photocopy items for internal or personal use is granted by Koninklijke Brill NV provided that the appropriate fees are paid directly to The Copyright Clearance Center, 222 Rosewood Drive, Suite 910, Danvers, MA 01923, USA. Fees are subject to change.

This book is printed on acid-free paper and produced in a sustainable manner.

Printed by Printforce, the Netherlands

Contents

Preface

This collection of papers is the result of a two-day conference held in August 2015 in St Aidan's College at Durham University, organised jointly by the Al-Mahdi Institute in Birmingham and Durham's research group Islam, Law and Modernity (ILM). It was an attempt to give a voice to the Shīʿī side of Islamic jurisprudence, since most of the discussions about Sharīʿa that is in the public domain these days, and has been for some time, are centered on the rich material provided over the centuries by Sunnī jurisprudence.

The majority of modern political Islamist teaching and rhetoric is in fact based on an often corrupt understanding of Sunnī scholars who mainly lived and taught centuries ago. Sunnī jurisprudence has been concerned to a large degree with the right balance between adhering to tradition and consensus on the one hand (*taqlīd* and *ijmāʾ*), and the need for adapting to modern times (*ijtihād*) on the other. This is frequently highlighted by the debate surrounding the closure of the "gate to ijtihād" in the 10th century. Adaptation to modern circumstances is seen by the more conservative section of the Sunnī *ʿulamā* as *bidʿa*, or unlawful innovation.

Shīʿī jurisprudence has a similarly long pedigree and is, of course, subject to similar conditions and struggles between the demands of modernisation and the reluctance of the traditional conservative spectrum. However, and this is something which becomes clear when discussing legal philosophy with Shīʿī scholars from the renowned schools of Iran in particular, there is an avid desire even among religiously traditional scholars to engage with ideas and concepts from foreign backgrounds. As one of the editors experienced personally when first attending a conference of Shīʿī scholars at Durham University, and later on a seminar at the Al-Mahdi Institute, the frequency, ease and mastery with which these scholars engaged with European thinkers such as Hegel, Kant, Schleiermacher, or Kierkegaard in order to make a comparative point, was breath-taking, and something he had not encountered to the same degree in similar venues with Sunnī colleagues.

Thus, it seems that a wider and better dissemination of Shīʿī thought has the potential of adding a new and exciting aspect to the intercultural and interreligious conversation about the *Sharīʿa*. The chapters in this volume are meant to be a contribution to the discussion about legal theory approaches that we hope will prove fruitful for the comparative field as well as those with a specific interest in Islamic legal thought.

We would like to express our deep gratitude to Dr Susan Frenk, Principal of St Aidan's College, for the generous additional support from the College.

Thanks are also due to Shaykh Arif Abdul Hussain and the Al-Mahdi Institute for their support throughout, and in particular during the somewhat arduous process of collecting and converting the conference papers in to the form presented here. We are also grateful for the assistance of Nazmina Dhanji and Mohsin Najafi.

Ali-Reza Bhojani
Laurens de Rooij
Michael Bohlander
Oxford, Chester, and Durham
August 2019

Notes on Contributors

Hashim Bata
is a lecturer and one of the directors at the Al-Mahdi Institute. He is also an associate lecturer in Islamic studies at the University of Birmingham. He completed seminary (*ḥawza*) studies at the Al-Mahdi Institute, attained a BA from the Islamic College, and an MA in Islamic Studies from the University of Warwick. His Ph.D. (University of Warwick, 2014) focused on legal epistemology in Modern Shīʿī *uṣūl al-fiqh* and forms the basis of a forthcoming monograph.

Hassan Beloushi
is a teacher at the Hawzat al-Muntadhar in Karbala, Iraq. He studied in the Hawzat al-Qa'im in Syria and received his Ph.D. in Islamic studies at Exeter University. His research focuses on ethics, secularism and Islamic law. He has published a number of books and articles, including the Arabic monograph *The History of Imāmī Legal Theory* (Dār al-Rafidayn, 2017).

Ali-Reza Bhojani
is Senior Lecturer in Islamic Studies at the Markfield Institute of Higher Education, Lecturer at the Al-Mahdi Institute, and Research Associate at the University of Oxford. His research focuses on theological and ethical issues in the Islamic intellectual traditions, with a particular interest in *Uṣūl al-fiqh*. He is author of *Moral Rationalism and Sharīʿa: A Study of Independent Rationality in Modern Shīʿī Uṣūl al-fiqh* (Routledge, 2015).

Michael Bohlander
is a Professor of Law at Durham University and was the International Co-Investigating Judge in the Extraordinary Chambers in the Courts of Cambodia from July 2015 to July 2019. His candidature was submitted to the United Nations by the German Government; he was subsequently nominated for the post by United Nations Secretary-General Ban Ki-moon. After the approval of the Cambodian Supreme Council of the Magistracy, King Norodom Sihamoni of Cambodia appointed him to the ECCC bench by Royal Decree of 31 July 2015. He continues to serve as a judge of the Kosovo Specialist Chambers in The Hague to which he was appointed in 2017. He had been a civil and criminal pre-trial, trial and appellate judge in the courts of the East German Free State of Thuringia prior to starting his academic career. He pursued his legal studies at the Faculty of Law of the University of the Saarland. From 2010–2014, Professor

Bohlander was the Visiting Chair in Criminal Law at the Rijksuniversiteit Groningen in the Netherlands. In 2012, he was the first non-Muslim visiting scholar ever to teach at the Faculty of Law of Al-Azhar University in Cairo. His interests lie in comparative and international criminal law.

Seyyed Mostafa Mohaghegh Damad
is a member of the Academy of Sciences of Iran and a professor in the Faculty of Law at Shahid Beheshti University. He studied at the Fayzieh School in Qom, and achieved the degree of *Ijtihād* (Ayatollah) in 1970. He received his Ph.D. in Law (Doctorat en Droit) at the Catholic University of Louvain-la-Neuve in 1996. He is the author of 27 published books and more than 50 academic journal articles.

Robert Gleave
is Professor of Arabic Studies at the University of Exeter, UK. He is principal investigator of the European Research Council advanced award "Law, Learning and Authority in Imami Shi'ite Islam". His publications include *Inevitable Doubt: Two Shīʿī Theories of Jurisprudence* (Brill, 2001), *Scripturalist Islam: The Thought and Doctrines of the Akhbari School of Imāmī Shiʿism* (Brill, 2007) and *Islam and Literalism: Literal Meaning and Interpretation in Islamic Legal Theory* (Edinburgh University Press, 2012).

Haider Ala Hamoudi
is the Vice Dean of the University of Pittsburgh School of Law. His scholarship focuses on Middle Eastern and Islamic Law. In addition to his numerous articles and book chapters in a wide variety of law school journals, university presses and other scholarly venues, he has coauthored a casebook on Islamic Law published by Aspen, and is under contract with West to author a nutshell on Islamic Law.

Rahim Nobahar
is Associate Professor at Shahid Beheshti University Law School, Tehran. He achieved the degree of *Ijtihād* from the seminaries (*Hawza*) in Qom and obtained his Ph.D. in Criminal Law and Criminology from Shahid Beheshti University. He has taught courses including Islamic Law, Qur'anic Exegesis, and Philosophy of Law in Mofid University and Shahid Beheshti University. His publications include more than 12 books and 60 academic articles across a range of subjects in Islamic studies.

Imranali Panjwani
is a Lecturer in Law at Anglia Ruskin University and Head of Diverse Legal Consulting where he writes expert reports for immigration and asylum tribunals on issues of persecution. He pursued legal studies at the University of Sheffield, University of Law, King's College London and Western Sydney University. He completed seminary (*hawza*) studies at Al-Mahdi Institute, Birmingham and Jami'at al-Mustafa, Mashhad, Iran. His interests lie in comparative Islamic & Western law, human rights, philosophy, education and mysticism.

Laurens de Rooij
is visiting Lecturer in Islamic Studies at University of Chester and conducts research into the practices of Islam in Europe and Africa. He has studied at the University of Cape Town, the University of Durham, and at University of Leuven. His interests lie in theology and anthropology of Islam, and media discourses of Islam and Muslims.

Visions of *Sharīʿa*: An Introduction

Ali-Reza Bhojani

Central to the Muslim scholarly visions of *Sharīʿa* are the disciplines of *uṣūl al-fiqh* (legal theory) and *fiqh* (juristic inference). Amongst Twelver Shīʿī scholars,[1] whose ideas are the focus of this volume, *uṣūl al-fiqh* entails the study of issues of method and methodology informing the inference (or justification) of *Sharīʿa* rulings. It is the applied discipline of *fiqh* that engages the actual process of relating rulings to their sources. Despite scholarship acknowledging that reducing Muslim normative discourse to these jurisprudential disciplines fails to account for "the human and historical phenomenon of Islam",[2] their significance to Muslim thought in general, and contemporary Shīʿī thought in particular, cannot be overstated. If the system of learning that continues to flourish within and beyond the Shīʿī seminaries of Najaf and Qum is understood as premised on the need to produce, and maintain, the authority of independent scholarly experts (*mujtahids*) capable of inferring the *Sharīʿa* in the absence of the Twelfth Shīʿī Imam, then it is unsurprising that the discourse of *uṣūl al-fiqh* has remained so pivotal. The most authoritative of contemporary Shīʿī scholarship continues to be expressed within a discourse that seeks to maintain continuity with tradition despite its aims of producing scholars who can independently infer *Sharīʿa* rulings in the contemporary age.[3] Yet, it is also a discourse that speaks far beyond the immediate concerns of law and legal theory. As several contributions to this volume demonstrate, its apparently abstract and arcane discussions are often the forum for some of the most sophisticated philosophical and theological deliberations that the rich and diverse traditions of Shīʿī scholarship have to offer.

1 The term Shīʿī itself has come to refer to a large number of different groups, most important of which are the Twelvers, the Zaidis and the Ismailis. The focus of this volume is exclusively the former. Accordingly, and purely for ease of reading, hereafter we employ Shīʿī as a shorthand that refers to the Twelvers alone. The legal thought of the Twelver Shīʿa is often referred to as Jaʿfarī in reverence to the role of the Sixth Shīʿī Imām, Jaʿfar al-Ṣādiq (d. 148/702).

2 Shahab Ahmed, *What is Islam? The Importance of Being Islamic* (Princeton: Princeton University Press, 2016).

3 For a discussion of how modern Shīʿī *uṣūl al-fiqh* acts as a forum for novel developments in Muslim thought positioned in continuity with historical tradition rather than as a break from it, see Robert Gleave, "Modern Shi'ite Legal Theory and the Classical Tradition" in Elisabeth Kendall and Ahmed Khan (eds.), *Reclaiming Islamic Tradition: Modern Interpretations of the Classical Heritage* (Edinburgh: Edinburgh University Press, 2016), 12–32.

© KONINKLIJKE BRILL NV, LEIDEN, 2020 | DOI:10.1163/9789004413948_002

Notwithstanding increasing interest in Shīʿī thought over recent decades,[4] sustained engagement with Shīʿī legal theory remains in its infancy. For Anglophone scholars, direct access to works of Shīʿī legal theory themselves was initially aided by the publication of two separate translations of the first volume of Muḥammad Bāqir al-Ṣadr's (d. 1400/1980) influential modern textbook *Durūs fī ʿilm al-uṣūl*.[5] This has been added to with the recent publication of a translation, alongside an Arabic critical edition, of a 14th Century introductory work by ʿAllāma al-Ḥillī (d. 726/1325), offering a glimpse into a more classical formulation of the genre.[6] Secondary literature has often focused on the role of legal theory within the interplay between Shīʿī legal thought and its authority structures: an approach initially spurred on by the events of the 1979 Islamic Revolution in Iran.[7] Dedicated published research on Shīʿī legal theory is now building on notable initial contributions by Gleave (2000)[8] and Dahlén 2003).[9] Furthering such work, the former is currently conducting a major five-year project on 'Law, Authority and Learning in Imāmī Shi'ite Islam' seeking to examine the emergence, development and operation of the Shīʿī legal system both "in the past and the contemporary period".[10] Such ambitious and broad-ranging projects are expected to supplement the emergence of more focused studies, such as those of Bhojani (2015)[11] and Heern (2015),[12] significantly adding to our knowledge of the substance and context of a legal theory that is central to one of the least understood of the major Muslim legal and intellectual traditions.

Before introducing how the contributions within this volume add to this growing field of scholarship, a brief note outlining the history of Shīʿī legal

4 For a review outlining general patterns in this scholarship, see Liyakat Takim, "The Study of Shīʿī Islam in Western Academia" in *Journal of Shi'a Islamic Studies* 9 (2016): 17–37.

5 Arif Abdul Hussain's translation was published as *Principles of Islamic Jurisprudence: According to Shi'i law* (London: Islamic College for Advanced Studies, 2003) and Roy Mottahedeh's as *Lessons in Islamic Jurisprudence* (Oxford: Oneworld, 2003).

6 Al-ʿAllamāh al-Ḥillī, *The Foundations of Jurisprudence: An Introduction to Imāmī Shīʿī Legal Theory.* Trans Sayyid Amjad H. Shah Naqavi (Leiden: Brill, 2017).

7 Notable examples include, Abdulaziz Sachedina, *The just ruler (al-sultān al-ʿadil) in Shī'ite Islam* (Oxford: Oxford Univeristy Press, 1988) and Ahmad Kazem Moussavi, *Religious Authority in Shi'ite Islam: From the Office of Mufti to the Instituition of Marjaʿ* (Kuala Lumpur: International Institute of Islamic Thought and Civilization, 1996).

8 Robert Gleave, *Inevitable Doubt: Two Theories of Shīʿī Jurisprudence* (Leiden: Brill, 2000).

9 Ashk P. Dahlén, *Islamic Law, Epistemology and Modernity* (London, Routledge, 2003).

10 Law, Authority and Learning in Imāmī Shi'ite Islam. "About". http://www.lawalisi.eu/ (accessed July 18, 2018).

11 Ali-reza Bhojani, *Moral Rationalism and Sharīʿa: Independent Rationality in Modern Shīʿī Uṣūl al-Fiqh* (London: Routledge, 2015).

12 Zackery M. Heern, The Emergence of Modern Shi'ism (London: Oneworld, 2015).

theory, as conceived of by one of the most influential of contemporary Shīʿī jurists, is well in place. In a preface to his transcribed lectures on legal theory, a translation of which is included as an appendix to this volume, al-Sayyid ʿAlī al-Ḥusaynī al-Sīstānī (b. 1930) discusses the independence of Shīʿī *uṣūl al-fiqh*, its originality, early development and importance within Shīʿī thought.[13] He then goes on to categorize the history of Shīʿī legal theory into three distinct phases. For al-Sīstānī, each phase is characterised by a distinct "intellectual struggle".[14] The first phase in this account, extending from the period of the Shīʿī Imams right up until the Safavid period, is shaped by the intellectual struggle Shīʿī scholars undertook in response to the ideas and influence of the prevalent theoretical trends in legal theory amongst broader Sunnī thinkers.

With the onset of the Safavid dynasty in the 11th/16th century and the political establishment of the Shīʿa, the intellectual struggle that was to drive Shīʿī legal theory forward would shift from being inter-school to becoming intra-school. According to al-Sīstānī, it was early in the Safavid period that the tendency describing itself as Akhbārī came to dominate Shīʿī visions of *Sharīʿa*.[15] Epitomised in the works of Mullā Aḥmad Amīn al-Astarabādī (d. 1036/1626–7), this trend emphasized a return to privileging the hadith reports of the *Ahl al-Bayt* (the family of the Prophet) as the key to knowledge of *Sharīʿa*. In the Akhbārī view, Shīʿī access to the pristine teachings of the family of the Prophet meant that there was no need to rely upon fallible scholars who employed conjectural human understanding and adopted Sunnī-inspired methods in their efforts to understand the *Sharīʿa*. It was this challenge to the *mujtahids* (the advocates of *ijtihād*), who described themselves as Uṣūli Shīʿa, that would ultimately see Shīʿī legal thought emerge from the shadow of Sunnī legal theory through the intellectual struggle that defines al-Sīstānī's second phase of Shīʿī legal theory.

The revival of an Uṣūlī method that would supplant the Akhbārī influence is often credited to Muḥammad Bāqir al-Biḥbaḥānī (d. 1207/1791). Yet the need for an intellectual response to Akhbārī concerns continued to drive Shīʿī *uṣūl al-fiqh* thereafter, influencing the ongoing development of an Uṣūlī system culminating in the hands of Murtaḍā al-Anṣārī (d. 1281/1864). The continued influence of a scholar whose works still form a key element in the training of *mujtahids* today is reflected in Hossein Modarressi's nuanced historical periodisation of Shīʿī legal theory culminating in what he terms simply as 'the school

---

13 Sayyid Alī al-Ḥusaynī al-Sīstānī, *al-Rāfid fī ʿilm al-uṣūl*, transcribed by Munīr Qaṭīfī (Qum: Maktabat Āyatullāh Sīstānī, 1414/1993), 12–18.

14 Ibid. 15.

15 Ibid. 17. For a comprehensive treatment of the Akhbārī trend see Robert Gleave, *Scripturalist Islam: The History and Doctrines of the Akhbārī Shīʿī School* (Leiden, Brill, 2007).

of Anṣārī'.[16] However, for al-Sīstānī, the post-Anṣārī era marks a third phase in the development of Shīʿī legal theory – one defined by a new intellectual struggle. The struggle that demarcates the current context is no longer seen as the need to respond to formative Sunnī influence or internal Shīʿī debates. Instead, it is the broader economic, political and cultural challenges impacting Islamic modes of living at various levels of society that calls for "the discipline of legal theory, and its form, to progress to a level appropriate to the conditions of contemporary life".[17]

It is within the context of such live debates in Shīʿī legal thought that we may situate the contributions to this volume. Bringing together authoritative voices and emerging scholars, trained both in 'traditional' seminaries and 'Western' academies, the distinct critical insider and emic accounts included here seek to expand a novel avenue in Islamic legal studies.[18] Contextualised through reference to contemporary juristic practice and socio-political considerations, the volume offers the first broad examination of how an established tradition of thought and ideas continues to be an important site of internal contestation regarding the assumptions, epistemology and hermeneutics of *Sharīʿa* in contemporary Shīʿī thought.

The volume commences with SEYYED MOSTAFA MOHAGHEGH DAMAD's treatment of how a theory of *ijtihād* that Shīʿī scholars typically, and somewhat polemically, associate with Sunnī scholars has influenced modern Shīʿī *uṣūl al-fiqh*. Legal theorists across Muslim schools of thought widely accepted that most of the relevant evidence for the vast majority of *Sharīʿa* rulings was merely conjectural (*ẓannī*) and that human effort (*ijtihād*) was required to properly understand such sources. An implication of this position was a necessity to accommodate some level of diversity in opinion. What Damad describes as 'factuality' theories of *ijtihād* were a response to such need. In the absence of incontrovertible or definitive evidence, factualists held that the *ijtihād* performed by every suitably qualified *mujtahid* is deemed correct. The contrasting 'fallibility' theories held that only one opinion can ever be correct; all scholarly opinion should be considered fallible. These fallible opinions may however be deemed valid if they are inferred in a procedurally sound and authoritative manner. Damad argues that, despite claims of an Imāmī Shīʿī consensus upon fallibility from as early as Abū Jaʿfar al-Ṭūsī (d. 460/1067), factuality theories of

16 Hossein Modarressi Tabātabā'ī, *An Introduction to Shīʿī Law: A Bibliographical Study* (London: Ithaca Press, 1984), 57–58.

17 Sīstānī, *al-Rāfid fī ʿilm al-uṣūl*, 17.

18 The approach taken here has precedent with the inclusion of many 'insider' voices in the broad range of essays on Shīʿī thought collected by Lynda Clarke ed., *Shīʾite Heritage: Essays on Classical and Modern Tradition* (New York: Global Publications, 2001).

ijtihād have exerted considerable influence on deliberations in modern Shīʿī *uṣūl al-fiqh*. This influence can be seen in the very core of the theory of *ijtihād* developed by 18th century al-Bihbahānī and is demonstrated with increasing starkness in subsequent generations of Shīʿī Uṣūlīs, including Murtaḍā al-Ansārī and Muḥammad Kāẓim al-Khurāsānī (d. 1329/1911).

Damad's concern for the influence of factuality in modern Shīʿī thought is, however, not merely historical. By demonstrating the influence of factuality, and the subtle accommodations to the fallibility position that this influence afforded, he emphasizes the continued openness of Shīʿī *uṣūl al-fiqh* to consider questions apparently settled long ago. For Damad, the potential relevance of Shīʿī Uṣūlīs revisiting this particular question also goes beyond an open approach to questions of philosophy of law. Exploring Mirzā al-Qummī's (d. 1231/1815–16) endorsement of a modified factuality theory in the realm of fundamental beliefs, Damad identifies important precedent for developing a theory of religious pluralism indigenous to Uṣūlī Shīʿī thought.

Assuming that *ijtihād* is inherently fallible naturally provokes deep reflection over what constitutes a valid individual effort to infer rulings from sources and methods that have largely been acknowledged as conjectural. The problem of conjecture (*ẓann*) has taken on particular significance in Shīʿī legal theory where the pragmatic necessity of relying upon such sources has periodically been challenged by those who claimed that the core Shīʿī claim of a distinctive access to knowledge (*ʿilm*) could only be preserved through rejecting the authority of conjecture. Murtaḍā al-Ansārī sought to resolve these tensions by grounding the authoritativeness, or probative force, of all sources in certainty (*qatʿ*). Authoritative sources and methods are those that are certainty-bearing, or – when only yielding conjecture – those that rely upon certain evidence for their authoritativeness (*ḥujjiyya*). HASHIM BATA highlights how the epistemic assumptions that underpin this theory justify the modern Shīʿī Uṣūlī preference for textual sources and methods of inferring *Sharīʿa* precepts. He argues that the assumed notion of certainty central to this system was not detailed by al-Ansārī, nor suitably justified by later theorists. A coherent legal theory demands coherent and justified philosophical premises; in Bata's view, reassessing the increasingly untenable conception of certainty that underpins modern Shīʿī Uṣūlī epistemology will open up the inference of *Sharīʿa* precepts to being informed by a wider spectrum of sources and hermeneutical methods.

In RAHIM NOBAHAR'S contribution our attentions are shifted from the potential epistemic underpinnings of a broad range of sources to the actual employment of a single source. His treatment of the role of the Quran within Shīʿī *ijtihād* is framed in terms of Uṣūli responses to an apparent Akhbārī side-lining of the Quran. Nobahar defends the Uṣūlī rhetoric of listing the Quran, not only as a pivotal source, but as the primary source of *Sharīʿa*. The fact that there is a case to be made regarding the role of the Quran speaks to the extent of influence that hadith reports have played in Uṣūlī elaborations of *Sharīʿa*. After engaging a wide range of assumptions informing the role of the Quran within Uṣūlī models of *ijtihād*, Nobahar discusses the existence of some 'problematic' features in the Uṣūlī approach, acknowledging the value in Akhbārī concerns over the difficulties involved in interpreting the Quran. However, unlike the Akhbārīs, this is not directed to elevating recourse to hadiths reported by the family of the Prophet; instead it is used to reinforce the typical Uṣūlī motif of the need for qualified scholarly interpretations of *Sharīʿa*.

In a comparative legal approach, IMRANALI PANJWANI's shifts focus towards the potential in *uṣūl al-fiqh* to facilitate greater theoretical deliberation over the subject of *Sharīʿa* rulings in his call for greater attention to the role of case law as an evidentiary tool in the derivation and operation of *Sharīʿa*. Muḥammad Bāqir al-Ṣadr's textbooks on *uṣūl al-fiqh* define the discipline as the study of "the common elements" in the inference of *Sharīʿa* rulings.[19] This definition accommodates not only theoretical deliberation over sources, their authority, and modes of application, but also the epistemic foundations upon which any given source theory is constructed and the very nature of *Sharīʿa* rulings themselves. It is within modern Shīʿī discussions over the nature of rulings and their relationship with what is referred to as the subject (*mawḍūʿ*) of the rulings that Panjwani identifies an entry point to considering the potential significance of case law methodology. He argues that it is the normative worth in what Shīʿī Uṣūlīs term the 'the practice of rational people' that offers scope for *uṣūl al-fiqh* to incorporate case law methodology as an evidentiary tool, opening up a range of broad-reaching and diverse implications for both the theory and practice of *Sharīʿa*.

If Panjwani seeks to make reference to how the role of case law within English common law may offer a model to inform shifts in the theory of *Sharīʿa* at the level of *uṣūl al-fiqh*, HAIDER ALA HAMOUDI explores how the application of modern law in the Iraqi state context is actually impacting the practice of Shīʿī religious authorities at the level of *fiqh*. Through examining contemporary dynamics centred on historical rulings regarding the blood price (*dīyya*) of non-Muslims, Hamoudi argues that Shīʿī jurists employ "strategic juristic omission" to manage the tensions that arise between the substance of such rulings and the popular political concerns of lay communities. However, jurists simply omitting reference to historical rulings that stand in tension with

19 Muḥammad Bāqir al-Ṣadr, *Durūs fī ʿilm al-uṣūl* (Qum: Markaz al-abḥāth wa al-dirāsāt al-takhaṣṣuṣiyya lil Imām al-Shahīd al-Ṣadr, 2003), 46–49.

the normative demands of political realities and popular sentiments is, for Hamoudi, not a long-term solution to the challenges facing *Sharīʿa* discourse in the contemporary period. If the jurists themselves are "ignoring inconvenient or embarrassing" rules, how can they expect absolute adherence from their followers. Furthermore, the failure of jurists to categorically reject interpretations of texts that have long been ignored gives extremists important ammunition for their cause, raising the question of just how strategic such omission actually is.

The final contributions of the volume examine two trajectories in contemporary Shīʿī thought that seek to develop systematic and coherent responses to the sorts of tension resulting in the strategic juristic omission noted by Hamoudi. Ali-Reza Bhojani focusses on leveraging the moral rationalism that is typically associated with Mu'tazilī thought, yet fundamental to classical Shīʿī theology. After arguing for the potential relevance of non-scriptural judgments of morality within the process of inferring *Sharīʿa* precepts, even if they are only conjectural, he outlines a three-stage hermeneutic for dealing with apparent conflicts between such judgments and the conjectural indication of texts. For Bhojani, apparently immoral rulings that rely on conjectural scriptural evidence cannot be attributed to a moral God without considering this tension. Accordingly, he argues that a potentially valid, non-scriptural judgment of morality may render an apparently immoral textual evidence as contextually specified, demand that it be read in a manner consistent with the non-scriptural evidence, or even be excluded from the inferential process altogether.

The importance of political realities in shaping emergent visions of *Sharīʿa* in changing societies is emphasized in Hassan Beloushi's account of *maqāṣid al-sharīʿa* in contemporary Shīʿī jurisprudence. Widely debated in modern Sunnī discussions of legal theory is the potential, and associated challenges, in seeking to privilege the 'objectives' or 'higher purposes' of *Sharīʿa* over specific historical formulations of *fiqh*. Beloushi's contribution introduces the main trends and ramifications of how analogous debates are emerging within Shīʿī contexts. He argues that the discourse of *maqāṣid* in contemporary Shīʿī thought emerges out of particular socio-political, cultural and epistemic constructions. Despite a theological framework that is arguably more conducive to a *maqāṣid* discourse than the Ashʿarī framework associated with much Sunnī thought, and the diversity of emergent approaches to integrating a *maqāṣidī* approach within Shīʿī thought, he ultimately argues that any such shifts are unlikely to impact mainstream Shīʿī jurisprudence for some time. For Beloushi, until such thinking is reflected in the ideas of the most authoritative of Shīʿī jurists, the impact of such ideas will remain tempered.

The contributions to this volume largely employ the discourse of *uṣūl al-fiqh* as a means of deliberating on the mechanisms and extent to which change can be accommodated within what continues to be the authoritative discourse of much Shīʿī Muslim scholarship. However, it is important to note that the discourse of *uṣūl al-fiqh* is simultaneously, and arguably more widely, being employed within Shīʿī thought to limit any such changes. In his epilogue, Robert Gleave thus describes the contributions within this volume as representing "some of the more adventurous elements of contemporary Shīʿī legal theory". His translation of a defence of a key element in the dominant post-Anṣārī legal epistemology by the influential Iranian jurist Jaʿfar Subhānī, challenged by a number of authors in this volume, reminds us of the intensity of such debates. It also reminds us that the breadth and scope of contemporary discussions in Shīʿī legal theory is not something that a single volume could do justice to. Nevertheless, this volume does offer a novel insight into how one of the most intellectually vibrant and developed discourses of Islamic thought continues to be a key forum for exploring visions of *Sharīʿa*.

Bibliography

Ahmed, Shahab, *What is Islam? The Importance of Being Islamic*. Princeton: Princeton University Press, 2016.

Bhojani, Ali-reza, *Moral Rationalism and Sharīʿa: Independent Rationality in Modern Shīʿī Uṣūl al-Fiqh*. London: Routledge, 2015.

Clarke, Lynda (ed.), *Shi'ite Heritage: Essays on Classical and Modern Tradition*. New York: Global Publications, 2001.

Dahlén, Ashk P., *Islamic Law, Epistemology and Modernity*. London, Routledge, 2003.

Gleave, Robert, *Inevitable Doubt: Two Theories of Shīʿī Jurisprudence*. Leiden: Brill, 2000.

Gleave, Robert, "Modern Shi'ite Legal Theory and the Classical Tradition" in Elisabeth Kendall and Ahmed Khan (eds.), *Reclaiming Islamic Tradition: Modern Interpretations of the Classical Heritage* (Edinburgh: Edinburgh University Press, 2016) 12–32.

Gleave, Robert, *Scripturalist Islam: The History and Doctrines of the Akhbārī Shīʿī School*. Leiden, Brill, 2007.

Heern, Zackery M., The Emergence of Modern Shi'ism. London: Oneworld, 2015.

Al-Ḥillī, al-ʿAllamāh, *The Foundations of Jurisprudence: An Introduction to Imāmī Shīʿī Legal Theory*. Trans Sayyid Amjad H. Shah Naqavi. Leiden: Brill, 2017.

Moussavi, Ahmad Kazem, *Religious Authority in Shi'ite Islam: From the Office of Mufti to the Institution of Marjaʿ*. Kuala Lumpur: International Institute of Islamic Thought and Civilization, 1996.

Sachedina, Abdulaziz, *The just ruler (al-sultān al-ʿadil) in Shīʾite Islam*. Oxford: Oxford Univeristy Press, 1988.

al-Ṣadr, Muḥammad Bāqir, *Durūs fī ʿilm al-uṣūl*. Qum: Markaz al-abḥāth wa al-dirāsāt al-takhaṣṣuṣiyya lil Imām al-Shahīd al-Ṣadr, 2003.

al-Sīstānī, Sayyid Alī al-Ḥusaynī, *al-Rāfid fī ʿilm al-uṣūl*, transcribed by Munīr Qaṭīfī. Qum: Maktabat Āyatullāh Sīstānī, 1414/1993.

Tabātabāʾī, Hossein Modarressi, *An Introduction to Shīʿī Law: A Bibliographical Study*. London: Ithaca Press, 1984.

Takim, Liyakat, "The Study of Shīʿī Islam in Western Academia" in *Journal of Shīʿa Islamic Studies* 9 (2016) 17–37.

CHAPTER 1

The Reception of Factuality (*taṣwīb*) Theories of *Ijtihād* in Modern Uṣūlī Shīʿī Thought

Seyyed Mostafa Mohaghegh Damad

1 Introduction

This study will examine the reception of factuality theories of *ijtihād* in modern Shīʿī *uṣūl al-fiqh*, largely through the treatment of Shaykh Muḥammad Kāẓim al-Khurāsānī (d. 1911) who describes an agreement among Imāmī jurists in advocating the contrasting theory of fallibility.[1] However, despite the concurrence on fallibility, this study will show that some influence of factuality-type thinking can been seen in modern Shīʿī Uṣūlī thought, not least in the work of al-Khurāsānī himself. Analysis of the work of Mīrza al-Qummī (d. 1816) will show that this influence is not restricted to the theoretical framework for understanding efforts to infer the Sharīʿa precepts that regulate human life, but that it is an influence that also extends to debates on factuality and fallibility in determining rational beliefs at the level of the principles of faith (*uṣūl al-din*), a debate with important implications for understanding religious diversity.

2 Framing the Debate

Notions of factuality (*taṣwīb*) and fallibility (*takhṭiʾa*) in the human inference of Sharīʿa precepts are key concepts informing theories of *ijtihād* discussed in works of *uṣūl al-fiqh* across the variety of Muslim schools including the Imāmī Shīʿa.[2] The treatment of the issue by Abū Jaʿfar al-Ṭūsī (d. 460/1067) confirms that it was a question that early Imāmī Shīʿī jurists considered seriously.[3] Beyond the formative period of Shīʿī jurisprudential thought, subsequent

1 Muḥammad Kāẓim al-Khurāsānī, *Kifāyat al-uṣūl* (Qum: Majmaʿ al-fikr al-islāmī, 2009), 2:330.

2 For a survey of how these two theories of *ijtihād* relate to differing theological presuppositions and their implications for the position of law with regards theology in classical Sunni formulations see Aron Zysow, *The Economy of Certainty: An Introduction to the Typology of Islamic Legal Theory* (Atlanta: Lockwood Press, 2013) 259–278.

3 Abū Jaʿfar Muḥammad ibn al-Ḥasan al-Ṭūsī, *al-ʿUdda fī uṣūl al-fiqh* (Qum: Maṭbaʿa Sattāra, 1996), 2:723–726.

© KONINKLIJKE BRILL NV, LEIDEN, 2020 | DOI:10.1163/9789004413948_003

presentations of the concept of fallibility and factuality can be found in the writings of al-Muḥaqqiq al-Ḥillī (d. 676/1277)[4] and his pupil, al-ʿAllāma al-Ḥillī (d. 726/1325).[5] However there is no considerable discussion of the concept in later works, with recent Imāmī scholars largely treating the question as a resolved issue, rather than an open debate.[6]

Proponents of factuality theories, referred to as factualists (*muṣawwiba*), are associated with the belief that the objective of their *ijtihād* was not to discover any actually existent intelligible divine rulings; rather that God's rulings are tantamount to whatever is reached through the efforts of authoritative experts (*mujtahids*). A suitably qualified and diligent *mujtahid* always discloses facts through his practice of *ijtihād*, and he is always correct. This view is associated with the Ashʿarī school and with some from amongst the Mu'tazila. On the other hand, fallibilists (*mukhaṭṭi'a*) are associated with the belief that divine rulings do actually exist and that they are intelligible. For proponents of fallibility, the *ijtihād* of a *mujtahid* may either accurately identify the intelligible divine rulings, or it may fail to do so. The theory of factuality seems to somehow invest mankind with the responsibility of divine legislation. Man has the authority to deduct religious law, and to relate his findings to the very opinion of God. Accordingly, factuality theories of *ijtihād* imply that religious truths are the same as one's interpretations, and a sense of infallibility is conferred upon the *mujtahid*. This is in contrast to fallibilists who do not directly relate their understanding to the opinion of God, they recognise that the *mujtahid*'s fallible understanding and the Divine rulings in the knowledge of God are not considered tantamount to one and the same thing.

The early origins of the debate are not clear, with the distinction between fallibility and factuality gaining momentum only through later theologians. Abū Ḥāmid al-Ghazālī (d. 505/1111) states that there is no concrete evidence to show whether the early eponyms Abū Ḥanīfa (d. 150/767) and al-Shāfiʿī (d. 204/820) were either fallibillists or factualists.[7] Al-Ghazālī, himself a proponent of factuality, gives a typology of differing views held on the issue that is a useful background to the examination of the reception of factuality in

---

4 Ja'far bin al-Ḥasan al-Muḥaqqiq al-Ḥillī, *Maʿārij al-uṣūl* (Qum: Muassasāt Āl al-bayt, 1983), 181–182.

5 Jamāl al-Dīn Abū Manṣūr Ḥasan ibn Yūsuf al-ʿAllāma al-Ḥillī, *Mabādī al-wūṣūl ilā ʿilm al-uṣūl* (Beirut: Dār al-aḍwā', 1986), 244–245.

6 See al-Khurāsānī, *Kifāyat al-uṣūl*, 2:330–32; Muḥammad Riḍā al-Muẓaffar, *Uṣūl al-fiqh* (Qum: Intishārāt Ismāʿīliyyān, 2000), 2:37.

7 Al-Ghazālī, Abū Ḥāmid Muḥammad ibn Muḥammad, *al-Mustaṣfā min ʿilm al-uṣūl* (Beirut: al-Maktabat al-ʿasrīyya, 2009), 2:311. For a contrasting view see Abū al-Ḥasan al-Baṣrī, *al-Muʿtamid fī uṣūl al-fiqh* (Beirut: Dār al-kutub al-ʿilmiyya, 1983), 2:949.

modern Uṣūlī Shīʿī thought. Even the brief conceptual analysis he offers for the spectrum of opinions demonstrates that a complex range of views is accommodated within each of the broader camps of factuality or fallibility. This will provide a backdrop for al-Khurāsānī's treatment, which in turn, demonstrates how this spectrum can be interpreted in a way that breaks the dual distinction altogether, offering some accommodation to the distinctive claims of both camps within a single theory.

Al-Ghazālī acknowledges that in general, people do advocate either one of two theories of *ijtihād*. Some hold that, "in conjectural issues (*ẓanniyyāt*)[8] every *mujtahid* is correct"; these are the proponents of factuality.[9] Others hold that "the correct is only one", these are the proponents of fallibility.[10] Al-Ghazālī then goes on to further clarify and distinguish between what he sees as the major trends within these two broad theories, where differences arose particularly around the question of "whether or not God has a specific precept (*ḥukm muʿayyin*), to be sought out by the *mujtahid*, in cases where there is no explicit source text (*allatī lā naṣṣa fīhā*)".[11]

Al-Ghazālī distinguishes between two types of factuality theory. The first type is described as being held by the "rightly discerning from amongst the factualists"; this is the view that al-Ghazālī himself endorses and subscribes to.[12] According to this conception, God has no specific precept in cases for which there is no explicit source text. Thus the conjectural process of *ijtihād* is not a means to discover any actually pre-occurring precept, "instead it is the precept that follows the conjecture".[13] Briefly clarifying, he continues by stating that "God, exalted, judges for every *mujtahid* that which is in accordance with the preponderance of his [i.e. the *mujtahid*'s] conjecture".[14]

Al-Ghazālī then contrasts this first view with an alternative factualist position. The second, somewhat softer, theory of factuality resonates with al-Khurāsānī's reconciliation discussed below and, theoretically at least, seems to stem from a similar concern with the hard factuality advocated by al-Ghazālī himself. For these theorists, there must be a specific precept towards which the search of *ijtihād* is directed, however the *mujtahid* is not responsible to

---

8 The qualification here of 'conjectural issues', demonstrates al-Ghazālī 's view that *ijtihād* and hence the debate regarding factuality and fallibility is not relevant to definitive or certain issues (*qaṭʿiyyāt*).

9 Al-Ghazālī, *Mustaṣfā*, 311.

10 *Ibid.*

11 *Ibid.*

12 *Ibid.*

13 *Ibid.*

14 *Ibid.*

discover this; he is only responsible to act in accordance with whatever his conjecture leads him to;

> … for a search, it is necessary that there be something which is sought (*lā budda li al-ṭalab, maṭlūb*), however the *mujtahid* is not responsible to correctly identify this specific precept, thus he is correct (*muṣīb*) even if he is mistaken with regards to that specific precept, for he has not been ordered to correctly identify it![15]

The *mujtahid* is responsible for whatever he finds in his search, thus, even when not discovering the specific precept towards which his *ijtihād* is directed, the *mujtahid* is still correct (*muṣīb*) "in the sense that he reaches that which he is responsible for, and correctly identifies that which is upon him".[16]

For the fallibilists discussed by al-Ghazālī the notion that God has specific precepts – the object sought in *ijtihād* – even for issues in which there are no explicit texts, is presumed. However, in his view, different fallibilist positions emerge based on different positions regarding the existence and nature of indicators towards the precepts that are not covered by explicit texts. Three groups emerge; those who believe that there are no indicators to these precepts, those who believe that there are conjectural indicators and those who believe that there are definitive or certain (*qaṭʿī*) indicators. Although this spectrum of fallibility may seem to be the obvious place within which to locate the admittedly varied and diverse Shīʿa tradition of *ijtihād*, as we shall see below, tendencies within modern Uṣūlī Shīʿa thought may actually be more easily located in al-Ghazālī's second factualist position.

3 The Modern Uṣūlī Shīʿī Reception of Factuality in Legislative Issues

In his famous text *Kifāyat al-uṣūl*, al-Khurāsānī's discussion of fallibility and factuality commences by initially distinguishing between fallibility in two areas; the domain of rational beliefs (*al-ʿaqliyyāt*) and the domain of legislative regulations (*al-sharʿiyyāt*). Al-Khurāsānī claims that fallibility in the domain of rational beliefs, an issue that will be explored further below, has not been seriously contested.[17] Accordingly, his treatment of the issue does not consider factuality and fallibility with respect to the principles of doctrine

15 *Ibid.*
16 *Ibid.*
17 Al-Khurāsānī, *Kifāyat al-uṣūl*, 2:330.

(*uṣūl al-dīn*) – the subject matter of rational beliefs – but rather focuses on the debate solely with regard to the human understanding of the *Sharīʿa* precepts intended to regulate the practical elements of religion (*furūʿ al-dīn*). As already noted, al-Khurāsānī states that the established Imāmī position is of fallibility, whereby God has "a judgment with regard to every issue; sometimes *ijtihād* [correctly] reaches this, and at other times it leads to other than this". He adds that "our counterparts (*mukhālifūnā*)" subscribe to a theory of factuality that apparently considers God to have normative judgments (*aḥkām*) to the extent of "the number of opinions of the *mujtahids*, such that whatever is attained through their *ijtihād* is His judgment, blessed and exalted be He".[18] To al-Khurāsānī this is "quite obviously" nonsensical, for "it is not possible to think of *ijtihād* regarding the precept for an issue, except that there be for that issue a real precept (*ḥukm wāqiʿī*) which the *mujtahid* seeks to reach by way of his inference from its indicators".[19] Accordingly he goes on to offer three possible explanations of what the proponents of factuality may have meant, refuting the first two of these possible explanations outright, whilst accommodating the third within his conception of the different levels of legislation and reconciling it with fallibility theory.

The first possibility that al-Khurāsānī proposes is that factualists may have believed that God has initiated a range of precepts – to the extent of the number of opinions held by *mujtahids* – for each issue, in actuality, such that the differing precepts reached through each individual act of *ijtihād* are all actual precepts (*aḥkām wāqiʿiyya*). For al-Khurāsānī, although such a phenomenon is not impossible, it must be rejected as false due to the existence of concurrently transmitted reports (*tawātur al-akhbār*) and the consensus of the Imāmiyya indicating that "He, blessed and exalted, has a judgement for every situation, which is commonly applicable to all".[20] Al-Khurāsānī is, of course, not the first Shīʿī scholar to have made such a case. Murtaḍā al-Anṣārī (d. 1864), al-Khurāsānī's teacher, traces the argument that religious precepts are commonly applicable to both learned and unlearned, based again on a claim to the presence of concurrently transmitted traditions to that effect, all the way back to al-Sayyid al-Murtaḍā (d. 436/1044) and al-Shaykh al-Ṭūsī.[21] Beyond the *tawātur*, al-Ṭūsī himself also cites the consensus of Imāmī scholars upon the

18 *Ibid.*
19 *Ibid.*
20 Al-Khurāsānī, *Kifāyat al-uṣūl*, 2:331.
21 See Murtaḍā al-Anṣārī, *Farāʾid al-uṣūl* (Beirut: Muʾassasat al-Nuʿmān, 1991), 1:44.

belief that both learned and unlearned are equal bearers of Sharīʿa responsibility as a justification for rejecting factuality theory.[22]

The second possibility proposed by al-Khurāsānī is that the factualist may have believed that God initiates precepts which are in accordance with the views of the authoritative scholars, *after* their *ijtihād*. This for al-Khurāsānī is still incomprehensible, for just as in the case of his initial conception of factuality, he feels it is impossible to search for "something that has no self, nor any effect".[23]

The third possibility is that factuality is concerned only with the level of actualisation of a precept (*fiʿliyyat al-ḥukm*). Thus, while a *mujtahid* is seeking to reach the reality of the divine precept, whatever he grasps in this process is effectively God's ruling for that *mujtahid*, despite the possibility of qualitative discrepancy between his findings and the actual precept.[24] This can be better understood in light of the modern Uṣūlī Shīʿī conception of the divine precept and its process of legislation being of four different levels: (1) necessitation (*iqtiḍāʾ*), (2) initiation (*inshāʾ*), (3) actualisation (*fiʿliyya*), and (4) activation (*munajjaziyya*). The level of 'necessitation' results from the occurrence of actual utility or detriment as the criteria of a precept and 'initiation' is the Divine Legislator's normative recognition of these actual criteria. Al-Khurāsānī believes that indicators have been laid down by the Divine Legislator to help people understand these initiated rulings. *Mujtahids* are in search of these initiated precepts, however the result of their *ijtihād* differs in accordance with the variety of opinions on any issue – opinions that do not always disclose the precept as initiated in line with the necessitation of the real criterion of utility or detriment. If in the process of attempted discovery, the one attempting to infer the initiated precept is successful, the legislation process reaches its third level and the initiated precept is deemed actualised and may subsequently be activated. However, if in the process of inference the *mujtahid* fails to grasp the initiated precept, the precept based on the real necessitated criterion never reaches the level of actualisation. Instead it is the ruling as appreciated by the *mujtahid* that proceeds to actualisation, and it is this precept that is subsequently activated for him as a duty to observe. Accordingly, al-Khurāsānī acknowledges that the actualised precept on any given issue may vary in accordance with the differing views of *mujtahids*, and that "self-evidently" it is a level of precept that is not commonly applicable to both learned and unlearned and that

22 Al-Ṭūsī, *al-ʿUdda fī uṣūl al-fiqh*, 2:725–726.

23 Al-Khurāsānī, *Kifāyat al-uṣūl*, 2:331.

24 *Ibid.*

"there is no impossibility of factuality (*taṣwīb*) in this sense".[25] This conception of the legislation process allows for some reconciliation between factuality and fallibility, for whatever the *mujtahid* attains to in his *ijtihād* becomes an actualised precept (*ḥukm fiʿlī*) for him, yet this actualised precept is not necessarily an accurate appreciation of the actual precept (*ḥukm wāqiʿī*) initiated in line with the real intended criterion of utility and detriment.

Traces of factuality in Shīʿī Uṣūl thought are not restricted to the space identified by al-Khurāsānī through this four-level conceptualization of divine precepts. A sense of factuality can also be identified within Uṣūlī Shīʿī discourse emerging from issues relating to a slightly earlier stream of thought that commenced with Muḥammad Bāqir al-Bihbahānī (d. 1207/1791) and the categorisation of the divine precept into apparent (*ẓāhir*) and real (*wāqiʿ*).[26] The apparent precept is observed by one who is in a situation of doubt (*shakk*) regarding the real precept. The apparent precept is the result of the conclusive and binding efforts of a *mujtahid* who has employed all categories of evidence available to him including what later scholars have termed "non-reality securing evidence"[27] such as the principle of presumed continuity (*istiṣḥāb*), the principle of exemption (*barāʾa*), the principle of optional choice (*takhyīr*), and the principle of precaution (*iḥtiyāṭ*). Prolific debates emerged amongst Uṣūlī Shīʿa's regarding the reconciliation of how and why God may have allowed us, or in fact demanded that we observe, apparent precepts – despite the known possibility of their error. One of the theories that emerged from this debate, referred to as the theory of instrumental utility (*maṣlaḥa al-sulūkiyya*) may be termed the Shīʿī factuality. The theory refers to a notion that there is an instrumental utility embedded in observing obedience to specific systems and evidence designated as valid by the Legislator, despite the possibility of their error. The 'instrumental utility' of observing the authoritative system of evidence is held to compensate for any elapsed benefits that may have been missed by following apparent precepts which in some cases would not secure the original necessitating factors (the actual utility or detriment) that were the criterion behind the real precept or missed truth.[28] Accordingly this compensatory instrumental utility implies that, so long as the *mujtahid* employs a valid means, he will never fail in his *ijtihād*, and in a sense, such a *mujtahid* is always successful.

---

25 Al-Khurāsānī, *Kifāyat al-uṣūl*, 2:331.

26 Muḥammad Bāqir al-Waḥīd al-Bihbahānī, *al-Fawāʾid al-ḥāʾiriyya* (Qum: Majmaʿ al-fikr al-islāmī, 2003), 399.

27 See Muḥammad Bāqir al-Ṣadr, *Durūs fī ʿilm al-uṣūl* (Qum: Markaz al-abḥāth wa al-dirāsāt al-takhaṣṣuṣiyya lil Imām al-Shahīd al-Ṣadr, 2003), 1:69 & 139–158.

28 See al-Anṣārī, *Farāʾid al-uṣūl*, 1:40–48.

Despite the apparent convergence or influence of factuality theories within the above mentioned streams of thought, we see that modern Shīʿī scholars continue to position themselves exclusively within a fallibilist framework. The insistence on this self-positioning may be better understood through recognition of how the modern Uṣūlī Shīʿa view the origins of the debate. The late grand Ayatollah Burūjirdī (d. 1961), one of the most famous students of al-Khurāsānī, cites intra-Muslim theological issues as the root concern that led to the development of factuality theory;

> The origin of the controversy in this matter is the controversy regarding the state of the companions of the Prophet, blessings of Allah be upon him and his family, and whether all of them were free from error and corruption (*fisq*) or not. Some theologians from the *Ahl al-Sunna* are of the view that whosoever can be given the term "companion" was amongst those who do not even err, never mind the possibility of any corruption coming from them. Accordingly, contradiction amongst the views and beliefs of the companions does not reveal that some of them must have been in error; for example, even Muʿāwiya is considered correct in his open contestation with ʿAlī, peace be with him, and likewise ʿAlī, peace be with him, [was correct] in his open contestation with Muʿāwiya. Whereas others have held that the correct (*muṣīb*) from amongst the companions are those whose opinions correspond with reality – everyone else is wrong, although they are excused, for they acted in accordance with that which was required by their *ijtihād*.[29]

It is clear that Burūjirdī believed that the origins of factuality theory lied with core Sunnī doctrinal concerns over the justice of the companions of the Prophet. In his view factuality theory, when applied to the early Muslim community, rendered all companions of the Prophet effectively infallible. Of course for Imamī scholars, infallibility is a quality held only by a number of spiritual figures from the family of the Prophet Muhammad. All others, even the closest companions to the Prophet, are considered capable of error and sin.

The Imāmī rejection of factuality and the adoption of fallibility cannot be seen in isolation of such theological claims regarding the origins of the debate. Although these theological origins may help explain the vigour and consistency with which Imāmī scholars have chosen to position themselves within the scope of fallibility, Burūjirdī argues that recognising these theological origins

29 Ḥusayn al-Muntaẓirī, *Nihāyat al-uṣūl: taqrīrāt al-Burūjirdī* (Qum: *Nashr tafakkur*, n.d.), 151–152.

allow for the question of factuality and fallibility to be treated as an open jurisprudential question – despite the claim of al-Khurāsānī, his teacher, that there is an Imāmī consensus upon fallibility.

> It has become popular amongst jurists and legal theorists that the invalidity of factuality is a matter of consensus. However the popularity of this opinion should not deceive you, rather you should refer to the history of the issue of fallibility and factuality, whence it would become clear to you that it is actually a rational issue (*mas'ala 'aqliyya*) and not a canonical devotional issue (*mas'ala shar'iyya ta'abbudiyya*) that can be based on consensus. The consensus claimed in this issue is [only] a consensus of Imāmī theologians as theologians (*bi mā hum mutakallimūn*) – and not a consensus of jurists or traditionists that is authoritative evidence amongst the [range of] authoritative juristic evidence.[30]

Shī'ī legal theorists hold that consensus is only considered authoritative evidence when it is a means to discovering the opinion of the Prophet or an impeccable from amongst his family. A consensus amongst jurists or traditionists can be a means to discovering such Sunna, if the consensus is based on some lost textual evidence or if it included the opinion of an impeccable himself. A consensus amongst theologians, on an issue of rational theological speculation has no such authority in itself and hence, Brūjurdī argues, the claimed Imāmī consensus regarding the invalidity of factuality has no binding authority.[31]

4 Factuality in Doctrinal Beliefs

Notwithstanding the theological origins of the debate, the core of the discussion over fallibility and factuality has been directed to framing an understanding of the nature of a *mujtahid*'s efforts in understanding the subsidiary canonical matters or practical elements of Sharī'a (*furū' al-dīn*), rather than discussing a framework for the human understanding of the fundamental doctrinal principles of Islam. Yet the implications of this debate for framing differing understandings of belief have not been entirely ignored by legal theorists

30 Al-Muntaẓirī, *Nihāyat al-uṣūl*, 151.

31 To support his argument that the Imāmī consensus against factuality is not jurisprudential in nature, but rather theological, Burūjirdī cites Abū Ja'far al-Ṭūsī's explicit statement, 'The *theologians* (*mutakallimūn*) of the truthful sect, early and contemporary, all of them agree that the people of the truth (*aṣḥāb al-ṣawāb*) are a single sect whilst all others are proponents of error (*mukhaṭṭi'ūn*)' [*emphasis added*] al-Muntaẓirī, *Nihāyat al-uṣūl*, 152.

and they are of particular relevance in light of contemporary debates regarding religious plurality.

Although recognising that fallibility and factuality theory may be considered with respect to either rational beliefs (*al-ʿaqliyyāt*) or the domain of legislative regulations (*al-sharʿiyyāt*), we have seen that al-Khurasānī's treatment focused exclusively on the latter claiming that fallibility in the realm of beliefs is uncontested. However debate on the issue and some influence of factuality type theories, in the realm of rational doctrinal beliefs, can be found in Shīʿī works of legal theory. Mīrzā al-Qummī dedicates an extensive section of the final volume of his *Qawānīn al-uṣūl* to the question of *ijtihād* in matters of doctrinal belief, followed by a discussion on factuality and fallibility that clearly demonstrate the influence of such thinking. Before examining his contribution in this regard, we will again frame the discussion by first outlining al-Ghazālī's much earlier comments on the issue.

We have seen that al-Ghazālī advocates a factuality theory of *ijtihād* in matters of legislative regulations that are not covered by a definitive text. He adopts the harder version of the two factuality theories described above, whereby "God, exalted, judges for every *mujtahid* that which is in accordance with the preponderance of his [i.e. the *mujtahids*] conjecture".[32] For al-Ghazālī the doctrines of fundamental belief are not within this remit for they are definitive issues (*qatʿiyyāt*), in which certainty can be attained, "and one who errs with regards to definitive issues is sinful".[33]

After outlining his advocacy for fallibility in matters of rational doctrinal belief, he cites and criticises two contrasting views. The first is attributed to Abū ʿUthman al-Baṣrī al-Jāḥiẓ (d. 255/869). According to al-Ghazālī, al-Jāḥiẓ categorizes those who hold beliefs contrary to the Muslims as falling into one of three groups. A person may oppose the Muslims out of obstinacy and in contradiction to their own beliefs – such a person is sinful. The second category consists of one who opposes Muslim beliefs after having searched for the truth but failing to reach it – such a person is excused and not sinful. The third category consists of those who have never even searched, due to not knowing that such a search was a duty upon them – like the second group, these people are also excused. For al-Jāḥiẓ;

> The only one who is sinful and punishable is the obstinate [unbeliever] (*Innamā al-āthim al-muʿadhdhab al-muʿānid*)' because Allah, exalted

32 Al-Ghazālī, *Mustaṣfā*, 311.

33 *Ibid.*, 304.

> [states] "Allah does not oblige a soul except with that which it is capable of" [2:286] whilst these [other two groups] have been unable to perceive the truth.[34]

Al-Ghazālī acknowledges that this position is plausible and not rationally incoherent, but accepting it as the correct view would depend upon the occurrence of devotional instructions from God confirming the position. Not only does he hold that no such confirmation exists, rather he argues for, and cites, the presence of transmitted evidence from both the Quran and Prophetic practice to the contrary.[35] He sees this evidence as extensive and amounting to a necessary feature of the faith;

> For just as the Prophet called to the canonical prayer and alms giving, necessarily, it is also known – necessarily – that he called the Jews and Christians to attain proper belief, and to follow him. Furthermore he blamed them for persisting in their beliefs, and it is for this [persistence] that he fought against all of them ...[36]

Al-Ghazālī continues by arguing that it is known with "certainty" that it was only the minority of these people who were "obstinate" rejecters of the Prophet, rather "the vast majority of those addressed were blind followers who believed in the way (*dīn*) of their forefathers through imitation".[37] Furthermore al-Ghazālī does not accept that the unbeliever may not have been capable of belief, and thus not responsible for their unbelief, for God has enabled them through their own minds and through sufficient evidence; evidence pointed to by the Prophets who themselves were assisted with miracles from God to make their arguments conclusive.[38]

Mīrzā al-Qummī's direct response to this line of thinking will be treated in what follows. At this point it is important to note that, in the manner presented by al-Ghazālī, al-Jāḥiẓ's argument does not seem to fully conform to a sense of a factuality theory. Despite his inclusivity, Jāḥiẓ maintains a fallibility theory regarding doctrinal beliefs, for he still believes that the correct understanding is one; whoever reaches it will be rewarded and those who fail to reach this

34 *Ibid.*, 306.

35 The Quranic verses al-Ghazālī cites in support of his position are 38:27, 41:23, 2:78, 58:18, and 2:10.

36 Al-Ghazālī, *Mustaṣfā*, 306.

37 *Ibid.*

38 *Ibid.*

truth are exempted – so long as they are not obstinate in their rejection of anything of the truth in so far as they perceive it.[39]

Accordingly al-Ghazālī goes on to cite, and again respond to, a further opinion. ʿAbd Allāh ibn al-Ḥasan al-Anbārī (d. 168/785) is quoted as holding that 'every *mujtahid* is correct (*mūṣīb*) in rational doctrinal issues, just as they are in subsidiary practical issues (*furūʿ*)'.[40] If this statement was intended to mean that people are only commanded to believe that which they have attained, in accordance with their capacity in seeking the truth, then according to al-Ghazālī this is not substantially different from the position of al-Jāḥiẓ. It is a position that is rationally possible, but shown to be invalid by way of the aforementioned evidence from the Quran and Sunna. However if what al-Anbārī intended was that;

> [T]he object of one's belief *is* in accordance with one's belief ... [then] this is a more dangerous position than that of al-Jāḥiẓ ... and in fact more dangerous than even the position of the sophists, for they deny the reality of things, whereas this affirms reality and then designates it as dependent upon belief.

To al-Ghazālī such a conception is not logically possible, for it would allow for the unity of contradictions. It implies that the world is both eternal and temporal, that God exists and does not exist, that the Prophets are true and yet are also false – all in line with the diversity of beliefs occurring in each case. Of course al-Ghazālī can still maintain the possibility of factuality when it comes to understanding regulative precepts at the level of the practical elements of Sharīʿa for "it is possible that a thing be prohibited for Zayd and permissible for Umar". Whereas theological designations at the level of the principles of belief are for him not "circumstantial (*waḍʿiyya*)", they relate to "essentialities (*umūr dhātiyya*)" and thus cannot depend on an individual's own understanding.[41]

It must be acknowledged that the original text of al-Anbārī is not available, and thus attempts to assess what he may have meant are rendered merely speculative. Nevertheless it is possible that al-Anbārī was pointing towards something that later became known as Immanuel Kant's antinomies. Kant believed that in probing transcendent reality, reason could arrive at two equally

39 *Ibid.*, 306–307.

40 *Ibid.*, 307.

41 Al-Ghazālī, *Mustaṣfā*, 307.

rational, but contradictory results.[42] Interestingly Abū al-Ḥusayn al-Baṣrī (d. 478/1085), whose proximity in time to al-Anbārī may give added strength to the weight of his opinion, mentions that al-Anbārī referred to apparently contradictory allegorical verses of the Quran to support his case; verses which for instance confirm both the visibility and the invisibility of God at the same time.[43] Another possibility is that al-Anbārī's views foreshadowed the religious pluralism advocated by the late John Hick,[44] further discussion of which is beyond the scope of this study.

Mīrzā al-Qummī, a leading student of the great Uṣūlī reviver al-Biḥbahānī and arguably the most significant scholar of his time in the Shīʿī centre of Qum, makes an important contribution to the foregoing debate within his work of legal theory. He too engages with the received views of al-Jāḥiẓ and al-Anbārī ultimately arguing for a more developed version of the formers ideas.[45] Mīrzā al-Qummī acknowledges that when it comes to rational beliefs at the level of the principles of religion "the majority of Muslims hold that which is correct (*al-muṣīb*) to be only one ... whilst one who rejects Islam is a proponent of error (*mukhṭiʾ*), sinful (*āthim*) and an unbeliever (*kāfir*) – whether he struggled to understand or not".[46] Al-Qummī maintains the fallibilist premise that there is actually one truth being sought out in *ijtihād*, be that *ijtihād* in doctrinal issues or legislative ones. However he contends against the latter part of the statement claiming that it may only be valid in the hypothetical case of two *mujtahids* who differ in their views despite being absolutely "complete" in the capacity and capability.[47] In terms of the general population, one who does not attain to the truth is only sinful and punishable if he is obstinate (*muʿānid*) in his unbelief and, going beyond al-Jāḥiẓ, only if he is wilfully negligent (*muqaṣṣir*) in his search for truth.

Mīrzā al-Qummī maintains that there is a distinction between the fundamental acceptance of the principles of belief and their specific details, and accepts that a conjectural and undetailed (*ijmālī*) belief may be sufficient in establishing the latter. Accounting for a degree of difference within Islam, he

---

42 See Immanuel Kant, 'Critique of Pure Reason' in Paul Guyer and Allen W. Wood (eds.), *Critique of Pure Reason* (Cambridge: Cambridge University press, 1999).

43 See Muḥammad ibn 'Alī Abū al-Ḥusayn al-Baṣrī *al-Muʿtamid fi uṣūl al-fiqh* (Beirut: Dār al-kutub al-ʿilmiyya, 1982), 2 vols.

44 See John Hick, 'A Philosophy of Religious Pluralism' in Paul Badham (ed.), *A John Hick Reader* (London: Palgrave Macmillan, 1990) 161–177.

45 al-Mīrzā Abū al-Qāsim al-Qummī, *al-Qawānīn al-muḥkama fī al-uṣūl al-mutqana* (Qum: Iḥyāʾ al-kutub al-islamiyya, 2010), 3:448–449.

46 *Ibid.*, 448.

47 *Ibid.*, 353.

argues that the nature and the detail of conviction on issues of doctrine such as the immateriality of God, the non-individuation of His attributes, or the modality of resurrection can not be equated to belief in the very existence of God, or the general notion of prophecy and the principle that there is an afterlife.[48] Explicitly incorporating an account of the "false" beliefs of non-Muslims into his framework, he introduces a further distinction in response to those who, like al-Ghazālī, claim that the non-Muslims whom the Prophet fought were largely simple people who were not obstinate in their rejection of true belief. He argues that the application of regulations of unbelief (*kufr*) on peoples in this world does not necessitate their punishment in the Hereafter.[49] Punishment in the Hereafter for erroneous beliefs, despite one's best efforts, would be an act of injustice by God and thus the sincere rejecter of Islam cannot be punished. According to Mīrzā al-Qummī treating an unbeliever with the regulations of unbelief in this world, does not have the same implication, and thus the Prophet may have treated some people as unbelievers in this world despite the possibility of their salvation in the next. As for textual evidence suggesting that the unbelievers are punishable in the hereafter, "the foremost understanding of these (*al-mutabādar minhā*)", according to al-Qummī, is that they only refer to those who are obstinate and wilfully negligent in the attainment of belief.[50] Accordingly, in a manner that resonates with al-Khurasāni's later accommodation of factuality within a fallibility framework at the level of practical Sharīʿa precepts, Mīrza al-Qummī maintains that doctrinal truth is only one, but that eschatological accountability is in accordance with one's understanding of the truth.

5 Conclusion

The foregoing account has introduced the reception of factuality theories of *ijtihād* within modern Uṣūlī Shīʿī thought. In contrast to fallibility theories of *ijtihād*, hard factuality theories give a sense of the *mujtahid*'s own understanding as being determinative of the actuality of that which the *mujtahid* seeks to understand. Imāmī scholars unequivocally rejected this type of theory of *ijtihād*. However, the foregoing analysis has demonstrated that some of the most influential modern Uṣūlī Shīʿa did develop theories that allowed for

48 *Ibid.*, 354.
49 *Ibid.*, 452.
50 *Ibid.*, 452.

mujtahids to be held accountable to the extent of their own understanding irrespective of whether they actually reached the truth or not. Although firmly positioned as fallibility theories, such positions are reconcilable with softer accounts of factuality.

In the case of *ijtihād* with regard to the legislative or practical elements of Sharīʿa, al-Khurāsānī acknowledged that a *mujtahid* is held accountable according to his own understanding. Al-Khurāsānī's teacher, Murtaḍā al-Ansarī, developed a theory of 'instrumental utility' which argued that the very following of fallible and potentially mistaken evidence, has an actual utility that in a sense ensures that every valid *ijtihād* is as good as being correct, even if it is not correct in actuality. Beyond such examples of factuality-type thinking in modern Imāmī thought, the theoretical space for factuality theories amongst Imāmī scholars was argued for by Burūjirdī when he identified the claimed consensus upon fallibility as being of an un-authoritative theological nature and thus not binding on jurisprudential deliberations.

In the author's view, the question of factuality and fallibility holds great relevance to understanding competing tensions and trajectories in the contemporary interpretation of *Sharīʿa* and deserves to be treated as an open question. This apparent epistemic question cuts to the heart of concerns over the nature of God's regulative framework, the scope of *Sharīʿa*, and what products of human understanding can be attributed to God. If factuality theories give a sense of devolving responsibility of legislation to humans, then they should not be seen without recognising that proponents of hard factuality were arguing for their theory only in the context of cases not covered by explicit texts. Accordingly, such theories may be suggestive of concerns to protect the boundaries and integrity of the *Sharīʿa* directly attributable to God, whilst opening the scope for human understanding – as human understanding – beyond such limits. Whereas proponents of fallibility, including those Imāmī thinkers treated in this chapter, emphasise the presumption that there is a precept of God for every instance, and fallible human understanding is deemed the necessary and authoritative means for disclosing this all encompassing normativity of God.

Moving beyond the questions of legal theory, serious appraisal of factuality theories in doctrinal issues may allow for Muslims to better engage with the influential modern philosophical products of thinkers such as Kant, in light of epistemological debates emerging from the Muslim tradition itself. As was the case with factuality in legislative issues, modern Uṣūlī Shīʿī thought has demonstrated some influence of factuality thinking as seen in Mīrza Qummī's account of doctrinal diversity – an account with important implications for contemporary debates on religious plurality.

Bibliography

al-Anṣārī, Murtaḍā, *Farā'id al-uṣūl*. Beirut: Mu'assasat al-Nu'mān, 1991.

al-Baṣrī, Abū al-Ḥasan, *al-Mu'tamid fī uṣūl al-fiqh*. Beirut: Dār al-kutub al-'ilmiyya, 1983.

al-Bihbahānī, Muḥammad Bāqir al-Waḥīd, *al-Fawā'id al-ḥā'iriyya*. Qum: Majma' al-fikr al-islāmī, 2003.

Al-Ghazālī, Abū Ḥāmid Muḥammad ibn Muḥammad, *al-Mustaṣfā min'ilm al-uṣūl*. Beirut: al-Maktabat al-'asrīyya, 2009.

Hick, John, 'A Philosophy of Religious Pluralism' in Paul Badham (ed.) *A John Hick Reader*. London: Palgrave Macmillan, 1990. 161–177.

al-Ḥillī, al-Muḥaqqiq Ja'far bin al-Ḥasan, *Ma'ārij al-uṣūl*. Qum: Muassasāt Āl al-bayt, 1983.

al-Ḥillī, al-'Allāma Jamāl al-Dīn Abū Manṣūr Ḥasan ibn Yūsuf, *Mabādī al-wūṣūl ilā'ilm al-uṣūl*. Beirut: Dār al-aḍwā', 1986.

Kant, Immanuel, 'Critique of Pure Reason' in Paul Guyer and Allen W. Wood (eds.), *Critique of Pure Reason*. Cambridge: Cambridge University press, 1999.

al-Khurāsānī, Muḥammad Kāẓim, *Kifāyat al-uṣūl*. Qum: Majma' al-fikr al-islāmī, 2009.

al-Muntaẓirī, Ḥusayn, *Nihāyat al-uṣūl: taqrīrāt al-Burūjirdī*. Qum: *Nashr tafakkur*, n.d.

al-Qummī, al-Mīrzā Abū al-Qāsim, *al-Qawānīn al-muḥkama fī al-uṣūl al-mutqana*. Qum: Iḥyā' al-kutub al-islamiyya, 2010.

al-Ṣadr, Muḥammad Bāqir, *Durūs fī 'ilm al-uṣūl*. Qum: Markaz al-abḥāth wa al-dirāsāt al-takhaṣṣuṣiyya lil Imām al-Shahīd al-Ṣadr, 2003.

al-Ṭūsī, Abū Ja'far Muḥammad ibn al-Ḥasan, *al-'Udda fī uṣūl al-fiqh*. Qum: Maṭba'a Sattāra, 1996.

Zysow, Aron, *The Economy of Certainty: An Introduction to the Typology of Islamic Legal Theory*. Atlanta: Lockwood Press, 2013.

CHAPTER 2

Reassessing the Pivotal Role of Certainty in Modern Shīʿī Uṣūlī Legal Method: A Case for Accepting a Wider Range of Evidence in the Inference of Sharīʿa Precepts

Hashim Bata

In modern Shīʿī Uṣūlī discourse,[1] the chief function of a jurist (*mujtahid*) is to infer the knowledge of Sharīʿa precepts (*aḥkām al-Sharīʿa*) from evidence that is considered as authoritative (*dalīl al-ḥujja*). A jurist attains the credentials to take part in the inference of Sharīʿa precepts only when he can master a range of Islamic sciences (*ʿulūm al-islāmiyya*). Accordingly, in addition to mastering sciences that specifically study the authenticity, compilation and reliability of the primary sources of Sharīʿa, that is the Quran and the *sunna*[2], a jurist is also required to master theology (*kalām*), logic (*manṭiq*), rules pertaining to Arabic grammar (*naḥw*) and morphology (*ṣarf*), and various historical works of juristic inference (*ijtihād*) of past jurists.[3] As each of these sciences

1 Modern Uṣūlī discourse refers to the period following the works of Shaykh Murtaḍā al-Anṣārī (d. 1864) to the present day. Al-Anṣārī can be described as the founding father of modern Shīʿī *uṣūl al-fiqh*, as he caused radical shifts in juristic discourse by introducing a range of newly developed elements from Muslim philosophy and logic. His works cemented the influence of the Shīʿī Uṣūlī School over the Shīʿī Akhbārī School within Shīʿī seminaries and intellectual circles. On the impact of al-Anṣārī's legal method on his contemporaries, see ʿAbd al-Hādī al-Faḍlī, *Durūs fi uṣūl fiqh al-imāmiyya*, 2 vols. (Beirut: Markaz al-Ghadīr, 2007) 1:81–83; M. Litvak, 'Madrasa and Learning in Nineteenth-Century Najaf and Karbalā'' in R. Brunner, et al (ed.) *The Twelver Shia in the Modern Times: Religious Culture and Political History* (Leiden: Brill, 2001) 71–74. For accounts of the historical origins and the methodological differences between Uṣūlīs and Akhbārīs, see Robert Gleave, *Inevitable Doubt: Two Theories of Shīʿī Jurisprudence* (Leiden: Brill, 2000); idem, *Scripturalist Islam: The History and Doctrines of the Akhbārī Shīʿī School* (Leiden: Brill, 2007); Andrew J. Newman, *The Formative Period of Twelver Shīʿism: Ḥadīth as Discourse between Qum and Baghdad* (Richmond: Curzon, 2000).

2 In the Shīʿī tradition, the term *sunna* refers to the words, actions and tacit endorsements of Prophet Muḥammad and his twelve descendants known as the Imams who are characterised as being *maʿṣūm* (impeccable), as they are unable to commit any mistakes or errors in transmitting knowledge of Sharīʿa precepts.

3 M. Litvak, 'Madrasa and Learning in Nineteenth-Century Najaf and Karbalā'', 105.

© KONINKLIJKE BRILL NV, LEIDEN, 2020 | DOI:10.1163/9789004413948_004

comprise unique subject matters and focus on very specific discussions, the conclusion(s) arrived at within each science forms basic assumptions (*mabādī taṣawwuriyya*) that are taken for granted in the science of legal method (*ʿilm uṣūl al-fiqh*).[4]

Uṣūl al-fiqh is defined as the study of general principles that provide a jurist with a method of 'how' to infer Sharīʿa precepts.[5] For instance, the contemporary Uṣūlī jurist, Muḥammad Bāqir al-Ṣadr (d. 1980), in his *Durūs fi ʿilm al-uṣūl*, compares the role and function of *uṣūl al-fiqh* to logic. He claims that just as logic provides general principles whose application ought to ensure a correct way of thinking and rational deduction, *uṣūl al-fiqh* provides general principles whose application ought to ensure a correct manner of juristic inference of Sharīʿa precepts.[6]

A unique discussion that finds its place within the subject matter (*mawḍūʿ*) or the remit of *uṣūl al-fiqh* relates to what is considered as evidence that can be utilised by a jurist to infer Sharīʿa precepts. Muḥammad Riḍā al-Muẓaffar (d. 1964), whose work entitled *Uṣūl al-fiqh* is widely studied at the intermediary (*suṭūḥ*) level by students training to become jurists in the traditional Shīʿī seminaries of Qum and Najaf, argues that 'anything' that is 'potentially competent'

4 See Muḥammad Riḍā al-Muẓaffar, *Uṣūl al-fiqh*, 2nd ed. 2 vols. (Beirut: Mu'assasat al-ʿilmī li-l Maṭbūʿāt, 1990) 2:10–11.

5 *Ibid.*, 1:5–6; Muḥammad Kāẓim al-Khurāsānī, *Kifāyat al-uṣūl*, 2 vols. (Qum: Majmaʿ al-fikr al-islāmī, 2009) 1:21–29; al-Faḍlī, *Durūs fi uṣūl fiqh al-imāmiyya*, 1:105–109; Muḥammad Bāqir al-Ṣadr, *al-Durūs fi ʿilm al-uṣūl*, 2 vols. (Qum: Mu'assasat al-nashr al-islāmī, 2006) 1:42–43.

6 *Ibid.* Commentators of Islamic legal studies have questioned the Uṣūlī understanding of the role and function of *uṣūl al-fiqh*. Since *uṣūl al-fiqh* historically emerged as an independent science subsequent to works on juristic inference (*fiqh*), commentators render its relevance as merely nominal by claiming that its primary purpose was to systematically justify and defend pre-occurring *sharʿī* precepts and prominent social practices of Muslim societies as opposed to prescribing a systematic framework of how Sharīʿa precepts ought to be inferred. See Joseph Schacht, *An Introduction to Islamic Law* (Oxford: Clarendon Press, 1964) 60; Sherman A. Jackson, 'Fiction and Formalism: Towards a Functional Analysis of *Uṣūl al-Fiqh*', in Bernard G. Weiss (ed.) *Studies in Islamic Legal Theory* (Leiden: Brill, 2002) 178. In this essay, I maintain the stance adopted by modern Uṣūlīs, which is that the discipline of *uṣūl al-fiqh* has relevance, insofar as it prescribes a method by which juristic inferences ought to be derived. The reason why I maintain this is not only because the insider account of modern Uṣūlīs is to consider *uṣūl al-fiqh* to have a prescriptive function, but also because, in the present context, there is a heightened demand on Muslim jurists and scholars to provide authentic responses that are grounded within a familiar tradition to contemporary issues. As past Muslim jurists and scholars for centuries have predominantly inferred Sharīʿa precepts operating within the bounds of traditional *uṣūl al-fiqh* – irrespective of whether the discipline is used as justificatory or prescriptive – Muslim communities are familiar with its style and theoretical rigour and thus find responses generated from the discipline as authentic and authoritative.

in providing knowledge of Sharīʿa precepts or revealing that which God intends must be considered as evidence whose authoritativeness (*ḥujjiyya*) ought to be evaluated within the science of *uṣūl al-fiqh*.[7] By having an inclusive definition of the subject matter of *uṣūl al-fiqh*, al-Muẓaffar creates space for the potential acceptance – subject to evaluation – of a wider range of evidence that a jurist may utilise in his inference of Sharīʿa precepts. Al-Muẓaffar is thus highly critical of his Uṣūlī counterparts who restrict the subject matter of *uṣūl al-fiqh* to the evaluation of *al-uṣūl al-arbaʿa*[8], which refers to the famously accepted fourfold categorisation of independent sources of evidence, namely the textual sources of the Quran and *sunna* and the non-textual sources of *ijmāʿ* (consensus) and *ʿaql* (reason). In accordance with al-Muẓaffar, the subject matter of *uṣūl al-fiqh* should not only include an evaluation of the authoritativeness of the fourfold sources of evidence, but also of the sources of evidence that have historically been rejected by Shīʿī jurists, such as *qiyās* (analogy), *istiḥsān* (juristic preference) and *maṣlaḥa* (public interest). Furthermore, in the spirit of including any evidence that is 'potentially competent' in revealing the knowledge of Sharīʿa precepts, al-Muẓaffar also classifies hermeneutical tools used to interpret the textual sources of the Quran and *sunna* as potential 'evidence' (*dalīl*). Accordingly, al-Muẓaffar, together with other modern Uṣūlīs, not only evaluates the authoritativeness of a wide range of independent sources of evidence, but also the foremost hermeneutical tool of the primacy of apparent meaning (*aṣālat al-ẓuhūr*), which maintains that when there is no valid evidence to suggest otherwise, the apparent meaning (*ẓāhir*) of textual evidence is treated as authoritative.[9]

Despite this theoretical acceptance of a wide range of evidence, it is found that jurists working within the bounds of the modern Uṣūlī framework primarily infer Sharīʿa precepts using textual sources of evidence and rarely refer to

---

7 Al-Muẓaffar, *Uṣūl al-fiqh*, 2:9.

8 For instance, see Mīrzā Abū al-Qāsim al-Qummī, *al-Qawānīn al-muḥkama fi-l uṣūl*, 2 vols. (Beirut: Dār al-Murtaḍā, 2009) 1:47–48.

9 On Uṣūlī argument for the authoritativeness of apparent meaning, and the certainty-bearing evidence presented to corroborate it, see al-Muẓaffar, *Uṣūl al-fiqh*, 2:121–136; Kamāl al-Ḥaydarī, *Uṣūl al-istinbāṭ al-fiqhī: al-Ẓann, Dirāsat fi ḥujjiyyati-hi wa aqsāmi-hi wa aḥkāmi-hi* (Qum: Dār al-Farāqid, 2008) 233–273; al-Faḍlī, *Durūs fi uṣūl al-fiqh al-imāmiyya*, 1:330–335; Hashim Bata, 'Towards the Utility of a Wider Range of Evidence in the Derivation of Sharīʿa Precepts: Paradigm Shift in Contemporary Uṣūlī Epistemology', PhD dissertation, University of Warwick, 2013, 207–208; for a comprehensive study of the Uṣūlī evaluation of a wide range of independent sources of evidence, see al-Muẓaffar, *Uṣūl al-fiqh*, 2:47–177; Muḥammad Taqī al-Ḥakīm, *al-Uṣūl al-ʿāmma fi-l fiqh al-muqārin* (Qum: Muʿāwiniyyat al-thaqāfiyya li-l majmaʿ l-ahl al-Bayt, 1997) 96–98.

non-textual sources. In this essay, I examine the fundamental underpinnings held in the modern discourse of *uṣūl al-fiqh* that determine whether a particular evidence – that is either an independent source or a hermeneutical tool – is authoritative (*ḥujja*). This examination will enable me to demonstrate how modern Uṣūlīs epistemologically justify their preference towards the literal interpretation of textual evidence over a wider range of non-textual evidence. Moreover, I will elucidate that the Uṣūlī presentation of the fundamental underpinnings and the epistemological reasoning given to justify their validity are centred on the pivotal assumption that it is possible to have access to 'certainty' (*qaṭʿ*). By clarifying that the assumption of certainty held by modern Uṣūlīs is derived rationally, as opposed to being a necessary theological article of Shīʿism, I will demonstrate how substituting this assumption with a more justifiable and defensible assumption would impact evidence that a jurist may utilise in his juristic inference (*fiqh*).

1 Fundamental Underpinnings Held in Modern Shīʿī *Uṣūl al-fiqh*

The foremost purpose of an Uṣūlī jurist is to infer Sharīʿa precepts that he attributes to and believes are ordained by God. In doing so, he must take exceptional care in only using evidence that is considered as authoritative (*ḥujja*). Uṣūlī legal method admits that although evidence may be deemed as authoritative, it does *not* necessarily mean that it corresponds in every particular way to the actual Sharīʿa precept that is in the knowledge of God or in the metaphysical objective reality (*wāqiʿ*). Rather, Uṣūlī legal method emphasises the utility of authoritative evidence because it safeguards a jurist from being held accountable in cases where his inference of Sharīʿa precepts does not correspond with the Sharīʿa precepts present in the objective reality. In other words, by acting on the basis of authoritative evidence, a jurist is granted with the right of excusability (*muʿadhdhariyya*) from error even if his inference does not correspond to the objective reality. Meanwhile, by acting contrary to authoritative evidence or by inferring Sharīʿa precepts from non-authoritative evidence, if the Sharīʿa precept does not correspond to the objective reality, then the jurist he would be held accountable (*munajjiziyya*) before God and may be subjected to punishment by God in the Hereafter.[10]

10 See al-Muẓaffar, *Uṣūl al-fiqh*, 2:7–12; al-Ṣadr, *Durūs fī ʿilm al-uṣūl*, 3:35–38; al-Ḥakīm, *Uṣūl al-ʿāmma*, 22; Abū al-Qāsim al-Khūʾī, *Miṣbāḥ al-uṣūl*, transcribed by Sayyid Muḥammad Surūr al-Wāʿiẓ, 2 vols. (Qum: Muʾassasat Imam al-Khūʾī, 2001) 1:14.

One of the major differences between various mainstream Muslim schools of law – whether Sunni or Shia – is the underpinnings that they hold to determine whether evidence is authoritative or not. By making an epistemological distinction between evidence that generates certainty (*qaṭʿ*) and evidence that generates conjecture (*ẓann*), some Muslim schools of law firmly insist on retaining underpinnings that advocate that knowledge of Sharīʿa precepts can only be inferred from evidence that generates certainty, whereas others retain underpinnings that are less firm and thus accept that knowledge of Sharīʿa precepts can be inferred from evidence that generates both certainty or conjecture – or at least a preponderant conjecture (*ghalabat al-ẓann*).[11]

The modern Shīʿī Uṣūlī school holds that evidence is only authoritative if it generates certainty. Any evidence that fails to generate certainty, or generates mere conjecture, is not deemed as authoritative and thus cannot be utilised in the juristic process of inferring Sharīʿa precepts (*ijtihād*). Despite the non-authoritativeness of conjecture, a hallmark of the modern Uṣūlī method is that it admits that there are specific conjectural (*ẓannī*) sources of evidence whose utility has been permitted in the juristic inference by God Himself. The Uṣūlī position on the evidence accepted is based on the following three fundamental underpinnings:

1.1 *First Underpinning: The Non-authoritativeness of Conjecture*

The underpinning of the non-authoritativeness of conjecture can be described as the primary axiom of the Shīʿī legal method. It holds a distinct significance because it was originally constructed in the formative era of the Shīʿī intellectual movement, which at the time was considerably preoccupied with a polemical encounter with mainstream Sunni schools. By claiming that mainstream Sunni schools inferred Sharīʿa precepts using evidence that generated mere conjecture, Shīʿī scholars of the formative era (late 10th and early 11th century CE) believed that such evidence was insufficient in revealing real knowledge of Sharīʿa precepts. Alternatively, they argued that such knowledge could only be inferred from evidence that generated certainty or knowledge (*ʿilm*).[12] Still, to the present day, the underpinning of the non-authoritativeness of conjecture is unwaveringly maintained and reinforced in modern Shīʿī Uṣūlī legal method.

---

11 For a detailed study of the underpinnings held by different Muslim schools, see Aron Zysow, *The Economy of Certainty; An Introduction to the Typology of Islamic Legal Theory* (Atlanta: Lockwood Press, 2013).

12 See Norman Calder, 'Doubt and Prerogative: The Emergence of Imāmī Shīʿī Theory of Ijtihād' in *Studia Islamica*, 70, 1989, 57–65.

Although modern Uṣūlīs present a range of different rational (*ʿaqlī*) and textual (*naqlī*) arguments to establish the non-authoritativeness of conjecture, the most popular (*mashhūr*) argument is based on the rational principle of *qubḥ al-ʿiqāb bi-lā bayān* (blameworthiness of punishment without explication).[13] In accordance with this principle, it is reprehensible for any rational master to punish his or her subordinate or hold them accountable without fully explicating his or her ordinance. As Shīʿa theological thought is centred on moral rationalism,[14] one of the key doctrines upheld by prominent modern Uṣūlīs is that God judges the moral properties of actions in the same way as rational agents, because God is the Chief of all rational agents (*raʾīs al-ʿuqalāʾ*).[15] Therefore, God, as a priori, acts in accordance with the rational principles that are set forth by rational agents. As a result, it is also reprehensible for God – who is accepted as the Master of all rational masters – to punish His subordinates without Him fully explicating their ordinance.

Therefore, by analogising the faculties possessed by God to the faculties possessed by a rational agent, the popular view held amongst modern Uṣūlīs is that God does not expect a jurist to utilise evidence that generates mere conjecture of Sharīʿa precepts in his juristic inference. God's lack of expectation is indeed due to the fact that conjectural evidence does not have the ability to provide full explication of what is in His knowledge. Accordingly, conjectural evidence is not considered as authoritative (*ḥujja*) by modern Uṣūlīs[16] insofar

---

13 The popularity of this opinion is claimed by Kamāl al-Ḥaydarī. See *al-Ẓann*, 27–32.

14 See ʿAllāma al-Ḥillī, *Kashf al-murād fī sharḥ tajrīd al-iʿtiqād: Qism al-ilāhiyyāt* (Beirut, Dār al-Amira, 2006) 279–283; Ali-Reza Bhojani, *Moral Rationalism and Sharīʿa: Independent rationality in modern Shīʿī uṣūl al-fiqh* (New York: Routledge, 2015) 147.

15 See al-Muẓaffar, *Uṣūl al-fiqh*, 1:184–200; Muḥammad Ḥusayn al-Iṣfahānī, *Nihāyat al-dirāya fī sharḥ al-kifāya*, 5 vols. (Beirut: Muʾassasat Ahl al-Bayt, 2008) 3:344; Abū al-Qāsim al-Khūʾī, *Dirāsāt fī ʿilm al-uṣūl*, 4 vols. (Qum: Muʾassasat Dāʾira Maʿārif al-Fiqh al-Islāmī, 1998) 1:285; al-Ḥakīm, *Uṣūl al-ʿāmma*, 276–280; Ṣādiq Ḥusaynī al-Shīrāzī, *Bayān al-uṣūl*, 9 vols. (Qum: Dār al-Ansār, 2006) 1:222; Jaʿfar al-Subḥānī, *al-Wasīṭ fī uṣūl al-fiqh*, 2 vols. (Qum: Ḥawza Imām Ṣādiq, 2009) 2:24–25; Muḥammad Ḥusayn al-Shīrāzī, *al-Wasāʾil ila-l rasāʾil*, 15 vols. (Qum: Muʾassasat al-ʿĀshūrāʾ, 2000) 2:310.

16 See Murtaḍā al-Anṣārī, *Farāʾid al-uṣūl*, 4 vols. (Qum: Majmaʿ al-Fikr al-Islāmī, 1991) 1:105; al-Khurāsānī, *Kifāyat al-uṣūl*, 2:88–97; Ḍiyāʾ al-Dīn al-ʿArāqī, *Minhāj al-uṣūl*, 5 vols. (Beirut: Dār al-Balāgha, 1990) 3:3–16 & 105–110; al-Iṣfahānī, *Nihāyat al-dirāya*, 3:399; al-Muẓaffar, *Uṣūl al-fiqh*, 2:12–19; Muḥammad Ḥusayn al-Naʾīnī, *Ajwad al-taqrīrāt*, transcribed by Abū al-Qāsim al-Khūʾī, 2 vols. (Qum: al-ʿIrfan Press, 1973) 2:106–144; al-Khūʾī, *Miṣbāḥ al-uṣūl*, 1:101–106; Rūḥallāh al-Khumaynī, *Tahdhīb al-uṣūl*, transcribed by Jaʿfar al-Subḥānī, 3 vols. (Qum: Dār al-Fikr, 2003) 2:130; al-Subḥānī, *al-Wasīṭ*, 2:50–52; al-Shīrāzī, *Bayān al-uṣūl*, 1:115–120; Nāṣir Makārim al-Shīrāzī, *Anwār al-uṣūl*, 3 vols. (Qum: Imām ʿAlī Press, 2007) 2:269–273. The only exception to this is Muḥammad Bāqir al-Ṣadr, who claims that it is inaccurate to analogise the mastership possessed by a human master to the mastership possessed by God. Accordingly, al-Ṣadr concludes that in theory (*maqām al-thubūt*) it is

as, for instance, if a jurist infers a Sharīʿa precept from evidence that generates mere conjectural knowledge, and if his inferred precept does not correspond to the precept that is actually in the knowledge of God, the jurist would then be held accountable for following and acting in accordance with an evidence that was never sanctioned by God.

The non-authoritativeness of conjecture has consequently led modern Uṣūlīs to abstain from utilising a wider range of evidence that is otherwise accepted by other non-Shīʿī schools of jurisprudence. Accordingly, the authoritativeness of independent sources of evidence, such as *ʿurf* (social custom), *maṣlaḥa* (public interest), *qiyās* (analogy) and *istiḥsān* (jurist preference) is rejected by modern Uṣūlīs for providing mere 'conjecture' of Sharīʿa precepts that are in the knowledge of God.

1.2 *Second Underpinning: The Authoritativeness of Certainty*

Following on from the first underpinning, the second underpinning up holds that knowledge of Sharīʿa precepts can only be inferred from evidence that generates certainty (*qaṭʿ*), as such evidence can provide full explication or disclosure (*bayān al-tāmm*) of that which is in the knowledge of God. Al-Shaykh Murtaḍā al-Anṣārī (d. 1864), who is described as one of the founding fathers of modern discourse on Shīʿī legal method,[17] claims that it is obligatory (*wājib*) to follow and act in accordance with certainty, as certainty is essentially a path towards the objective reality (*wāqiʿ*).[18] Following al-Anṣārī, modern Uṣūlīs generally agree that certainty is authoritative (*ḥujja*) and that it is obligatory for jurists to utilise evidence that generates certainty in their inference of Sharīʿa precepts;[19] however, they vary on their explanations to establish

possible for God to postulate authoritativeness (*ḥujjiyya*) to conjecture, although in practice (*maqām al-ithbāt*) this would never be the case. For further understanding of al-Ṣadr's theory, see Bata, 'Towards the Utility of a Wider Range of Evidence', 86–95; Muḥammad Hāshimī al-Shāhrūdī, *Buḥūth fī ʿilm al-uṣūl*, 7 vols. (Beirut: Mu'assasat dā'ira maʿārif al-fiqh al-islāmī, 2005) 4:186–187; al-Ṣadr, *Durūs*, 2:35–38; al-Ḥaydarī, *al-Ẓann*, 26–32.

17 See Abdulaziz Abdulhussein Sachedina, *The Just Ruler in Shi'ite Islam: the comprehensive authority of the jurist in Imamite jurisprudence* (New York: Oxford University Press, 1988) 22–23; Kamāl al-Ḥaydarī, *Uṣūl al-istinbāṭ al-fiqhī: al-Qaṭʿ, dirāsat fi ḥujjiyyati-hi wa aqsāmi-hi wa aḥkāmi-hi* (Qum: Dār al-Farāqid, 2006) 22; al-Faḍlī, *Durūs fi-l ʿilm al-uṣūl al-imāmiyya*, 1:101–102.

18 al-Anṣārī, *Farāi'd al-uṣūl*, 1:29.

19 For instance, see al-Khurāsānī, *Kifāyat al-uṣūl*, 2:11; Ḍiyā' al-Dīn al-ʿArāqī, *Minhāj al-uṣūl*, 3:12; al-Iṣfahānī, *Nihāyat al-dirāya*, 3:76–78; al-Na'īnī, *Ajwad al-taqrīrāt*, 2:6–9; Rūḥallāh al-Khumaynī, *Tanqīḥ al-uṣūl*, transcribed by Ḥusayn al-Taqvī al-Ishtihārdī, 4 vols. (Tehran: Mu'assasat Imam al-Khumaynī, 1997) 3:17–18; al-Shīrāzī, *Anwār al-uṣūl*, 2:273–281; al-Shīrāzī, *Bayān al-uṣūl*, 1:22; al-Ḥakīm, *Uṣūl al-ʿāmma*, 25–28; al-Muẓaffar, *Uṣūl al-fiqh*, 2:21; al-Ṣadr, *Durūs*, 2:35–38; al-Khū'ī, *Miṣbāḥ al-uṣūl*, 2:16; al-Ḥaydarī, *al-Qaṭʿ*, 126–128;

authoritativeness (*ḥujjiyya*) and the obligatory nature of following and acting in accordance with certainty. The following are thus the different explanations provided by prominent modern Uṣūlīs:

1. The popular position is primarily attributed to Muḥammad Kāẓim al-Khurāsānī (d. 1911), who claimed that in the realm of jurisprudence the property of authoritativeness is *essential* (*dhātī*), whereby it necessarily correlates to the essence of certainty (*lawāzim al-dhat*).[20] In other words, whenever certainty exists, it exists with the property of authoritativeness. Therefore, the obligation of following and acting in accordance with certainty is intrinsic to its existence.
2. The second position, primarily attributed to Muḥammad Ḥusayn al-Iṣfahānī (d. 1945), is that the property of authoritativeness is *postulated* (*majʿūl*) to the essence of certainty by the convention of rational people (*banāʾ al-ʿuqalāʾ*).[21] This is because the convention popularly comprehends and acknowledges the obligation of following and acting in accordance with certainty, as this regulates and ensures the preservation of a functioning of social structure (*ḥifẓ al-niẓām*).
3. The third position is attributed to Abū al-Qāsim al-Khūʾī (d. 1992), who believed that the property of authoritativeness is *existential* (*amr azalī*), as it is existentially related to the essence of certainty. By this, he means that whenever certainty exists, reason existentially comprehends the praiseworthiness of following and acting in accordance with it and the blameworthiness of failing to do so.[22] As mentioned, in line with the Uṣūlī thought, God also judges the actions considered praiseworthy by rational agents as praiseworthy. This correlation between human and Divine judgment makes it obligatory upon God, the Chief of all rational agents, to enact any action judged as praiseworthy (*ḥasan*) and conversely prohibit the enactment of any action that is judged as blameworthy

---

Muḥammad Isḥāq al-Fayyāḍ, *al-Mabāḥith al-uṣūliyya*, 13 vols. (Qum: Dār al-Huda, 208) 7:22.

20 al-Khurāsānī, *Kifāyat al-uṣūl*, 2:11; al-ʿArāqī, *Minhāj al-uṣūl*, 3:10–11; al-Naʾīnī, *Ajwad al-taqrīrāt*, 2:5; The popularity of the belief within the Uṣūlī school regarding the property of authoritativeness being necessarily correlated to the essence of certainty is expounded by Kamāl al-Ḥaydarī see al-Ḥaydarī, *al-Qaṭʿ*, 128–129; also, al-Naʾīnī, *Ajwad al-taqrīrāt*, 2:6–9; al-Khumaynī, *Tanqīḥ al-uṣūl*, 3:17–18; al-Khūʾī, *Miṣbāḥ al-uṣūl*, 1:15.

21 al-Iṣfahānī, *Nihāyat al-dirāya*, 3:22; in line with al-Iṣfahānī's understanding, al-Muẓaffar categorically states that the obligatory nature (*wujūb*) of following and acting in accordance with *qaṭʿ* is something that is unanimously concurred by the rational people; see al-Muẓaffar, *Uṣūl al-fiqh*, 2:21.

22 Abū al-Qāsim al-Khūʾī, *Mabānī al-istinbāṭ*, commentary by Abū al-Qāsim al-Kawkabī, 4 vols. (Najaf: al-Adāb, n.d.) 1:46

(*qabīḥ*).[23] Therefore, by using the Shīʿī theological understanding of moral rationalism as a basis, al-Khūʾī establishes the obligatory nature of following and acting in accordance with evidence that generates certainty.

4. The fourth position is primarily attributed to Muḥammad Bāqir al-Ṣadr, who claimed that God essentially possesses the absolute *right of obedience* (*ḥaqq al-ṭāʿa*), irrespective of whether He chooses to fully disclose His ordinances or not. Accordingly, al-Ṣadr claims that in both theory (*maqām al-thubūt*) and practice (*maqām al-ithbāt*), if one is to have certainty regarding a particular ordinance of God, then it is obligatory for him/her to follow and act in accordance with it.[24]

Despite the varying explanations proposed by modern Uṣūlīs, it is upheld that certainty is authoritative and that it is obligatory to follow and act in accordance with it. Therefore, if a jurist were to follow and act in accordance with evidence that generates certainty, he is then granted the right of excusability, even if his inference or 'certainty' is contrary to that which is in the knowledge of God. Conversely, if a jurist were to abstain from following and acting in accordance with evidence that generates certainty, God would hold him accountable and may subject him to punishment in the Hereafter. Modern Uṣūlīs claim that sources of evidence that generate certainty and must be utilised in the juristic process of inference are the textual sources of the Quran and a handful of reports (*aḥādīth*) that form the tradition (*sunna*) of the Prophet and Imams. The reason for this is that it is believed that both of these textual sources are widely reported (*mutawātir*), since there is no doubt of any fabrication or error. Although there may be no doubt regarding the authenticity of the widely reported textual sources, their indication or content does not generate certainty, except in instances when there is explicit indication (*naṣṣ*).[25] Therefore, in theory, modern Uṣūlīs accept that it is obligatory for a jurist to utilise any evidence that generates certainty of Sharīʿa precepts. In practice, however, the rigidity held by modern Uṣūlīs in the form of the second underpinning restricts authoritative evidence to textual sources that are widely reported and include content that explicitly indicate Sharīʿa precepts.

---

23 See Bhojani, *Moral Rationalism and Sharīʿa*, 41.

24 Al-Ṣadr, *Durūs*, 2:35–44; al-Shāhrūdī, *Buḥūth fī ʿilm al-uṣūl*, 4:28; al-Ḥaydarī, *al-Qaṭʿ*, 136; This view is also maintained by Muḥammad Isḥāq al-Fayyāḍ (b. 1930). See al-Fayyāḍ, *al-Mabāḥith al-uṣūliyya*, 7:66.

25 See al-Faḍlī, *Durūs fī ʿilm al-uṣūl al-imāmiyya*, 1:326–330.

1.3 *Third Underpinning: The Authoritativeness of Special Conjecture*

Restricting the inference of Sharīʿa precepts to evidence that generates certainty limits the access that a jurist has to the range of evidence that he can utilise. Limited access to evidence implies that it becomes rather difficult for jurists to offer guidance on what Sharīʿa responsibilities (*al-takālīf al-sharʿiyya*) a Shīʿī Muslim is required to enact. Despite this restriction, it is found that in their works of juristic inference (*fiqh*), Uṣūlī jurists largely rely on inferring Sharīʿa precepts from evidence that are *essentially* deemed as conjectural (*ẓannī*). Much of the juristic inference of Sharīʿa precepts within the modern Uṣūlī camp – like most other Muslim schools of jurisprudence – is undertaken using evidence such as isolated reports (*khabar al-wāḥid*) and the primacy of apparent meaning (*aṣālat al-ẓuhūr*). The former is an independent source of evidence that conveys the tradition (*sunna*) of the Prophet and Shīʿī Imams, whereas the latter is a hermeneutical tool that allows a jurist to interpret the indication of an isolated report or any other textual evidence in a particular manner. Uṣūlīs admit that an isolated report generates mere conjecture because there always exists a possibility that it may be fabricated, as its chain of transmission (*sanad*) does not produce certainty (*qaṭʿ*) and that its content (*matan*) may not actually reveal the tradition of the Prophet or the Imams.[26] Uṣūlīs also admit that the hermeneutical principle of the primacy of apparent meaning generates mere conjectural knowledge because although textual evidence is open to several interpretations, in the absence of any valid counter evidence, the apparent meaning of a text is taken as its intended meaning.[27] The question that arises here is that, considering the primary axiom of the Uṣūlī thought regarding the non-authoritativeness of conjecture, how is it possible for Uṣūlī jurists to rely on conjecture to infer Sharīʿa precepts?

In response to this, a hallmark of the modern Uṣūlī thought is that it argues that although a particular source of evidence or hermeneutical principle may generate conjecture, it is excluded from the primary axiom in cases where there is certainty-bearing (*qaṭʿī*) evidence, which indicates that God permits its utility in the juristic process of inferring Sharīʿa precepts. Consequently, the conjectural knowledge of Sharīʿa precepts generated from such evidence is categorised as *special* conjecture (*al-ẓann al-khāṣṣ*). Therefore, in the modern Uṣūlī discourse, evidence that generates special conjecture is on the same epistemic pedestal as evidence that generates certainty, as both are deemed as

---

26 See al-Muẓaffar, *Uṣūl al-fiqh*, 2:61–63; al-Ḥakīm, *Uṣūl al-ʿāmma*, 197–198; al-Faḍlī, *Durūs fi-l ʿilm al-uṣūl al-imāmiyya*, 1:279–282.

27 See al-Muẓaffar, *Uṣūl al-fiqh*, 2:121–135; al-Faḍlī, *Durūs fi ʿilm al-uṣūl al-imāmiyya*, 1:323–365.

being authoritative (*ḥujja*). The only difference is that the latter is popularly described as essentially authoritative, whereas the former is described as accidentally authoritative, as its authoritativeness (*ḥujjiyya*) is postulated by God.[28] In his response to the criticism posed by Shīʿī Akhbārīs, al-Muẓaffar explains that the Uṣūlī position is harmonious with the Shīʿī legal heritage of the non-acceptance of conjecture:

> At this point, the answer to the slander from a group of Akhbārīs towards the Uṣūlīs is apparent, [regarding] them taking some evidence that is specifically conjectural such as the isolated report (*khabar al-wāḥid*) and its likes. They have slandered them for taking recourse to conjecture that does not reveal the truth of a thing.
>
> They have accused the Uṣūlīs of taking recourse to particular conjectures (*ẓūnūn*). However, [in defence of the Uṣūlīs,] they do not take recourse to conjectures because they are conjectural. Rather, they take recourse to them on the basis that their authoritativeness (*ḥujjiyya*) is substantiated with certainty. Thus, taking recourse to them is like taking recourse to certainty (*qaṭʿ*) or assented certainty (*yaqīn*).[29]

Therefore, a jurist belonging to the modern Uṣūlī camp is required to infer Sharīʿa precepts from evidence such as the isolated reports and hermeneutical primacy of apparent meaning, as the special conjecture generated from such evidence is authoritative. Accordingly, he is granted with the right of excusability, even if the indication of such evidence leads to the inference of Sharīʿa precepts that are actually in contrast to those that are in the knowledge of God. Conversely, if a jurist intentionally abstains from utilising evidence that generates special conjecture and, as a result, fails to infer Sharīʿa precepts that are in the knowledge of God, he would then be held accountable and possibly subjected to punishment by God in the Hereafter.

2 The Modern Uṣūlī Textual Dependency

It becomes apparent from the restrictions imposed by the fundamental underpinnings of modern Shīʿī *uṣūl al-fiqh* that a jurist is permitted to infer Sharīʿa precepts only from evidence that generates either certainty or special

28 See al-Ḥaydarī, *al-Qaṭʿ*, 128–129; al-Iṣfahānī, *Nihāyat al-Dirāya*, 3:76–78; al-Naʾīnī, *Ajwad al-taqrīrāt*, 2:6–9; al-Khumaynī, *Tanqīḥ al-uṣūl*, 3:17–18; al-Khūʾī, *Miṣbāḥ al-uṣūl*, 1:14–15.

29 Al-Muẓaffar, *Uṣūl al-fiqh*, 2:16–17.

conjecture. By remaining committed to the primary historical Shīʿī axiom of the non-authoritativeness of conjecture *qua* conjecture, Uṣūlī works on juristic inference (*fiqh*) display a strong dependency upon textual sources of evidence for inferring knowledge of Sharīʿa precepts. Therefore, despite modern Uṣūlīs insisting that the subject matter of *uṣūl al-fiqh* is to examine the authoritativeness of any – or a wide range of – evidence that can potentially disclose knowledge of Sharīʿa precepts, in practice, Sharīʿa precepts are largely – and rather defensively – inferred from the textual sources of the Quran and *sunna* (mainly using isolated reports), and both sources are interpreted using the hermeneutical tool of the primacy of apparent meaning.

This overriding textual dependency displayed by modern Uṣūlīs raises the important question of why Uṣūlīs historically categorised reason within their famous fourfold categorisation of evidence but refrained from utilising it in their juristic process of inferring Sharīʿa precepts?

In response, modern Uṣūlīs theologically maintain that the judgment of reason correlates with the judgment of God, as God is the Chief of all rational agents (*raʾīs al-ʿuqalāʾ*). Accordingly, reason is included as an independent source of evidence alongside the textual evidence of the Quran and *sunna*. However, it is maintained that it is only possible to know that an independent judgment of reason correlates with the judgment of God, if, and when, it generates certainty.[30] For instance, al-Muẓaffar proposes that a method of knowing whether a correlation exists between a rational judgment and the judgment of God with 'certainty' is if there is unanimous concurrence by all rational people on a particular rational judgment. Thus, if all rational people judge that 'justice is good' then it can be said that God, too, agrees and judges that 'justice is good'.[31] Considering the Uṣūlī understanding, it is thus theoretically possible that reason, as an independent source of evidence, can outweigh the apparent indication of the textual sources of the Quran and *sunna*. Nevertheless, in practice, such occurrence is rare, as it is extremely difficult to obtain certainty or unanimous concurrence on any rational judgment. It seems that al-Muẓaffar also accepts this difficulty as in his final analysis of examining the authoritativeness of utilising reason as an independent source of evidence, he concludes that:

> There is no way in which reason (*ʿaql*) can know, without referring [to textual evidence], that its judgment regarding an action is consistent with [the judgment of] the Divine Legislator. The reason for this is clear,

---

30 See Bhojani, *Moral Rationalism and Sharīʿa*, 123–128; al-Muẓaffar, *Uṣūl al-fiqh*, 2:107–118.

31 *Ibid.*, 114–18.

> for indeed the precepts (*aḥkām*) of Allah are dictated (*tawqīfiyya*), and it is not possible to know them [by any other means] except by hearing them from the presenter of the precepts who is approved by the Almighty to deliver them.[32]

In the Uṣūlī thought, the role of certainty is pivotal in determining what evidence is utilised in the juristic inference of Sharīʿa precepts. All three fundamental underpinnings of modern Uṣūlīs are contingent up on the assumption that certainty exists and is accessible. Indeed, if it is found that there is no certainty, or that it is inaccessible, then it would imply that it is impossible to infer Sharīʿa precepts. This is evident because Sharīʿa precepts cannot be inferred from evidence that generates mere conjecture; nor can they be inferred from evidence that supposedly generates special conjecture, as the lack of certainty would imply that there is no certainty-bearing evidence that could substantiate special conjecture. It is thus critical to understand how modern Uṣūlīs justify the assumption of certainty. Is the assumption of certainty considered a necessary theological aspect of the Shīʿī faith, whereby a Shīʿī Muslim is only considered to be one if he or she is to believe in the existence of certainty? Or conversely, is the assumption of certainty rationally derived? If so, is its derivation discussed within the discourse of *uṣūl al-fiqh*? Or is it discussed in another science and thus taken as a basic assumption in *uṣūl al-fiqh*?

3 The Nature of Certainty in Modern *Uṣūl al-Fiqh*

The pivotal role of certainty in the juristic process of inferring Sharīʿa precepts was originally crystallised in the works of Shaykh al-Anṣārī.[33] In his *Farāiʾd al-uṣūl*, al-Anṣārī mentions,

> There is no problem [regarding] the obligatory nature of following certainty and acting upon it if it is existent … for indeed it by itself is a path (*ṭarīq*) towards the objective reality (*al-wāqiʿ*), and its path cannot be affirmed or negated by the Divine Legislator.[34]

32 *Ibid.*, 111.

33 For the lasting influence of Shaykh al-Anṣārī within modern Shīʿī seminaries and intellectual circles, see Bata, 'Towards the Utility of a Wider Range of Evidence', 41–47.

34 al-Anṣārī, *Farāiʾd al-uṣūl*, 1:29.

Although al-Anṣārī concludes that certainty is a path (*ṭarīq*) towards the objective reality or towards knowing what is in the knowledge of God, he does not detail how he arrives at this conclusion. Post-Anṣārī, modern Uṣūlīs have thus taken the onus to explain and defend this stance.

In *Durūs uṣūl al-fiqh al-imāmiyya*, ʿAbd Hādī al-Faḍlī (d. 2013) explains that post-Anṣārī, modern Uṣūlīs seem to be perplexed when it comes to defining certainty (*qaṭʿ*). On the one hand, they accept that certainty is synonymous with *jazm*, which is a psychological state acquired by a person who possesses certainty that creates utmost belief in a particular proposition being true, with no remaining doubt of any contradictory proposition being true. On the other hand, when it comes to discussing the authoritativeness of certainty in the inference of Sharīʿa precepts, post-Anṣārī Uṣūlīs define certainty as being synonymous with *ʿilm* (knowledge) and *yaqīn* (assented certainty).[35]

Al-Faḍlī explains that the reason for this confusion is due to al-Anṣārī's claim that certainty is a 'path (*ṭarīq*) towards the objective reality'. Indeed, if certainty is defined as *jazm*, its potency is then reduced, since such a definition does not support the notion that certainty always corresponds to the objective reality. Thus, although there may be no doubt regarding a particular proposition being true in the mind of an individual, this does not necessarily mean that such a proposition exists in the objective reality or in the knowledge of God.[36] Alternatively, by defining certainty as being synonymous with *ʿilm* and/or *yaqīn*, modern Uṣūlīs remain loyal to al-Anṣārī's claim, as both *ʿilm* and *yaqīn* by their very nature correspond to the objective reality. Therefore, if an individual is to possess certainty regarding a particular proposition, such a proposition then corresponds to the objective reality or to that which is in the knowledge of God.

Muḥammad Ḥusayn al-Iṣfahānī discusses that when al-Anṣārī claims that certainty is the 'path towards the objective reality', he means that it is a 'reflective' path, whereby certainty has the property of reflecting the objective reality. Al-Iṣfahānī explains that similar to the way in which a mirror accurately reflects an object's reflection, certainty accurately reflects the objective reality; therefore, if one is to follow and act in accordance with it, there is no possibility of erring in acquiring knowledge of what is in the knowledge of God.[37] Following al-Iṣfahānī's discussion, modern Uṣūlīs concur that certainty, like knowledge (*ʿilm*), is made up of the essential properties of reflection

35 See al-Faḍlī, *Durūs fi uṣūl al-fiqh al-imāmiyya*, 1:260; also see al-Muẓaffar, *Uṣūl al-fiqh*, 2:20.
36 al-Faḍlī, *Durūs fi uṣūl al-fiqh al-imāmiyya*, 1:260–261.
37 See al-Iṣfahānī, *Nihāyat al-dirāya*, 3:18.

(*ṭarīqiyya*)[38] and/or disclosure (*kashfiyya*); therefore, just as knowledge essentially reflects or discloses the objective reality, so does certainty. Since 'reflection' and/or 'disclosure' are deemed to be essential properties of certainty, they establish and define the very existence of it. In other words, when certainty is created, so are the properties of reflection and/or disclosure, because certainty could never be devoid of these properties and if it were, certainty *qua* certainty would then not be defined as certainty. To clarify this explanation, the existence of certainty can be analogised with the existence of a human being. In Muslim metaphysics, a human being (*insān*) is defined as a rational animal (*ḥaywān nāṭiq*) because when he is created, he is created with the essential properties of rationality (*nāṭiqiyya*) and animality (*ḥaywāniyya*). If the existence of a human being were to be devoid of any of these two properties, then he would no longer be defined as a human being *qua* human being.

Considering this, modern Uṣūlīs explain that when al-Anṣārī claims that the path of certainty 'cannot be negated or affirmed by the Divine Legislator', he means that the property of 'reflection' is an essential property of certainty and cannot be treated as being postulated to the essence of certainty.[39] The distinction between essential properties and postulated properties signifies that the nature of certainty wholly differs to the nature of special conjecture. The reason for this is that the properties of 'reflection' and/or 'disclosure' are essential to the nature of certainty, whereas they have been postulated by God to the nature of special conjecture. The modern Uṣūlī understanding of the nature of certainty is summarised by al-Iṣfahānī, who concludes that:

> Certainty (*qaṭʿ*) is an illuminating pure reality whose nature is of reflection (*ṭarīqiyya*) in that it reflects the objective reality (*wāqiʿ*). It is not that certainty is one thing and its necessary correlatives are another thing; rather [the properties of] disclosure (*kashfiyya*) and reflection (*ṭarīqiyya*) are among the essential properties of certainty itself.[40]

The popular Uṣūlī understanding of the nature of certainty is problematic, for if it is accepted that the properties of reflection and disclosure are essential properties of certainty, this then necessarily implies that certainty always accurately discloses and reflects the objective reality. However, there are many

38 The term *ṭarīqiyya* is literally translated as instrumentality. However, in line with al-Iṣfahānī's explanation, I will translate *ṭarīqiyya* in its technical usage as the property of reflection.

39 See al-Ḥaydarī, *al-Qaṭʿ*, 128–129; al-Iṣfahānī, *Nihāyat al-dirāya*, 3:76–78; al-Na'īnī, *Ajwad al-taqrīrāt*, 2:6–9.

40 Al-Iṣfahānī, *Nihāyat al-dirāya*, 3:18.

instances where something that one believes to be a certain truth does not, in fact, correspond to the objective reality. If so, then, contrary to the popular Uṣūlī claim, certainty by its very nature does not always disclose the objective reality or that which is in the knowledge of God. In *Tahdhīb al-uṣūl*, Sayyid Rūḥullāh al-Khumaynī (d. 1989) lends support to this view by claiming that:

> Those who say that reflection (*ṭarīqiyya*) and disclosure (*kāshifiyya*) are from the essentialities (*dhātiyāt*) of certainty (*qaṭʿ*) and not through the postulation (*jaʿal*) of a postulator (*jāʿil*), [do so] because there cannot be a real synthetic [or composite] postulation (*al-jaʿal al-tālīfī*) between an object and its essentialities… [Therefore,] an object cannot be removed or be separated from its essentialities. [However,] it is found that certainty is sometimes accurate and sometimes inaccurate. Thus, how is it possible to assert that [properties of] reflection and disclosure are amongst the essentialities of certainty? It can be said that this [i.e. disclosure and reflection being essential properties of certainty] is only true from the [subjective] perspective of a person who possess certainty (*qāṭiʿ*).[41]

Al-Khumaynī then describes that in order to explain what al-Anṣārī meant when he stated that certainty is a 'path (*ṭarīq*) towards the objective reality, and its path cannot be affirmed or negated by the Divine Legislator', modern Uṣūlīs have referred to the discourses of philosophy and logic. However, it is clear from al-Khumaynī's criticism that modern Uṣūlīs have not dwelled deep enough as to be able to decipher further implications of their explanation that are purely epistemological in nature. Al-Khumaynī thus reminds us that rather than discussing and debating the nature of certainty, scholars of *uṣūl al-fiqh* should stay within their remit and be solely concerned with establishing its authoritativeness (*ḥujjiyya*) in the inference of Sharīʿa precepts. Accordingly, as opposed to claiming that disclosure and reflection are essential properties of certainty, al-Khumaynī explains that if certainty exists, a rational person who possesses it would follow and act in accordance with it because he or she would believe that their certainty is reflecting or disclosing the objective reality.[42]

Irrespective of al-Khumaynī's criticism, the modern Uṣūlī explanation of the authoritativeness of certainty is contingent upon its nature, since certainty

41 See al-Khumaynī, *Tahdhīb al-uṣūl*, 2:84.

42 *Ibid.*; note that al-Khūʾī also admits that discussions on the nature of certainty are outside the remit of *uṣūl al-fiqh* – see al-Khūʾī, *Miṣbāḥ al-uṣūl*, 1:4.

is only deemed authoritative because of the assumption that, by its very essence, it accurately discloses and reflects the objective reality. Although most modern Uṣūlīs accept this assumption as a fact and do not find it necessary to explain why and how certainty accurately corresponds to the objective reality, Kamāl al-Ḥaydarī, in his work entitled *al-Qaṭʿ*, goes to great lengths to defend the Uṣūlī assumption. By dwelling further into the realm of epistemology, al-Ḥaydarī endeavours to respond to the criticism posed by al-Khumaynī.

Al-Ḥaydarī argues that knowledge possessed within the mind of a human being can either be at the level of concept (*taṣawwur*) or at the level of assent (*taṣdīq*). At the level of concept, the mind comprehends immaterial forms or quiddities of external objects without giving a judgment on their objective reality. Meanwhile, at the level of assent, the mind not only comprehends the immaterial forms or quiddities of external objects but also gives a judgment on their objective reality. Al-Ḥaydarī explains that our minds are only able to comprehend the immaterial form or the quiddity of an external object via sensory organs. Sensory organs, or the faculty of sense perception, allow the mind to extract the immaterial form or the quiddity of an external object, until it is present or imprinted within the mind as a simple concept.[43]

For instance, the mind, via its faculty of sense perception, can comprehend or extract the immaterial form of a 'pen' or the colour 'blue', which exists in the external world or the objective reality, as the immaterial form of both a 'pen' and the colour 'blue' become existent within the mind as simple concepts (*taṣawwur*). It is not possible to assent (*taṣdīq*) or assign a truth value to simple concepts; therefore, one cannot say that the simple concept of a 'pen' that exists in one's mind is accurate or inaccurate, nor can one say that the concept of the colour 'blue' is accurate or inaccurate. Al-Ḥaydarī explains that it is only possible to assent or assign a truth value of accuracy or inaccuracy to simple concepts if the mind is to conjoin simple concepts in the form of propositions.[44] For instance, if the mind was to conjoin the simple concepts of 'pen' and 'blue' and arrive at the proposition that 'the pen is blue', then this proposition can now be assented to, as it is only at this point that it becomes possible for the mind to judge the accuracy or inaccuracy of the proposition against the external world or the objective reality.

Al-Ḥaydarī criticises al-Khumaynī's claim that 'certainty is at times accurate and at other times inaccurate' in corresponding to the objective reality by elucidating that al-Khumaynī fails to make, or overlooks, a distinction between

---

43 See al-Ḥaydarī, *al-Qaṭʿ*, 114–119.

44 *Ibid.*, 119–120.

certainty at the level of the mind's concept and at the level of the mind's assent. According to al-Ḥaydarī, certainty at the level of concept always corresponds to the objective reality, as sense perception is always accurate in comprehending the external world or the objective reality. Al-Ḥaydarī adds that the possibility of misjudgement or inaccuracy of certainty occurs only at the level of assent, when the mind decides to assign a truth value to a comprehended concept. At this point, the mind's faculty of imagination may overpower its faculty of sense perception, resulting in an inaccurate judgment being made with respect to what the mind accurately comprehended.[45] Therefore, al-Ḥaydarī's distinction between concept and assent allows him to defend the mainstream modern Uṣūlī understanding of the nature of certainty, and accordingly lend support to the view that certainty has the essential properties of accurately disclosing and reflecting the objective reality.

4 The Epistemic Assumption of the Infallibility of Sense Perception

Al-Ḥaydarī's defence of the mainstream modern Uṣūlī position regarding the nature of certainty hinges up on the epistemic assumption that sensory organs – or the mind's faculty of sense perception – are always accurate or infallible in comprehending the immaterial forms or quiddities that are existent in the external world or the objective reality. This is a bold claim, given that it is widely accepted that sense perception can at times be deceiving. For instance, a commonly cited example given to demonstrate the fallibility of sense perception is the hypothetical situation where a person cools one hand and warms the other hand and then places both hands in a tub of lukewarm water; the water would feel warm to the cold hand and cold to the warm hand. This example clearly indicates that the faculty of sense perception does not always provide an accurate representation of reality. Al-Ḥaydarī's defence of the Uṣūlī position can thus be described as akin or comparable to the epistemological theory of naïve realism. Advocates of naïve realism believe that sense perception has the capacity to provide direct awareness of the external world or the objective reality.[46] One of the first proponents of naïve realism was Aristotle,

---

45 *Ibid.*, 122–123.

46 On naïve realism, see Lee Braver, *A Thing of This World: A History of Continental Anti-realism* (USA: Northwestern University Press, 2007); Michael Williams, *Unnatural Doubts: Epistemological Realism and the Basis of Scepticism* (UK: Princeton University Press, 1996).

and therefore, it is possible to claim that the naïve realist tendency was introduced within Shīʿī sciences during the 8th/14th century, when aspects of Greek philosophy, in particular Aristotle's formal logic, first appeared in the science of Shīʿī jurisprudence.[47] It is evident from al-Ḥaydarī's argument – or the lack of objection towards al-Ḥaydarī's argument by his Uṣūlī associates – that the Uṣūlī school, until today, continues to uphold or subscribe to a view that is very similar to Aristotelian naïve realism. For instance, the prominent philosopher and Uṣūlī jurist, Muḥammad Ḥusayn al-Ṭabāṭabāʿī (d. 1981), in his deliberation on Muslim metaphysics, draws a link between sense perception and knowledge (*ʿilm*). After explaining that knowledge of the external world is attained through the faculty of sense perception, al-Ṭabāṭabāʿī explains that if one is to deny the accuracy of sense perception, he or she effectively denies the possibility of acquiring any knowledge. He accordingly categorises such a person as a sceptic or a sophist.[48]

However, more recently, philosophers have increasingly rejected naïve realism, arguing instead for a variety of alternative epistemological theories of how the mind acquires knowledge of the external world or the objective reality. For instance, one such theory is that of representative realism. This theory holds that the mind is not able to directly perceive objective reality or the external world through its faculty of sense perception, and perceptions mediated by the sensory organs provide the mind with only ideas or a 'representation' of what may exist in the objective reality. This theory is based on the notion that the mind's faculty of sense perception is in fact fallible; however, instead of taking a sceptical approach and wholly denying the possibility of attaining *any* knowledge of the objective reality, representative realism considers the mind as able to obtain knowledge of the objective reality by constantly interpreting representations that it derives from its faculty of sense perception.[49]

---

47 See Terence H. Irwin, *Aristotle's First Principle* (Oxford: Clarendon, 1988) 26; For the influence of Aristotle's philosophy within the Muslim world and particularly in Islamic jurisprudence see Bata, 'Towards the Utility of a Wider Range of Evidence in the Derivation of Sharīʿa Precepts', 28–29 & 264–265; Majid Fakhry, 'Greek Philosophy: Impact on Islamic Philosophy', in Edward Craig ed. *Routledge Encyclopedia of Philosophy*, 10 vols. (London: Routledge, 1998) 4:155–159; Devin J. Stewart, *Islamic Legal Orthodoxy: Twelver Shiite Responses to the Sunni Legal system* (Salt Lake City: University of Utah Press, 1998) 60.

48 See Muḥammad Ḥusayn al-Ṭabāṭabāʿī, *Bidāyat al-Ḥikma* (Qum: Mu'assasat al-nashr al-islāmī, 2004) 176–178.

49 On representative realism, see Frank Jackson, 'Representative Realism', in Jonathan Dancy *et al* (eds.) *A Companion to Epistemology* (Oxford: Blackwell, 1996) 445–448; George Berkeley, *Principles of Human Knowledge and Three Dialogues* (UK: Oxford University Press, 1996).

As *Uṣūl al-fiqh* is defined as the study of the general principles whose application ensures a correct manner of juristic inference of Sharīʿa precepts, its underpinnings and assumptions must be defensible and justifiable. In light of the overwhelming criticism of naïve realism, it is vital that modern Uṣūlīs are able to provide a stronger defence to justify the authoritativeness of certainty and al-Anṣārī's claim that certainty 'is a path towards the objective reality'. Accordingly, modern Uṣūlīs are faced with the challenge to provide a more robust explanation for how and why sense perception is infallible in comprehending the external world or offer an alternative epistemological theory that proves that certainty exists and is accessible.

A much-debated question that arises at this juncture is whether discussions regarding the existence, nature and accessibility of certainty *qua* certainty should be present in the discourse of *uṣūl al-fiqh*, or whether such discussions ought to be analysed in external sciences – such as philosophy or epistemology – and thus be accepted within the discourse of *uṣūl al-fiqh* as basic assumptions. Prominent post-Anṣārī jurists such as al-Khumaynī and al-Khūʾī have extensively argued that the discussion of the existence and nature of certainty are beyond the scope or subject matter of *uṣūl al-fiqh*.[50]

Nevertheless, by being unable to justify the infallibility of sense perception – at the level of the mind's conception – and by failing to propose an alternative epistemic theory, the modern Uṣūlī bases for the justification of certainty being authoritative is compromised. With this being the case, it is apparent that there is no difference between certainty and conjecture, as both certainty and conjecture are on the same epistemic pedestal, and can potentially fail to accurately reflect the objective reality. The obvious implication of this is that there is no evidence that generates certainty (*qaṭʿ*), nor is there any certainty-bearing (*qaṭʿī*) evidence that can substantiate special conjecture (*ẓann al-khāṣṣ*). Thus, a jurist only has access to evidence that generates conjecture from which he can infer Sharīʿa precepts. Indeed, following or acting in accordance with conjectural knowledge means that a jurist would be acting contrary to the primary axiom of Shīʿī jurisprudence of the non-validity of conjecture *qua* conjecture. Consequently, a jurist is left with two options: either he simply ignores the primary axiom and accepts inferring Sharīʿa precepts from conjectural evidence, or he stays true to the primary axiom and takes a sceptical approach, whereby he discards following and acting in accordance with all Sharīʿa precepts on the basis that he can attain only conjectural knowledge of them.

---

50 See al-Khumaynī, *Tahdhīb al-uṣūl*, 2:84; al-Khūʾī, *Miṣbāḥ al-uṣūl*, 1:3.

5 Pre-Anṣārī Uṣūlī Discourse of Inaccessibility of Certainty

The option of discarding Sharīʿa precepts due to conjectural or ambiguous knowledge seems to have been considered by certain pre-Anṣārī scholars, as it is found that in his *Farāiʾd al-uṣūl*, al-Anṣārī devotes extensive arguments to counter claims of discarding Sharīʿa precepts. Al-Anṣārī explains that it is evident from the works on juristic inference (*fiqh*) of past and present Uṣūlīs that they have indirectly formed a consensus (*ijmāʿ*), which holds that it is impermissible to discard following and acting in accordance with Sharīʿa precepts simply because we only have access to conjectural knowledge of them.[51] Al-Anṣārī points out that the majority of Shīʿī scholars are in fact of the opinion that conjecture (*ẓann*) replaces certainty (*qaṭʿ*) in cases where there is no – or limited – access to knowledge of Sharīʿa precepts. In addition to this, Abū Ḥasan al-Mishkīnī (d. 1939) in his notes on Muḥammad Kāẓim al-Khurāsānī's *Kifāyat al-uṣūl*, makes reference to the 'great teachers' of Shīʿī Islam, such as al-Shaykh al-Ṣadūq (d. 991), al-Muḥaqqiq al-Ḥillī (d. 1277) and al-ʿAllāma al-Ḥillī (d. 1325), who in spite of admitting that the majority of Sharīʿa precepts are unknown, claim that discarding them is akin to exiting from the folds of religion (*khurūj ʿan al-dīn*).[52] In other words, a person would not be considered a Muslim if he or she were to discard following and acting in accordance with Sharīʿa precepts simply because they are unknown, or known through mere conjecture.

Owing to the overwhelming emphasis on the impermissibility of discarding Sharīʿa precepts, prior to al-Anṣārī, various arguments were given by certain pre-modern Uṣūlīs to establish the former option, that is, the authoritativeness of conjecture *qua* conjecture (*ḥujjiyyat al-ẓann al-muṭlaq*).[53] Among such arguments, the most popular one given to establish the authoritativeness of conjecture was the theory or evidence (*dalīl*) of *insidād*. This theory is founded upon the following four fundamental premises (*muqaddimāt*),[54] and it is principally accepted by pre/post-Anṣārī Uṣūlīs that reason would necessarily conclude the authoritativeness of conjecture if all four premises are established or proven:

---

51 al-Anṣārī, *Farāiʾd al-uṣūl*, 1:403–404.

52 Abū Ḥasan al-Mishkīnī, *Kifāyat al-uṣūl maʿa ḥawāshī al-Mishkīnī*, 5 vols. (Qum: Dār Luqmān, 1992) 3:388.

53 See al-Anṣārī, *Farāiʾd al-uṣūl*, 1:367–385; Bata, 'Towards the Utility of a Wider Range of Evidence in the Derivation of Sharīʿa Precepts', 262–301.

54 For a detailed discussion on the fundamental premises of the theory of *insidād*, see *ibid.*, 283–301; al-Anṣārī, *Farāiʾd al-uṣūl*, 1:386–435.

1. The first premise of the theory of *insidād* is that in the current era, a jurist has no access to detailed knowledge of Sharīʿa precepts due to the 'closure of the door of knowledge and substantiated knowledge (*insidād bāb al-ʿilm wa-l ʿilmī*)'. By claiming that the door of knowledge is closed (*insidād bāb al-ʿilm*), proponents of this theory advocate that there is no direct access to acquiring knowledge of Sharīʿa precepts from the Divine Legislator (*shāriʿ*) or his appointed representatives – the Prophet and Shīʿī Imams. Furthermore, together with a lack of direct access to knowledge, there is limited access to and an insufficiency of certainty-bearing (*qaṭʿī*) evidence from which it is possible to infer knowledge of Sharīʿa precepts. By claiming that the door of substantiated knowledge is closed (*insidād bāb al-ʿilmī*), proponents of this theory advocate that there is no certainty-bearing evidence that is able to substantiate evidence that produces conjecture, thereby denying the possibility of there being any evidence that generates special conjecture (*al-ẓann al-khāṣṣ*) whose utility is permitted by God.
2. The second premise is built on the first premise. If it is accepted that a jurist has no access to detailed knowledge of Sharīʿa precepts, it then implies that he is left with mere ambiguous knowledge (*ʿilm ijmālī*). Here, a jurist has overall knowledge that God wants man to live by following and acting in accordance with Sharīʿa precepts; however, knowledge of each individual Sharīʿa precept is ambiguous, as it emanated from evidence that generates mere conjecture (*ẓann*). As mentioned, due to the consensus of Shīʿī jurists and the notion of 'exiting from the folds of religion', the second premise holds that a jurist cannot dissolve ambiguous knowledge by discarding it completely and not accepting such Sharīʿa precepts.
3. The third premise holds that if a jurist cannot discard following and acting in accordance with ambiguous knowledge of Sharīʿa precepts, then he must take a cautious (*iḥtiyāṭ*) approach and follow it for him to be sure that he has fulfilled his duty or responsibility (*taklīf*) towards God. Based on the logical notion of whenever one has conjecture (*ẓann*) of a thing, he or she has doubt (*shakk*) of its opposite, a cautious approach would imply that when a person has ambiguous knowledge, he or she would need to act in accordance with both conjecture and doubt. For example, a jurist knows that *ṣalāt* (prayer) is obligatory; however, he is unsure of whether on Friday afternoon he is required to pray two units of *ṣalāt al-jumuʿā* (Friday congregational prayers) or four-units of *ṣalāt al-ẓuhr* (afternoon prayers). If it is supposed that he has conjecture that he is required to pray two units, then it necessarily follows that he has

doubt that he may be required to pray four units. A cautious approach in this instance would imply that he must pray both the two units and the four units. However, the problem with taking a cautious approach across the entire scope of Sharīʿa precepts is that it would result in a person experiencing hardship (*ḥaraj*) and difficulty (*ʿusr*). Such experience implies that he or she is acting contrary to juristic maxims, which all Shīʿa jurists accept stem from the Divine Legislator, such as 'there is no hardship in religion' (*lā ḥaraj fi-l dīn*) or 'there is no difficulty in religion' (*lā ʿusr fi-l dīn*). In other words, taking a cautious approach and acting in accordance with both conjecture and doubt effectively results in facing hardship and difficulty, which implies going against widely accepted juristic maxims.

4. Since the jurist is neither able to discard acting in accordance with ambiguous knowledge nor take a cautious approach, he thus acts in accordance with ambiguous knowledge. The fourth and final premise of the theory of *insidād* effortlessly concludes that a jurist is left with no option but to follow and act in accordance with conjecture (*ẓann*). Therefore, the fourth premise establishes – by default – that evidence that generates conjecture *qua* conjecture is authoritative (*ḥujja*) and can be utilised in the juristic inference of Sharīʿa precepts. The only exception to this rule is a conjectural evidence that is explicitly abhorred by God due to there being certainty-bearing evidence proving its non-authoritative nature. Accordingly, if by using conjectural evidence a jurist is to infer a Sharīʿa precept that is contrary to that which is in the objective reality, or in the knowledge of God, then he is granted with excusability and cannot be held accountable by God in the Hereafter.

The theory of *insidād* demonstrates that it is possible to overturn the primary axiom of the non-authoritativeness of conjecture in cases where recourse to evidence that generates certainty of Sharīʿa precepts is restricted or inaccessible. Al-Anṣārī and his contemporaries criticised the theory of *insidād* by contending with its first or foundational premise. They argued that the first premise was not entirely correct as the 'door of substantiated knowledge' (*bāb al-ʿilmī*) is open, and this effectively led them to reject the entire theory of *insidād*.[55] As a result, modern Uṣūlīs by and large remain loyal to the primary axiom of the non-authoritativeness of conjecture *qua* conjecture (*al-ẓann al-muṭlaq*) and, alternatively, accept the juristic utility of evidence that generates special conjecture (*al-ẓann al-khāṣṣ*).

55 See *ibid.*, 1:438–552; al-Muẓaffar, *Uṣūl al-fiqh*, 2:27–29; al-Khurāsānī, *Kifāyat al-uṣūl*, 1:68; al-Naʾīnī, *Ajwad al-Taqrīrāt*, 2:19; al-Khumaynī, *Tanqīḥ al-uṣūl*, 3:86; al-Iṣfahānī, *Nihāyat al-dirāya*, 3:259; al-Khūʾī, *Miṣbāḥ al-uṣūl*, 1:109.

At this juncture, it is important to note that amongst the post-Anṣārī jurists, the only exception to this can be found in the works of the highly influential Ayatollah Mūsā Shubayrī al-Zanjānī (b. 1928). Al-Zanjānī criticises the lack of scholastic efforts within esteemed Shīʿī seminaries in discussing the theory of *insidād*. In contrast to the popular modern Uṣūlī belief, al-Zanjānī suggests that al-Anṣārī's argument against the theory of *insidād* in his *Farāʾid al-uṣūl* is unclear and analytically under researched by his contemporaries. Rather, al-Zanjānī argues that that a closer reading of al-Anṣārī's work on juristic inference, entitled *Kitāb al-Makāsib*, gives the impression that he too accepted the theory of *insidād*, and thereby the authoritativeness of conjecture qua conjecture. Following his understanding of al-Anṣārī's view, al-Zanjānī goes through extensive argumentation to prove the validity of the theory of *insidād* and the authoritativeness of conjecture qua conjecture. He argues that there is no certainty-bearing evidence that suggest that conjecture generated from evidence such as isolated reports (*khabar al-wāḥid*) or the hermeneutical primacy of apparent meaning (*aṣālat al-ẓuhūr*) is 'special,' insofar as it has been substantiated and authorised by the Divine Legislator. Instead, he upholds that the authoritativeness of conjecture generated from such forms of evidence can only be substantiated through the theory of *insidād*. Despite admitting to the authoritativeness of conjecture qua conjecture, al-Zanjānī, like pre-Anṣārī Uṣūlīs, admits that there is access to explicit certainty-bearing evidence that clearly indicates that the Divine Legislator abhors the juristic utility of particular types of evidence such as *qiyās*.[56]

---

56 See Mūsā Shubayrī al-Zanjānī, *Insidād az Dīdgāh-i Ayatullah al-ʿUẓmā Shubayrī Zanjānī*, retrieved 12th February 2019, from http://zanjani.net/index.aspx?pid=99&articleid=70681&itemid=70536. Comparably, in the lecture notes (*taqrīr*) of Sayyid ʿAbd al-Ṣāḥib al-Ḥakīm entitled *Muntaqā al-uṣūl*, the late Sayyid Muḥammad Ḥusayn al-Ruwḥanī (d. 1997) gives the impression that he accepts some parts of the theory of *insidād*, however, he does not explicitly mention that he accepts the authoritativeness of conjecture qua conjecture. Instead he suggests that there is no certainty-bearing evidence that substantiates the authoritativeness of isolated reports, as such he accepts that out of precaution (*iḥtiyāṭ*) all isolated reports that signify either prohibitions or obligations are to be accepted as authoritative. Interestingly, both al-Zanjānī and al-Ruwḥanī suggest that if an evidence generates surety (*iṭmʾinān*) or confidence in one's mind then it can be used in the juristic inference of Sharia precepts. However, neither scholar gives further explanation or detail of the epistemic value of surety in relation to certainty and conjecture; what forms of evidence generate surety and how they ought to be utilised in the practical juristic inference of Sharia precepts; and what processes a jurist must undertake to resolve conflict between two mutually conflicting forms of evidence that both generate surety see *Ibid.*; Sayyid Muḥammad Ḥusayn al-Ruwḥanī, *Muntaqā al-uṣūl*, annotated by Sayyid ʿAbd al-Ṣāḥib al-Ḥakīm, 7 vols. (Qum: Office of Ayatollah Sayyid Muḥammad Ḥusayn al-Ruwḥanī, 1992), 4:32–36, 186, 232, 361.

Nevertheless, apart from the eccentric opinion of al-Zanjānī, it seems that the major difference between the pre-Anṣārī and post-Anṣārī Uṣūlī discourse is that the former deems that certainty-bearing evidence that can substantiate conjectural evidence is inaccessible, whereas the latter deems otherwise. A question that arises here is that in the absence of any defensible justification for the existence and nature of certainty, can the modern Uṣūlī school revert to the theory of *insidād* and thus infer Sharīʿa precepts from a wider range of evidence that generates mere conjectural knowledge? As shown, in accordance with the theory of *insidād*, every evidence that can potentially reveal the objective reality or that which is in the knowledge of God is authoritative (*ḥujja*), except evidence that is explicitly abhorred by God via certainty-bearing evidence. Proponents of the theory of *insidād* primarily used it to substantiate the authoritativeness of the isolated report (*al-khabar al-wāḥid*). However, they held that additional evidence used by mainstream Sunni schools of jurisprudence, such as *qiyās* (analogy), *istiḥsān* (juristic preference), *maṣlaḥa* (public interest), *ʿurf* (social custom), etc., could not be substantiated by the theory because there exists certainty-bearing evidence that prohibits the utilisation of such evidence in the juristic inference of Sharīʿa precepts.[57] Therefore, although proponents of *insidād* claim that certainty is mostly inaccessible, they do acknowledge that it exists. Accordingly, simply reverting to the pre-Anṣārī theory of *insidād* does not deal with the epistemic issues that post-Anṣārī modern Uṣūlīs are faced with regarding the existence and nature of certainty.

6 Conclusion

It is clear from what has been discussed that the concept of certainty plays a pivotal role in the modern Shīʿī legal method (*uṣūl al-fiqh*). This is because the fundamental underpinnings held by post-Anṣārī modern Uṣūlīs to determine the authoritativeness (*ḥujjiyya*) of evidence that can be utilised in the juristic process of inferring Sharīʿa precepts, gravitate around the Uṣūlī assumption of the existence of certainty and its authoritative nature. Modern Uṣūlīs thus conclude that a jurist can only infer Sharīʿa precepts from evidence that either generates certainty (*qaṭʿ*) or special conjecture (*al-ẓann al-khāṣṣ*) that is substantiated by a certainty-bearing (*qaṭʿī*) evidence. Thus, the notion of certainty determines – or more precisely, curtails – the range of evidence used to infer knowledge of Sharīʿa precepts. By following and acting in accordance with

57 See al-Anṣārī, *Farāʾid al-uṣūl*, 1:209–211; al-Muẓaffar, *Uṣūl al-fiqh*, 2:28.

evidence that is deemed authoritative (*ḥujja*) a jurist is safeguarded, since he is granted with the right of excusability and protected from accountability, even if his inference of Sharīʿa precepts is contrary to that which is in the objective reality (*wāqiʿ*) or in the knowledge of God.

The authoritativeness of certainty is due to the belief that it, by its very nature or essence, accurately reflects and discloses the objective reality or that which is in the knowledge of God. However, as shown, modern Uṣūlīs have struggled to defend and justify this belief, to the extent that the likes of al-Khumaynī and al-Khūʾī have concluded that discussions pertaining to the nature of certainty fall outside the remit of *uṣūl al-fiqh*. Kamāl al-Ḥaydarī is one of the few modern Uṣūlīs who has taken the arduous task of defending the Uṣūlī position. He argues that at level of the mind's conception, certainty is always accurate in reflecting and disclosing the objective reality or the external world. Al-Ḥaydarī's argument hinges on the epistemic assumption that sensory organs – or the mind's faculty of sense perception – are always accurate or infallible in comprehending immaterial forms or quiddities of external objects. As suggested, al-Ḥaydarī's defence of the Uṣūlī understanding of the nature of certainty is reminiscent of Aristotelian naïve realism, which, due to several compelling objections, has been widely repudiated by a vast number of contemporary philosophers.

As stated, since modern Uṣūlīs explain that the purpose of *uṣūl al-fiqh* is to provide a jurist with a well-justified systematic framework that enables him to infer knowledge of Sharīʿa precepts precisely, it is vital that its fundamental underpinnings are justifiable and defendable. Thus, Uṣūlīs have no choice but to find a newer justification to defend their understanding of the existence and nature of certainty, or conversely, accept an alternative epistemological theory of knowledge as a basic assumption (*mabādiʾ taṣawwuriyya*). The former option seems to be difficult and conceivably outside the remit of *uṣūl al-fiqh*, whereas the latter option of accepting an alternative theory would almost certainly imply accepting an epistemological theory that denies the existence of certainty and, thus, effectively goes against the primary axiom of the non-authoritativeness of conjecture (*ẓann*).

Since the arguments presented by modern Uṣūlīs to establish their legal method are rational or epistemological as opposed to being theological or religiously based, the Shīʿī tradition is not restricted from accepting an alternative epistemological theory of knowledge. Indeed, if an alternative theory that denies the existence, or the accessibility, of certainty is accepted within the Shīʿī tradition, then this substantially impacts the fundamental underpinnings held by modern Uṣūlīs. The denial of certainty means that there is no access to evidence that generates either certainty-bearing or special conjectural knowledge of Sharīʿa precepts; thus, juristic inference of knowledge of Sharīʿa precepts is only possible from evidence that generates mere conjecture. The precedent of acting in accordance with conjecture has previously been established within the Shīʿī tradition by certain pre-Anṣārī jurists who, using the theory of *insidād* and other alternative theories, argued for the authoritativeness of conjecture *qua* conjecture (*ẓann al-muṭlaq*) in the juristic inference of Sharīʿa precepts.[58]

In conclusion, the range of evidence considered as authoritative in the juristic inference of knowledge of Sharīʿa precepts is largely limited to the textual sources due to a precarious conception of certainty held within the modern Uṣūlī school. The question that evidently arises here is that since an Uṣūlī jurist prefers using textual sources of evidence due to an indefensible conception of certainty, is he safeguarded and protected from accountability if his inference is contrary to that which is actually in the knowledge of God?

It can thus be suggested that it is necessary that the current underpinnings held within the discourse of *uṣūl al-fiqh* must be re-evaluated so that a jurist is provided with a defensible and justified systematic framework that enables him to infer knowledge of Sharīʿa precepts precisely. A possible means of achieving this is by introducing a modified theory of *insidād*, which does not rely on an unjustified Aristotelian assumption of knowledge and certainty, but rather is rooted along the lines of contemporary, or more justifiable, findings of epistemology. Owing to the non-existence or non-accessibility of certainty, a modified theory of *insidād* would deem every evidence that potentially reveals knowledge of Sharīʿa precepts as authoritative. Therefore, in addition to the utility of the fourfold categorisation of evidence, a modified theory of *insidād* would also legitimise the juristic utility of historically controversial sources of evidence such as *qiyās* (analogy), *maṣlaḥa* (public interest), *istiḥsān* (juristic preference), *ʿurf* (social custom), etc. Furthermore, it would also legitimise the juristic utility of what may be described as contemporary sources of evidence, such as current findings and discoveries in various areas of natural and social sciences. In addition to legitimising the juristic utility of independent sources of evidence, a modified theory of *insidād* would also impact the hermeneutical tools used to interpret the textual sources such as the Quran and sunna. Accordingly, together with legitimising traditional hermeneutical tools such as

58 As mentioned, although the theory of *insidād* is by and large rejected by post-Anṣārī jurists, an odd exception to this is Ayatollah Mūsā Shubayrī al-Zanjānī, who explicitly backs the theory of *insidād*, and thereby upholds the authoritativeness of conjecture qua conjecture.

the primacy of apparent meaning (*aṣālat al-ẓuhūr*), it would also legitimise the juristic utility of modern hermeneutical tools, which are proposed by Muslims to interpret the Quran and Sunna, such as Fazlur Rahman's (d. 1988) double movement theory[59] or Mahmoud Mohamed Taha's (d. 1985) theory of reversing the concept of abrogation in the Quran.[60]

Although a modified theory of *insidād* may be more epistemologically defensible than the current underpinnings held in modern Uṣūlī legal method, it's premature inauguration within the discourse of Shīʿī jurisprudence can lead to chaos. As a modified theory of *insidād* legitimises the authoritativeness of a wide range of evidence on an equal epistemological pedestal, there always remains a possibility that the indication of a particular evidence conflicts the indication of another. For example, the indication of an isolated report may conflict with the indication of a scientific discovery, or two different hermeneutical tools used to interpret the Quran may give two conflicting indications. Indeed, due to such conflicting indications, a jurist would face great difficulty in his process of inferring Sharīʿa precepts and would be left with no choice but to give preference to an indication that generates more conjecture, or more probability, of a Sharīʿa precept. However, how is it then possible for a jurist to decipher which conflicting evidence generates more conjecture of a Sharīʿa precept? What criteria does a jurist employ to justify a preference towards one particular conjectural evidence over another?

A detailed answer to this question is undoubtedly beyond the scope of this essay. Nevertheless, it can be suggested that the inauguration of a defensible modified theory of *insidād* would require the development of a contemporary discourse of *uṣūl al-fiqh*, that (re)considers, and is founded on, theological insights into deeper questions dealing with the nature of God and the purpose of Sharīʿa and religion. A contemporary discourse of *uṣūl al-fiqh* would accordingly provide a jurist with criteria, or a systemic method of grading levels of conjecture produced from conflicting evidence.

Bibliography

al-Anṣārī, Murtaḍā, *Farāʾid al-uṣūl*, 4 vols. Qum: Majmaʿ al-Fikr al-Islāmī, 1991.
al-ʿArāqī, Ḍiyāʾ al-Dīn, *Minhāj al-uṣūl*, 5 vols. Beirut: Dār al-Balāgha, 1990.

59 See Fazlur Rahman, *Islam and Modernity; Transformation of an intellectual tradition* (Chicago: University of Chicago Press, 1982).

60 See Mahmoud Mohamed Taha, *The Second Message of Islam*, translation and introduction by Abdullahi Ahmed An-Na'im (Syracuse: Syracuse University Press, 1987).

Bata, Hashim, 'Towards the Utility of a Wider Range of Evidence in the Derivation of Sharī'a Precepts: Paradigm Shift in Contemporary Uṣūlī Epistemology', PhD dissertation, University of Warwick, 2013.

Berkeley, George, *Principles of Human Knowledge and Three Dialogues*. UK: Oxford University Press, 1996.

Bhojani, Ali-Reza, *Moral Rationalism and Sharī'a: Independent rationality in modern Shī'ī uṣūl al-fiqh*. New York: Routledge, 2015.

Braver, Lee, *A Thing of This World: A History of Continental Anti-realism*. USA: Northwestern University Press, 2007.

Calder, Norman, 'Doubt and Prerogative: The Emergence of Imāmī Shī'ī Theory of Ijtihād' *Studia Islamica*, 70, 1989, 57–65.

al-Faḍlī, 'Abd al-Hādī, *Durūs fi uṣūl fiqh al-imāmiyya*, 2 vols. Beirut: Markaz al-Ghadīr, 2007.

Fakhry, Majid, 'Greek Philosophy: Impact on Islamic Philosophy', in Edward Craig ed. *Routledge Encyclopedia of Philosophy*, 10 vols. London: Routledge, 1998.

al-Fayyāḍ, Muḥammad Isḥāq, *al-Mabāḥith al-uṣūliyya*, 13 vols. Qum: Dār al-Huda, 208.

Gleave, Robert, *Inevitable Doubt: Two Theories of Shī'ī Jurisprudence*. Leiden: Brill, 2000.

Gleave, Robert, *Scripturalist Islam: The History and Doctrines of the Akhbārī Shī'ī School*. Leiden, Brill, 2007.

al-Ḥakīm, Muḥammad Taqī, *al-Uṣūl al-'āmma fi-l fiqh al-muqārin*. Qum: Mu'āwiniyyat al-thaqāfiyya li-l majma' l-ahl al-Bayt, 1997.

al-Ḥaydarī, Kamāl, *Uṣūl al-istinbāṭ al-fiqhī: al-Qaṭ', dirāsat fi ḥujjiyyati-hi wa aqsāmi-hi wa aḥkāmi-hi*. Qum: Dār al-Farāqid, 2006.

al-Ḥaydarī, Kamāl, *Uṣūl al-istinbāṭ al-fiqhī: al-Ẓann, Dirāsat fi ḥujjiyyati-hi wa aqsāmi-hi wa aḥkāmi-hi*. Qum: Dār al-Farāqid, 2008.

al-Ḥillī, 'Allāma, *Kashf al-murād fi sharḥ tajrīd al-i'tiqād: Qism al-ilāhiyyāt*. Beirut, Dār al-Amira, 2006.

Irwin, Terence H., *Aristotle's First Principle*. Oxford: Clarendon, 1988.

al-Iṣfahānī, Muḥammad Ḥusayn, *Nihāyat al-dirāya fi sharḥ al-kifāya*, 5 vols. Beirut: Mu'assasat Ahl al-Bayt.

Jackson, Frank, 'Representative Realism', in Jonathan Dancy, et al (eds.) *A Companion to Epistemology*. Oxford: Blackwell, 1996.

Jackson, Sherman A., 'Fiction and Formalism: Towards a Functional Analysis of *Uṣūl al-Fiqh*', in Bernard G. Weiss (ed.) *Studies in Islamic Legal Theory*. Leiden: Brill, 2002.

al-Khū'ī, Abū al-Qāsim, *Miṣbāḥ al-uṣūl*, transcribed by Sayyid Muḥammad Surūr al-Wā'iẓ, 2 vols. Qum: Mu'assasat Imam al-Khū'ī, 2001.

al-Khū'ī, Abū al-Qāsim, *Dirāsāt fī 'ilm al-uṣūl*, transcribed by 'Alī Hāshimī al-Shāhrūdī, 4 vols. Qum: Mu'assasat Dā'ira Ma'ārif al-Fiqh al-Islāmī.

al-Khū'ī, Abū al-Qāsim, *Mabānī al-istinbāṭ*, commentary by Abū al-Qāsim al-Kawkabī, 4 vols. Najaf: al-Adāb, n.d.

al-Khumaynī, Rūḥallāh, *Tanqīḥ al-uṣūl*, transcribed by Ḥusayn al-Taqvī al-Ishtihārdī, 4 vols. Tehran: Mu'assasat Imam Khumaynī, 1997.

al-Khumaynī, Rūḥallāh, *Tahdhīb al-uṣūl*, transcribed by Ja'far al-Subḥānī, 3 vols. Qum: Dār al-Fikr, 2003.

al-Khurāsānī, Muḥammad Kāẓim, *Kifāyat al-uṣūl*, 2 vols. Qum: Majma' al-fikr al-Islāmī, 2009.

Litvak, M., 'Madrasa and Learning in Nineteenth-Century Najaf and Karbalā" in R. Brunner, et al (ed.) *The Twelver Shia in the Modern Times: Religious Culture and Political History*. Leiden: Brill, 2001.

al-Mishkīnī, Abū Ḥasan, *Kifāyat al-uṣūl ma'a ḥawāshī al-Mishkīnī*, 5 vols. Qum: Dār Luqmān, 1992.

al-Muẓaffar, Muḥammad Riḍā, *Uṣūl al-fiqh*, 2nd ed. 2 vols. Beirut: Mu'assasat al-'ilmī li-l Maṭbū'āt, 1990.

al-Na'īnī, Muḥammad Ḥusayn, *Ajwad al-taqrīrāt*, transcribed by Abū al-Qāsim al-Khū'ī, 2 vols. Qum: al-'Irfan Press, 1973.

Newman, Andrew J., *The Formative Period of Twelver Shī'ism: Ḥadīth as Discourse between Qum and Baghdad*. Richmond: Curzon, 2000.

al-Qummī, Mīrzā Abū al-Qāsim, *al-Qawānīn al-muḥkama fi-l uṣūl*, 2 vols. Beirut: Dār al-Murtaḍā, 2009.

Rahman, Fazlur, *Islam and Modernity; Transformation of an intellectual tradition*. Chicago: University of Chicago Press, 1982.

al-Ruwḥanī, Sayyid Muḥammad Ḥusayn, *Muntaqā al-uṣūl*, annotated by Sayyid 'Abd al-Ṣāḥib al-Ḥakīm, 7 vols. Qum: Office of Ayatollah Sayyid Muḥammad Ḥusayn Ruwḥanī, 1992.

Sachedina, Abdulaziz Abdulhussein, *The Just Ruler in Shi'ite Islam: the comprehensive authority of the jurist in Imamite jurisprudence*. New York: Oxford University Press, 1988.

al-Ṣadr, Muḥammad Bāqir, *al-Durūs fi 'ilm al-uṣūl*, 2 vols. Qum: Mu'assasat al-nashr al-islāmī, 2006.

Schacht, Joseph, *An Introduction to Islamic Law*. Oxford: Clarendon Press, 1964.

al-Shāhrūdī, Muḥammad Hāshimī, *Buḥūth fī 'ilm al-uṣūl*, 7 vols. Beirut: Mu'assasat dā'ira ma'ārif al-fiqh al-islāmī, 2005.

al-Shīrāzī, Muḥammad Ḥusayn, *al-Wasā'il ila-l rasā'il*, 15 vols. Qum: Mu'assasat al-'āshūrā', 2000.

al-Shīrāzī, Nāṣir Makārim, *Anwār al-uṣūl*, 3 vols. Qum: Imām 'Alī Press, 2007.

al-Shīrāzī, Ṣādiq Ḥusaynī, *Bayān al-uṣūl*, 9 vols. Qum: Dār al-Ansār, 2006.

Stewart, Devin J., *Islamic Legal Orthodoxy: Twelver Shiite Responses to the Sunni Legal system*. Salt Lake City: University of Utah Press, 1998.

al-Subḥānī, Ja'far, *al-Wasīṭ fī uṣūl al-fiqh*, 2 vols. Qum: Ḥawza Imām Ṣādiq, 2009.

al-Ṭabāṭabāʾī, Muḥammad Ḥusayn, *Bidāyat al-Ḥikma*. Qum: Muʾassasat al-nashr al-Islāmī, 2004.

Taha, Mahmoud Mohamed, *The Second Message of Islam*, translation and introduction by Abdullahi Ahmed An-Naʾim. Syracuse: Syracuse University Press, 1987.

Williams, Michael, *Unnatural Doubts: Epistemological Realism and the Basis of Scepticism*. UK: Princeton University Press, 1996.

al-Zanjānī, Mūsā Shubayrī, *Insidād az Dīdgāh-i Ayatullah al-ʿUẓmā Shubayrī Zanjānī*, retrieved 12th February 2019, from http://zanjani.net/index.aspx?pid=99&articleid=70681&itemid=70536.

Zysow, Aron, *The Economy of Certainty; An Introduction to the Typology of Islamic Legal Theory*. Atlanta: Lockwood Press, 2013.

CHAPTER 3

The Role of the Quran in Legal Reasoning (*Ijtihād*): A Shīʿī Perspective

Rahim Nobahar

This chapter discusses the importance and centrality of the Quran in legal reasoning within the dominant Uṣūlī trend of Twelver Shīʿī scholarship. It commences with the discussion of basic assumptions regarding the nature of Quranic revelation that allow for it to be understood and interpreted by jurists. These assumptions are that the Quran is divine in terms of its origin yet revealed in a very normal form of language, and that there has been no substantive alteration to the text of the Quran – what we have in our hands today can be relied upon as that which was revealed to the Prophet Muḥammad. After a brief introduction to Twelver Shīʿī literature dedicated to the legally-relevant verses of the Quran, the chapter moves on to discuss the primacy of the Quran in Shīʿī jurisprudential thought before examining debates over the authoritativeness of employing the apparent meaning of the Quran as actual evidence in legal reasoning. These debates are largely set within a context internal to Shīʿī scholarship where the dominant Uṣūlī position is set against Akhbārī views that seem to limit, if not entirely exclude, the Quran from directly informing legal reasoning. Although the analysis here supports and advocates Uṣūlī claims regarding the central importance of the Quran in legal reasoning, in the concluding comments I do note some problematic features, or limits, to the dominant Uṣūlī method and recognise the value in some of the Akhbārī concerns.

1 The Nature of Quranic Revelation; Divine Speech and Ordinary Language

Discussion on the quality and quantity of revelation has not been a serious concern for jurists (*fuqahā*ʾ). As for the quantity of revelation, it is often acknowledged that the Quran was revealed two times; first it was revealed in its entirety during the night of destiny (*qadr*) into the heart of the Prophet and then it was revealed gradually over twenty three years in response to different

© KONINKLIJKE BRILL NV, LEIDEN, 2020 | DOI:10.1163/9789004413948_005

occasions and circumstances.[1] Some scholars, however, deny this repetition and reject its evidence. According to them the Quran was revealed only once; gradually over time in response to different contexts.[2] Regardless of this debate, it is often accepted that the contexts in which the Quran was revealed can play an important role in bettering the understanding of the message of the Quran in legal issues.

The nature of revelation has principally been conceived of as a matter of theology and philosophy. Some recent jurists have engaged with the question to some extent in their writings on Quranic studies.[3] The dominant trend, even in theology, is that the nature of revelation is not intelligible to ordinary people who have had no experience of revelation.[4] In other words, it is often assumed to be a personal and mysterious experience. According to Muḥammad Ḥusayn al-Ṭabāṭabā'ī (d. 1981), many statements about the nature of revelation raised by scholars are stemming from an unjust comparison between unseen issues (*al-umūr al-ghabiyya*) and material events.[5] Some relevant debate over the nature of revelation has taken place in theology when discussing the attribution of 'Speaker' (*mutakallim*) to God. The importance of such debate is reflected in it often being said that Islamic theology was named *kalām* because of the controversy over the issue of God's speech.[6] Shī'ī theologians often accept that God might have a material voice, despite the fact that God Himself is a completely immaterial entity. For this to happen, of course, they require a medium between such material speech and His immaterial self. They deny spiritual speech (*al-kalām al-nafsī*); a concept associated with Ash'arite theologians.[7] According to Shī'ī scholars it is difficult or even impossible to imagine spiritual speech as something different from God's will and/or knowledge.[8] Sharīf

1 See Muḥammad Ḥusayn al-Ṭabāṭabā'ī, *al-Mīzān fī tafsīr al-Qur'an* (Qum: Mu'assasat maṭbū'āt Ismā'īliyyān, 1973), 18:83.

2 See Ni'matullāh Sālihī NajafĀbādī, 'Nazarīiyeīī dar Bārey-e Keyfiyat-e Nozool-e Quran', *Keyhān-e Andīsheh*. No. 32, (1990) 58–83. For a critique of the idea see Mohammad Hadi Moazzen Jāmi, 'Barrasī-e Nazarīye-e Keyfiyat-e Nozool-e Quran', *Keyhān-e Andīsheh*. No. 37 (1991), 41–55.

3 See for example, Muḥammad Hādī Ma'rifat, *al-Tamhīd fi 'ulūm al-Qur'an* (Qum: Mu'assasat al-Tamhīd, 2007), 1:26.

4 See for example al-Ṭabāṭabā'ī, *al-Mīzān*, 18:83. See also, Muḥammad Husayn al-Ṭabāṭabā'ī, *Quran dar Islam* (Tehran: Dār al-kutub al-islāmiyya, 1974), 149.

5 Al-Ṭabāṭabā'ī, *al-Mīzān*, 15:319.

6 Ḥusayn al-Burūjirdī, *Nihāyat al-uṣūl*, dictated by Ḥusayn 'Alī Montaẓerī (Qum: Dār Tafakkur, 1995), 89.

7 Ḥasan al-Ḥillī, *Kashf al-murād fī sharḥ tajrīd al-i'tiqād* (Qum: Mu'assasat al-nashr al-islāmī, 2012).

8 Al-Burūjirdī, *Nihāyat al-uṣūl*, 90.

al-Murtaḍā (d. 436/965), a great Shīʿī theologian, however, believes that the description of God as speaker is not for any rational reason, but that scholars unanimously accept the description simply because this attribute of God has been mentioned in scriptural (*naqlī*) evidence.[9] Although the attribute has been established by way of a consensus amongst the Muslims, this does not mean that Sharīf al-Murtaḍā denies that God having speech is rationally intelligible, because for Shīʿī theologians something irrational cannot be accepted simply because of scriptural evidence. Rather, as the plain or apparent meaning (*ẓāhir*) of his words suggests, Murtaḍā simply insists that there is no rational reason requiring God to be a speaker; thus differentiating His speech, from other attributes such as His knowledge and power.

When talking about the nature of revelation scholars agree that this spiritual and, at the same time ambiguous, human experience has different levels and is comprised of various hierarchical degrees. Ibn Sīnā (d. 428/1037) and Nasīr al-Dīn al-Ṭūsī (d. 672/1274), for example, agree that the experience of revelation is something gradational.[10] At one level it may simply be a beautiful mode of seeing and hearing, and, at its peak, it may be hearing from God Himself directly.[11] In legal reasoning, however, such a gradational difference in revelation is either rejected[12] or not taken seriously as a potential cause for any variation in approaching different verses of the Quran. Differences that are taken seriously are linguistic, such as the difference between explicit (*naṣṣ*) and apparent (*ẓāhir*) meaning, or circumstantial, such as the differentiation between Meccan and Medinan verses. Such linguistic and circumstantial differences amongst the verses of the Quran are not construed in relating to different grades of a revelation, which for legal purposes is treated as being of a single and undifferentiated nature.

Muḥammad Ḥusayn al-Ṭabāṭabāʾī insists that speech as an act of God, mentioned in Quranic verses like: "*And God talked to Moses*" (4:163) or "*Among the prophets God talked to some of them*" (2:253), is actual speech, but in a particular mode. Speech (*kalām*) from God is not identical to the speech of humans, for God's speech does not rely upon sound coming from the larynx and lips. Also, the indication in God's speech is not of a contractual nature (*iʿtibārī*).

9 ʿAlī ibn al-Ḥusayn al-Mūsawī (Sharīf al-Murtaḍā), *Sharḥ jumal al-ʿilm wal-ʿamal* (Qum: Dār al-uswa, 1994), 89.

10 Ḥusayn ibn ʿAbd Allāh ibn Sīnā, *al-Ishārāt wa al-tanbīhāt* (Qum: Daftar-e nashr-e ketāb, 1983), 3:408–409.

11 Ibid., 409.

12 For further clarification on such a view, see Muḥammadī Zarandī Abū al-Faḍl, *Buḥūth fī tārīkh al-Qurʾān wa ʿulūmihi* (Qum: Muʾassasat al-nashr al-islāmī, 1999), 9.

God, most exalted, is too great to be described by imaginary and contractual claims. However, His speech is real speech in the sense that it has the very effects and function of actual speech and is not a matter of metaphor or simile.[13] Real or actual speech has different levels and grades, and God's speech is a level of real or actual speech, even though it differs from the speech that we use in our human relationships.[14] al-Ṭabāṭabā'ī believes that construing references to God's speech as something metaphorical, or as a simile, would lead to the destruction of all religious concepts and would open the door to interpret them materially.[15] A discussion raised by some contemporary jurists, however, opens the door to considering the nature of the Quran as being the expression of concepts delivered to the heart of the Prophet. Mūsawī Ardabīlī (d. 2016) believed that it is possible that the Quran was sent to the Prophet in two ways: via concept and sense (*mafhūm wa maʿnā*), and through words and letters. Some Quranic verses, according to him, are more compatible with the descent of concepts; while others are more consistent with the descent of letters and words.[16]

In practice, however, despite such philosophical and theological debates, Shīʿī jurists – in their process of juristic inference (*ijtihād*) – treat the word of God as a very ordinary form of language and like any other human text. They apply almost all the typical grammatical and philological rules and principles employed for understanding and interpreting any ordinary, humanly composed text. The structures and methods employed for understanding the Quran in *uṣūl al-fiqh* are categorically based on the assumption that the language of the Quran operates like human language. They do believe that the Quran contains equivocal (*mutashābih*) verses, metaphorical usage (*majāz*) and un-clarified (*mujmal*) concepts. However, those Quranic verses considered to have legal or *Sharʿī* relevance, referred to as *āyāt al-aḥkām*, are generally considered clearer than others, scarcely containing metaphor or allegory. The *āyāt al-aḥkām* might, however, contain some ambiguities, and be un-clarified (*mujmal*) in the sense of lacking the specific details of the precepts being

13 Al-Ṭabāṭabā'ī, *al-Mīzān*, 2:315–316.

14 Ibid., 2:320.

15 Ibid., 2:314.

16 ʿAbd al-Karīm Mūsawī Ardabīlī, *Dar Partow-e Vaḥy* (Qum: Daneshgāh-e Mofīd, 2009), 1:69. For an opinion on the nature of revelation and the impossibility of attributing any word or speech to God, see: Mohammad Mojtahed Shabestarī, at: [http://www.mohammadmojtahedshabestari.com/articles.php], accessed 3rd June 2013. The author, however, has hardly raised any philosophically or theologically convincing arguments to prove his claim. The arguments are mostly linguistic.

referred to by the Quran. This is basically because the Quran is not considered to get deeply involved in the details of laws and legal issues.[17]

One aspect of the assumed normality of Quranic speech is that, despite its divine origin, its language is not considered to be far from the everyday human language of seventh century Arabia. For any text to successfully communicate with its audience requires that it be deeply rooted in the structure of the language, and even the culture of its audience. In fact, it might be impossible for a text not be influenced by the prevalent literature at the time of authorship, irrespective of whether the text is ordinary or divine. It is such thinking that has led to the importance of the notion of intertextuality in modern linguistics where each and every text is considered to be under the influence of previous texts of the same historical and/or geographical context, and any text may influence future texts particularly when considered a prominent piece. Intertextuality might be at the level of words, structures and even the concepts employed. As far as the Quran is concerned, one may find that many expressions, proverbs and phrases are in common with the prevalent literature and language of the recipients of revelation. Similarly, it is quite clear that literature subsequent to the Quran has been deeply influenced by the Quranic text. Notable sources influential in Shīʿī thought, such as the 'The Peak of Eloquence (*Nahj al-Balāgha*)' attributed to Imām ʿAlī and the Ṣaḥīfa *Sajjādīyya* attributed to Imām al-Sajjād, are unsurprisingly and quite obviously imbibed with the literary influence of the Quran. Despite such interactions, the Quran describes itself in several places as the word of God, *not* taken from any other human sources.[18] The Quran quotes the disbelievers as insisting that a particular person was teaching Muḥammad, but the Quran states that this idea is categorically false, attributing the origins of the Quran's revelation to none other than God Himself (16:103).

From what has preceded, we see that the operating assumption is that the Quran is divine on the one hand yet normal, ordinary and intelligible on the other, at one and the same time. The Quran, despite containing some equivocal and ambiguous verses (3:7, 16:44), describes itself as a clear light (*nūr mubīn*)(4:174) and as a criterion (*furqān*) (25:1). It is the human and understandable aspect of the Quran that is assumed as the basis for allowing the Quran to act as a source of inference in juristic issues. Of course the legitimacy of recourse to the Quran is not considered to be without qualifications. One such qualification that implicitly recognises some level of the aforementioned

17 As discussed below, such a view has become an excuse for Shīʿī Akhbārīs to deny the authoritativeness of the Quran as a source for legal issues.

18 For example, see Quran 9:6, 16:103 and 43:4.

intertextuality is the insistence that a considerable level of acquaintance with Arabic language and philology are among the necessary prerequisites to attempting any inference of legal issues from the Quran.

2 The Authenticity of the Quran

The overwhelming majority of Shīʿī scholars believe that there is no substantive alteration (*taḥrīf*) in the text of what is nowadays known among Muslims as the Quran. They divide alterations into two types: conceptual and literal. Conceptual alterations are said to occur when the interpretations of the Quran are deemed unauthoritative or unsound. Normally no one is able to deny the occurrence of such alterations; Shīʿī scholars accept that there has been, and still are, many "false" interpretations of the Quran advocated by "unqualified people".[19] Literal alterations might be of two basic types; additions or omissions. There is overwhelming agreement, almost to the point of consensus that nothing has been added to the text of the Quran. This means that what we now refer to as the Quran is – in its entirety – all Quranic revelation sent down from God to the Prophet Muhammad. However, due to certain historical facts, additions to the Quran in the sense of adding dots and diacritical marks to distinguish letters and syntax, or differences with regard to recitations, is something undeniable and accepted by all.[20]

With regard to omissions, there are some narrations in the compendiums of Shīʿī hadiths suggesting that some revealed verses have been omitted from the Quran that is found in current circulation.[21] Narrations of this type have often been evaluated as weak and unreliable by the dominant Uṣūlī trend amongst Shīʿī scholars. Some suggest that the majority of these narrations were forged by exaggerators (*ghulāt*), a tendency in the Shīʿī community that exaggerates the status and virtues of the infallible Imams, with arguments that include claims of some Quranic verses regarding the virtues of the progeny of the Prophet (*Ahl al-Bayt*) as having been removed from the Quran. It seems that the first controversial Shīʿī text discussing alteration in the Quran is the *Kitāb al-qirāʾāt* of Ahmad b. Muhammad al-Sayyārī. While the book is considered an evidence

19 Abū al-Qāsim al-Khūʾī, *al-Bayān fī tafsīr al-Qurʾān* (Beirut: Dār al-Zahrā, 1975), 1:197.

20 Ibid., 197.

21 *Aḥādīth* of this type, however, are not limited to Shīʿī narrations. To see the same narration in the Sunni traditions, see: ʿAlī al-Kūrānī, *Tadwīn al-Qurʾān* (Qum: Dār al-Qurʾān al-karīm, 1997), 67; also, Muḥammad Hādī Maʿrifat, *Ṣīyanat al-Qurʾān min al-taḥrīf* (Qum: Muʾassasat al-Tamhīd, 2007), 135.

for alteration of Quran in Shīʿa belief,[22] it is almost always marginalized by main stream Shīʿī scholars. Āyatullāh al-Burūjirdī (d. 1961), for example, insists that two-thirds of the *ḥadīths* across the Shīʿī hadith corpus that indicate, implicitly or explicitly, that the Quran has been altered have been narrated through Aḥmad ibn Muḥammad al-Sayyārī, a reporter considered corrupt in belief. A quarter of the hadith are from the *Tafsīr* of Furāt ibn Ibrāhīm al-Kūfī who, according to al-Burūjirdī, is like al-Sayyārī in corruption, weakness and unreliability. Moreover, most of these traditions are disconnected (*mursal*) in their chain of transmission, and therefore, not considered authoritative.[23]

It seems that there were genuine socio-political concerns that may have led to the claim that the Quran had been subject to alterations. Indeed, it seems that the claim is a reaction to the unfortunate treatment of the household of the Prophet (*Ahl al-Bayt*), whom the Shīʿa believe to be the rightful and authoritative commentators of the Quran. The insistence of some non-Shīʿī trends that the Quran is enough for the guidance of the Muslim community, a move perceived as belittling the rightful position of the Imams of the *Ahl al-Bayt*, may have provoked some of the extreme Shīʿa to respond with the claim that in fact, the Quran is not enough, because it has been altered. Employing competing narratives about the compilation and authenticity of the Quran to strengthen claims for leadership of the Muslim community ran both ways. Āyatullāh al-Burūjirdī suggests that on the one hand some extreme Sunnis exaggerated the role of the Caliphs in the compilation of different parts of the Quran,[24] whilst on the other hand some extreme Shīʿa, interested in belittling and criticizing this compilation project, argued that the original Quran was with Imam ʿAlī and that the Caliphs did not do their job properly.[25]

Accordingly, ʿAllāma Ṭabāṭabāʾī, author of what is arguably the most important Quranic commentary of recent generations, argues that a lot of the hadiths suggesting alteration in the Quran are forged.[26] He insisted that the motivation for fabricating hadith and including false traditions within the true legacy of the Prophet and Imams was not limited to legal subjects; and that in fact the motivation to fabricate in creedal issues, the life of previous prophets

22 See for instance Etan Kohlberg and Mohammad Ali Amir-Moezzi, *Revelation and Falsification The Kitāb al-qirāʾāt of Ahmad b. Muhammad al-Sayyārī* (Leiden: Brill, 2009); for a critique of the book and its content see Mohammad Saeed Bahmanpour, 'Book Reviews', *Journal of Shīʿa Islamic Studies*. No. 2 (Spring 2010), Vol. III 231–233.

23 Al-Burūjirdī, *Nihayat al-uṣūl*, 483.

24 Ibid., 483.

25 Ibid., see also Ḥossain Modarresī, 'Early Debates on the Integrity of the Qur'an: A Brief Survey', *Studia Islamica*. No. 77 (1993), 5–39.

26 Al-Ṭabāṭabāʾī, *al-Mīzān*, 12:104–133.

and nations, characteristics of the principle of unity (*tawḥīd*) and 'the last day' is much greater than the motivation to fabricate hadith with regard to legal issues.[27] More importantly, the narrations suggesting alteration in the Quran contradict Quranic verses indicating that the Quran is under the protection of God (15:9), and such a contradiction is enough to make any hadith of this type implausible.[28]

One of the most controversial Shīʿī texts regarding the alteration of the Quran in recent centuries is *Faṣl-al-khiṭāb fī taḥrīf Kitāb Rabb al-arbāb* (The Decisive Discourse regarding the Alteration of the Book of the Lord of lords) by Mīrzā Ḥusayn Nūrī (d. 1902). As the title suggests, the author is certain that the Quran has indeed been altered. In polemical sectarian debates between Shī īs and Sunnis, the status and value of this book, and its credibility amongst Shīʿī scholars, has been greatly exaggerated. While the book has been marginalized and seriously criticized by many Shīʿī scholars, in sectarian debates it is often introduced in a manner suggesting that it is the only book reporting the Shīʿī opinion regarding the status of the Quran. The disdain with which the book is held amongst mainstream Shīʿī scholarship can be seen from the following personal testimony. I was informed by one of my professors who was a direct student of Āyatullāh al-Burūjirdī, arguably the most important Shīʿī religious authority (*marjaʿ*) of his day, that when Āyatullāh al-Burūjirdī came to Qum he spent religious alms to buy copies of Nūrī's book with the sole purpose of destroying them! The book has received many strong, critical and independent refutations including: *Ḥifẓ al-kitāb al-sharīfʿan shubhat al-qawl bi al-taḥrīf* (The Protection of the Noble Book from the Doubt of Alteration) by Muḥammad Ḥusayn Shahristānī, *Kashf al-irtīyābʿan taḥrīf al-kitāb* (Removal of Doubt from the Lack of Alteration of the Book) by Maḥmūd al-Muʿarrab al-Ṭahrānī, *Ṣīyānat al-Qur'ān 'an al-taḥrīf* (The Protection of the Quran from Alteration) by Muḥammad Hādī Maʿrifat,[29] *Tadwīn al-Quran* (Compilation of the Qur'an) by 'Alī al-Kūrānī, and *Ukdhūbat taḥrīf al-Qur'ān bayn al-Shīʿa wa al-Sunna* (The Lie of Alteration of the Quran between Shīʿa and Sunni) by Rasūl Jaʿfarīyān. Moreover, many long discussions have been allocated by Shīʿī scholars to prove the non-alterability of the Quran in general exegetical works such as *Tafsīr ālā' al-Raḥmān* by Muḥammad Jawād Balāghī (d. 1933),[30] *al-Bayān fī*

27 Ibid., 108.

28 Ibid., 115.

29 The book is also translated into Persian under the title of *Maṣūnīyat-e Qur'ān az taḥrīf*, by Muḥammad Shahrābī (Qum: Daftar-e tablīghāt-e islāmī, 1997).

30 Muḥammad Jawād Balāghi, *Tafsīr ālā' al-Raḥmān* (Beirut: Dar iḥyā' al-turāth al-ʿarabī, 1989), 25–29.

tafsīr al-Qur'ān by Abū al-Qāsim al-Khū'ī[31] and *al-Mīzān fī tafsīr al-Qur'ān* by 'Allāma al-Ṭabāṭabā'ī.[32]

3 *Āyāt al-Aḥkām* in Shī'ī Scholarship

Before discussing evidence for the centrality of the Quran in the actual process of legal reasoning within Shī'ī thought, a brief note on the sub-field of Quranic exegesis known as *āyāt al-aḥkām* is well in place. Due to the significant role of the Quran in legal reasoning, Shī'ī scholars started writing on *āyāt al-aḥkām* – verses of the Quran with legal relevance – from as early as the second century Hijri. Muḥammad ibn Sā'īd Kalbī (d. 146/763) and Muqātil ibn Sulaymān (2nd/8th century) who have both been described as Shī'a, are, along with al-Shāfi'ī, reported to have been the foremost scholars in this field.[33] Although the study of the Quranic verses with legal relevance continued to be an important subfield throughout the formative and classical periods of Imāmī Shī'ī legal thought, Quṭb al-Dīn al-Rāwandī (d. 573/1177) offered an explanation as to why independent Shī'ī works on *āyāt al-aḥkām* up to his period were limited in number. In the introduction to his important dedicated treatment of the *āyāt al-aḥkām*, penned under the title *Fiqh al-Qur'ān*, he explains that Imāmī Shī'ī scholars had been largely relying upon the consensus (*ijmā'*) of scholars within the school as the authority (*ḥujja*) in matters of non-rational *Sharī'a* responsibilities (*al-takālīf al-sam'iyya*).[34] As al-Rāwandī notes, this was based on the theory that any consensus of Imāmī scholars contained, and thus revealed, the opinion of the impeccable (*ma'sūm*) Imam and thus acted as a definitive proof.[35] Therefore, there was no need to add to this consensus any evidence from the book of God or other sources. Reference to the Quran and other sources were simply supplementary; an advantage, adding an indicator to another.[36]

As the tradition matured, the number of dedicated works dealing with the *āyāt al-aḥkām* increased. Important examples include *al-Nihāya fī tafsīr khams mi'a āya* by Ibn Mutawwaj al-Baḥrānī (d. 820/1417), *Kanz al-'irfān fī fiqh al-Qur'ān*, by al-Miqdād al-Suyūrī (d. 826/1422), *Zubdat al-bayān fī*

31 al-Khū'ī, *al-Bayān fī tafsīr al-Qur'ān*, 197–235.
32 Al-Ṭabāṭabā'ī, *al-Mīzān*, 12:104–133.
33 Āqā Buzurg Tehrānī, *al-Dharī'a ilā taṣānīf al-shī'a* (Beirut: Dār al-Aḍwā', 1983), 1:40.
34 Quṭb al-Dīn al-Rāwandī, *Fiqh al-Qur'ān* (Qum: Maktabat Āyatullāh Mar'ashī Najafī, 1985), 1:4.
35 Ibid.
36 Ibid.

aḥkām al-Qur'ān by Mawlā Aḥmad Ardabīlī (d. 1101/1689.), *Āyāt al-aḥkām* by Muḥammad Ḥusaynī Astarābādī (d. 1028/1618), *Masālik al-afḥām ilā āyāt al-aḥkām* by al-Fāḍil al-Jawād al-Kāẓimī (d. 1065/1654) and *Fiqh al-Qur'ān* by Muḥammad Yazdī (b. 1310/1931).[37] In addition to independently written, dedicated treatments of the *āyāt al-aḥkām*, many Shīʿī commentators paid attention to the legal aspects of Quranic verses in their general exegeses. Shaykh Tūsī in *al-Tibyān*, Ṭabrisī in *Majmaʿ al-bayān fī tafsīr al-Qur'ān*, Ṭabāṭabā'ī in *al-Mīzān fī tafsīr al-Qur'ān*, Muḥammad Ṣādiqī Tehrānī in *al-Furqān fī tafsīr al-Qur'ān* and ʿAbd Allāh Jawādī Āmulī in *Tafsīr al-Tasnīm*, are just a few examples of those who have made important contributions in this regard. In turn, Persian writings on *āyāt al-āḥkām* also constitute a long list of valuable works.[38]

4 The Primacy of the Quran in the System of Jurisprudential Reasoning

Understanding the position that jurists have given the Quran, compared with other sources such as Sunna, *ʿaql* (reason) and *ijmāʿ* (specific juristic consensus), is critical in determining the role of the Quran in the particular method of legal reasoning adopted by each jurist or school of *fiqh*. In light of what has preceded, it should be clear that the dominant trend within Shīʿī thought has always regarded the Quran as a reliable and pivotal source. In what follows, it will be argued that despite some internal tension, the dominant Uṣūlī trend in Shīʿī scholarship is justified in listing the Quran as their primary source of legal reasoning, giving it supremacy over any other source.

The jurisprudential supremacy of the Quran can be seen in scholars of *uṣūl al-fiqh* invoking the Quran to prove,[39] or to support, the credibility and authority of all other sources of *Sharīʿa* knowledge. This is most notable in the case of the second major source of *Sharīʿa*; the Sunna – understood in Shīʿī

37 For a longer list of *Āyāt al-aḥkām*, see ʿAbbās, *al-Tarjumān*, in his preamble on *Fiqh al-Qur'ān* by Muḥammad Yazdī (Qum: Ismāʿīlīyyān, 2007), 1:7–18; Muḥammad ʿAlī Ayāzī, *Feqh pazhūhī-e Qur'ani* (Qum: Būstān-e Ketāb, 2007); Muḥammad Fākir Meibodī, *Bāzpazhūhī-e āyāt-e feqhī-e Qur'ān* (Qum, Pazhūheshgāh-e farhang va andīsheh-e eslāmī, 2007), 377–382.

38 Muḥammad Taqī Fakhlaʿī, 'Jostārī dar tārīkh-e tafsīr-e āyāt al-aḥkām', *Majalleh-e Moṭāleʿāte Eslāmī*. No. 49 & 50, (2000) 374–393.

39 Reason (*ʿaql*) is, of course, an exception, although Quranic references are employed to support its authority. The authority of reason is described within the Uṣūlī tradition as essential, nothing can prove the authority of something that is authoritative *per se*; see Muḥammad Kāẓim al-Khurāsānī, *Kifāyat al-usūl* (Qum: Mu'assasat al-nashr al-islāmī, 2006), 2:233.

thought to be the words, actions and tacit approvals of the Prophet and the infallible Imams from his household. The authority of the Sunna is often proved by recourse to Quranic verses like the 'Role Model Verse' (*āyat al-uswa*) (33:21) which describes the Prophet Muḥammad as a beautiful example. Many discussions about Quranic verses have been undertaken to determine whether or not an isolated report (*khabar wāhid*) regarding an element of the Sunna is credible or not.[40] The Quran is not only employed within justifications for the authoritativeness (*ḥujjiyya*) of other sources of evidence, it is also used to undermine the credibility of some sources of evidence deemed unacceptable. For instance, the credibility of almost every evidence or proof that is deemed to yield a less-than-certain conjecture (*ẓann*) has been rejected on the basis of Quranic verses such as (10:36).[41] So whilst the Quran is employed by jurists to justify recourse to some evidence and restrict recourse to other forms of evidence, the Quran itself has been considered a source of *Sharīʿa* without the necessity of referring to any other proofs.

Beyond the role of the Quran in establishing the authority of the Sunna per se, the Uṣūlī tradition sees the Quran as a decisive criterion for determining the credibility of dubious hadith. A hadith that contradicts the Quran is in no way acceptable. The idea stems from many reliable hadith.[42] There are also epistemic grounds for holding that hadith have no capacity to contradict the Quran, because from the issuance point of view, the Quran is certain (*qaṭʿī*) and the vast majority of hadith are considered conjectural (*zannī*). In addition to a literal or atomistic consistency, a 'spiritual consistency' (*al-mūwāfaqa al-rūḥīyya*) with the entirety of the Quranic message has been deemed a necessary test of the validity of hadith relaying Sunna.[43] According to this view, when evaluating the content of a hadith with respect to the Quran, it does not suffice to determine that its content does not contradict a particular part of the Quran concerning the same subject. Rather, the jurist must make sure that the hadith is consistent with the whole spirit and core message of the Quran.[44]

---

40 Murtaḍā Anṣārī, *Farā'id al-uṣūl* (Qum: Majmaʿ al-fikr al-islāmī,, 2003), 1:255–310.

41 See for example, Anṣārī, *Farā'id al-uṣūl*, 1:125; Muḥammad Riḍā Muẓaffar, *Uṣūl al-fiqh* (Qum: Mu'assasat al-nashr al-islāmī, 2002), 2:18.

42 Muḥammad al-Ḥurr al-ʿĀmilī, *Wasā'il al-Shīʿa ilā tafṣīl masā'il al-sharīʿa* (Tehran: Dār al-kutub al-islamiyya, 2007), 18:75–89.

43 ʿAlī al-Ḥusaynī al-Sīstānī, *al-Rāfid fī ʿilm al-uṣūl*, transcribed by Munīr Qaṭīfī (Qum: Maktabat Āyatullāh Sīstānī, 1994), 12.

44 This should make plain the complexity of *ijtihād*. A great deal of general knowledge and a holistic approach are needed for a sound and comprehensive *ijtihād*. It is not only a matter of technicality and an art to be compared with engineering, as has recently been argued. In other words a jurist is more than a simple technician. He, ideally, should be fully aware of the spirit of the Quran and general approaches of the *Sharīʿa*.

Consistency with the Quran is also relevant in the process of identifying and reconciling apparent or actual conflicts between different hadiths. In the case of two apparently conflicting hadiths of soundly-transmitted (*ṣaḥīḥ*) chains, when neither is considered to contradict the explicit sense of the Quran, jurists consider consistency with the apparent (*ẓāhir*) sense of the Quran as a preferential factor (*murrajjiḥ*). Having said this, the ranking of 'consistency with the Quran' amongst the other preferential factors considered by jurists within their system of reconciliation is not so clear. This system of reconciliation can be described as containing four distinct categories of preferential factors. The category usually referred to first deals with the denotation (*dalāla*), or indication, of any conflicting evidence (*al-murajjiḥāt al-dalāliyya*). When a hadith is, for example, clearer in its denotation because of its being explicit (*naṣṣ*) whilst the other is only apparent (*ẓāhir*), the explicit one would be given priority over the other because of its strength of denotation. The second category of preferential factors are those that relate to the strength of the chain (*sanad*) of reporters that narrate the hadiths in question. So for example, when the transmitters of one hadith are deemed more reliable than those of another conflicting hadith, the preference would be given to the one reported by a more reliable chain. The third kind of preferential factor is that which pertains to the perspective (*jihat*) from which the two conflicting hadiths have been issued. When, for example, the possibility of dissimulation (*taqīyya*) – dispensation from the requirements of religious teachings under a serious threat – exists in one, but not in the other, preference would be given to the latter. The fourth category of preferential factors relates to the content of the conflicting evidence, and it is here that consistency with the Quran, and for some, consistency with the well-known opinion amongst the scholars, becomes relevant. Shīʿī scholars are, of course, not all agreed upon the order of application of these preferential factors. The majority of them, however, as Anṣārī reports, agree that preferential factors concerning denotation take priority over others as far as they are being applied within the framework of reasonable and acceptable denotative resolution.[45] This is because room for accepting two seemingly conflicting pieces of evidence by construing them together in a reasonable way, leaves no justifiable way to reject either one or both of them.

In addition to the Quran being a basis for the authority of other sources of juristic evidence and its relevance in reconciling hadith literature, its supremacy amongst the sources can also be seen in Shīʿī jurists' perspectives on

---

45 Anṣārī, *Farāʾid al-uṣūl*, 3:80.

abrogation (*naskh*).[46] It is generally argued that a part of the Quran can only be abrogated by another part of the Quran, with some Shīʿī jurists being very minimalistic in their acceptance of even this type of abrogation.[47] No other evidence is believed to have the authority to abrogate any part of the Quran, not even hadith considered extensively transmitted (*mutawātir*). The importance of preserving the centrality of the Quran within the mindset of Shīʿī jurists is also demonstrated in their arguments for this position – arguments that include the claim that the possibility of abrogating the Quran by hadith would open the door for evil people to destroy the Quran, the very basis of Islam and the miracle of the Prophet, and hence it is a possibility that must be rejected.[48] Some Shīʿī jurists, however, do believe that an extensively transmitted (*mutawātir*) hadith protected by the consensus of the Muslim community can abrogate a Quranic verse.[49] Similarly, the consensus of scholars (*ijmāʿ*) might abrogate, according to some, Quranic teachings when the consensus represents the view of the infallible, such that the abrogation can be attributed, ultimately, to the infallible himself.[50] But consensus in its Sunni sense, i.e. the consensus of jurists *per se*, has no authority according to Shīʿī jurists' view.[51]

The discussion of the supremacy of the Quran in Uṣūlī Shīʿī thought does, however, need to acknowledge and explain why Shīʿī scholars allow for the particularization (*takhṣīṣ*) of general verses or the qualification (*taqyīd*) of unconditional Quranic verses by hadith – subject to the hadith reaching the requirements of authoritative evidence. It is believed that the Prophet, and in the Shīʿī tradition also his infallible successors, are the interpreters of the Quran, and that particularization and qualification are examples of interpretation and clarification. Accordingly, sound hadith, even an isolated single report (*khabar wāhid*), relaying Sunna are considered capable of particularizing and qualifying the generality and/or unqualified nature of any Quranic verse. The argument is that the authoritativeness (*ḥujjiyya*) of a single report has its own proofs – including some Quranic verses, none of which are more important than (6:49), referred to as the 'verse of news (*āyat al-nabaʾ*)'.[52] The

46 For a discussion on different aspects of *naskh* from a Shīʿī perspective, see Maʿrifat, *al-Tamhīd fī ʿulūm al-Qurʾān*, 2:268.

47 See Abū al-Qāsim al-Khūʾī, *al-Bayān fī tafsīr al-Qurʾān*, 286.

48 Muḥammad Taqī al-Ḥakīm, *al-Uṣūl al-ʿāmma li al-fiqh al-muqāran* (Qum: Muʾassasat Āl al-Bayt, 1979), 247.

49 See Maʿrifat, *al-Tamhīd fī ʿulūm al-Qurʾān*, 2:293.

50 See Abū al-Qāsim al-Khūʾī, *al-Bayān fī tafsīr al-Qurʾān*, 286.

51 Anṣārī, *Farāʾid al-uṣūl*, 1:224.

52 This dominant position has, however, not been entirely unchallenged from within the Shīʿī juristic tradition such that a denial of this position, either theoretically or both theoretically and practically, has been attributed to some great jurists such as Muhaqqiq

extensively-transmitted reports indicating that no hadith contradicting the Quran can be accepted, are not seen as covering cases of possible particularization or qualification; because when the relation between two pieces of evidence is generality and particularity, they are not reasonably construed as contradictory.[53] In the realm of legality, it is very common to issue a general law and then particularize or qualify it. Due to the great role given to the Prophet, and his successors, as being infallible in law-making and the theological assumption of a concomitance between the Quran and the purified household of the Prophet (*ʿitra*), Shīʿī jurists easily accept that a sound hadith can particularize or qualify Quranic verses. However, due to the aforementioned primacy of the Quran within the hierarchy of sources, this does not mean that every single hadith, even though authoritative and reliable for inferring detailed legal issues, should be considered capable to particularize the generality or unconditionality of a Quranic verse.[54]

5 The Debate between *Akhbārīs* and *Uṣūlīs* on the Authoritativeness of the Quran as Evidence in Legal Reasoning

Uṣūlī jurists argue for employing the Quran in legal reasoning, not just as a basis for the authority of other sources, but also as evidence in its own right. This is in contrast to some from within the Akhbārī trend who argued that the Quran was only authoritative for, or through, the Prophet and Imams. Uṣūlī jurists tend to draw distinctions between different categories of verses, creating room for the employment of at least some of these categories by suitably trained *mujtahids* within the process of legal reasoning.

A four-fold categorisation of Quranic verses suggested by al-Shaykh al-Ṭūsī in the preamble of his Quranic exegesis *al-Tibyān* continues to be instructive for many Uṣūlī jurists. The first category are those verses whose meaning only God knows, and no one is allowed to try to take on the responsibility of explaining these, nor will an understanding of them ever be reached. Second are those that are so clear and evident that their literal sense and outward meaning are consistent with the intended content, such that whoever is familiar with

al-Ḥillī (d. 676). See Abū al-Qāsim Kalāntarī Tehrānī, *Maṭāriḥ al-anẓār: Taqrīrāt al-Sheikh Murtaḍā Anṣārī* (Qum: Majmaʿ al-fikr al-islāmī, 2007), 2:219.

53 See, for instance, Mīrzā Ḥusayn Nāʾinī, *Fawāʾid al-uṣūl* (Qum: Muʾassasat al-nashr al-islāmī, 1984), 1:561.

54 For examples of the criterion necessary for deeming that an authoritative hadith is capable of particularizing the Quran, see Muḥammad Ḥusayn Beheshtī, *Ravesh-e bardāsht az Quran* (Tehran: Rowzaneh Publications, 2011), 39.

the language of the Quran is capable of understanding them. The third category is of those that are undetailed (*mujmal*) and the literal apparent meaning does not indicate the detailed intended sense (*mufassal*). And the fourth category are those that include words that are homonymous (*mushtarak*), with more than one possible meaning. According to al-Ṭūsī, when it comes to such verses no one is allowed to say that God has meant this or that, unless based on authoritative reports from the Prophet or infallible Imams, or unless based on other sound evidence.[55] According to such distinctions, Uṣūlis argue that there are verses within the Quran that can be referred to directly within the actual process of legal reasoning, and from looking at the index of almost any Shīʿī work of *fiqh* it is obvious that many Quranic verses have been referred to within jurisprudential and juristic discourse.

Some arguments for this dominant Uṣūlī approach stem from the Quran itself. It is argued, for example, that God himself gave the Quran such credibility by introducing the Quran as a source and means for conflict resolution within the Muslim community (4:59).[56] Reference to the Quran to determine solutions for legal disputes can be seen as an instance of this imperative. Furthermore, God condemns those who research the content of equivocal verses (*mutashābihāt*) and not the univocal (*muḥkam*) ones (3:6), implying that reference to the univocal verses is legitimate. God strongly commands people to contemplate upon the content of the Quran and strongly blames those who ignore such reflection (47:24). This implies that the results of such contemplation and reflection must be credible. As noted earlier, the Quran also describes itself as being revealed in clear Arabic language (16:103). Many Shīʿī scholars have followed al-Shaykh al-Ṭūsī's treatment of the question, which goes beyond the above four-fold categorisation of verses, directly arguing in favour of the authoritativeness of the plain meaning of the Quran by way of both rational and scriptural evidence. According to al-Ṭūsī, since God describes His book as 'clear' and 'evident', strongly commanding people to contemplate upon it, then it makes no sense to believe that the Quran in its entirety is ambiguous and can only be understood through hadith received from the infallibles.[57]

Uṣūlī scholars, again in line with Shaykh Ṭūṣī's approach, also refer to many hadith traditions that assume the Quran to be a source of legal reasoning. For example, the famous hadith from the Prophet known as the 'tradition of the two weighty things (*ḥadīth al-thaqalayn*) states: "I have left among you two

55 Abū Jaʿfar Muḥammad ibn al-Ḥasan al-Ṭūsī, *Tafsīr al-Tibyān al-jāmiʿ lil-ʿUlūm al-Qurʾān*, (Qum: Muʾassasat al-nashr al-islāmī, 2006), 1:4.

56 Muḥammad al-ʿĀmilī, *al-Fawāʾid al-Ṭūsiyya* (Qum: Maktab al-Maḥallātī, 2002), 163.

57 al-Tūsī, *al-Tibyān*, 1:4–7.

weighty things; God's book and my household."[58] As referred to earlier, there are also a large number of very well known hadith suggesting that when there is doubt in the authority of a hadith, its content should be checked against the Quran. These numerous hadith, known as the hadiths of comparison (*akhbār al-ʿarḍ*), must assume that the Quran itself is understandable. Likewise numerous hadith condemn those who stray from behaving according to Quranic principles – principles that undoubtedly include reference to the regulative and legal issues of *Sharīʿa*. In fact it has been argued that if the Quran had not been a source for legal issues, then there would not have been any way to resolve disagreements amongst the Muslim community at large, and consequently the door would have been open for every form of bad innovation (*bidʿa*) within the system of Islamic laws and precepts.[59]

Hadith literature also suggests that the Imams themselves taught and encouraged their companions to infer legal issues from the Quran. In a hadith narrated by ʿAbd al-Aʿlā Mawlā Āl al-Sām, Imām al-Bāqir is asked about the proper method for ritual purification (*wuḍūʾ*) when a finger is bandaged due to injury. The Imam is reported to have said, 'Questions of this type can be understood from the plain meaning of God's book. God says: "*God made no hardship in religion*" (22:78). Touch the bandage and that is enough.'[60]

Akhbārī Shīʿī jurists, however, believe that the apparent meaning (*ẓāhir*) of the Quran cannot be relied upon as a source for inferring *Sharīʿa* precepts. Uṣūlīs try to argue that such views regarding the non-authoritativeness of the apparent meaning of the Quran have only emerged in recent centuries, and that the Uṣūlī position has the historic precedent – as demonstrated in their continued reliance on the likes of Shaykh Ṭūṣī within these debates. Yet the Akhbārīs also argue that they are advocating the historically authentic approach. They claim that it is their method of reliance upon the hadith tradition, to the exclusion of direct reference to the Quran, that was the method prevalent amongst the early well-known Shīʿī scholars, citing the works of Kulaynī (d. 328–329/941), Ṣadūq (d. 381/991), his father, Ibn Bābawayh (d. 327/939), and others as support for their claim.[61]

---

58 Muḥammad ibn ʿIsā al-Tirmidhī, *Jāmiʿ al-Tirmidhī* (Rīyāḍ: Dār al-Salām, 1999), 859, hadith no. 3788.

59 ʿĀmilī, *al-Fawāʾid al-Ṭūsiyya*, 165.

60 Muḥammad ibn Yaʿqūb al-Kulaynī, *al-Kāfī* (Tehran: Dār al-kutub al-islāmiyya, 2008), 3:33. For further clarification on the way that the infallible Imams treated the Qur'an see: Hammūd al-Arājī Sattār Jabbār, *Taʾsīs al-Aʾimma li uṣūl manhaj fahm naṣṣ al-Qurʾānī* (Qum: Markaz al-Risāla, 2011), 71–74.

61 Muḥammad Amīn al-Astarabādī, *al-Fawāʾid al-Madaniyya* (Qum: Muʾassasat al-nashr al-islāmī, 2005), 91.

Akhbārī arguments on the issue can be classified into different categories and all these arguments have been seriously criticized by Uṣūlīs. The criticism of the Akhbārīs for this opinion has become a part of almost all Uṣūlī books when discussing the authoritativeness of the apparent meaning of the Quran in general, and legal verses in particular.[62] Above all, the Akhbārīs rely upon some hadiths indicating that the Quran is not understandable for everybody. Obviously they do not refer to the Quran itself as the basis for this position – reference to Quranic verses to prove that the Quran is not a source for legal reasoning, according to Akhbārīs or at least some of them, is a circular argument – for it relies upon the very evidence that they seek to undermine.[63] They do, however, sometimes refer to Quranic verses interpreted by the infallible Imams to suggest that the Quran is beyond the perception of ordinary people.[64]

Accordingly, their main evidence is made by reference to hadith literature. For instance, Ḥurr al-ʿĀmilī argues that there are extensively-transmitted (*mutawātir*) traditions, consisting of over two hundred hadith indicating that it is not allowed to infer deductive precepts (*al-aḥkām al-naẓariyya*) from the literal meaning of the Quran. Reliance on the Quran is allowed only in the case of a thorough understanding of the verse – a level of understanding only achieved when it has been interpreted by the Prophet or Imams – even by way of a single isolated hadith. This reliance on interpretation through the Prophet and the Imams is considered necessary to ensure that there is no abrogation, particularization, qualification or similar issue – all of which are very common in the Quran. These narrations, according to Ḥurr al-ʿĀmilī, are explicit in their indication and do not carry any possibility of dissimulation (*taqīyya*). He claims that it is in fact the hadiths that seem to contradict these explicit reports that are the ones issued in a context of dissimulation. Moreover, they are apparent (*ẓāhir*), and therefore not capable of contradicting explicit text (*naṣṣ*).[65] Yet it is hard to believe that hadiths regarding the methodology of understanding the Quran would have been issued in a context of fear necessitating dissimulation.

Moderate Akhbārīs like Yūsuf al-Baḥrānī (d. 1186/1772) and al-Jazāʾirī (d. 1128/1701) agree that these hadith do contradict some other hadith. Although the hadith prohibiting reliance upon the Quran in inferring legal

62 See, for example, al-Khurāsanī, *Kifāyat al-uṣūl*, 2:291–296.
63 ʿĀmilī, *al-Fawāʾid al-Ṭūsiyya*, 186.
64 Muḥammad Bāqir al-Ṣadr, *Durūs fī ʿilm al-uṣūl* (Qum: Dār al-Ṣadr, 2010), 2:309.
65 ʿĀmilī, *al-Fawāʾid al-Ṭūsiyya*, 200.

issues are more numerous and more authentic according to al-Baḥrānī,[66] he adds that the majority of Quranic verses regarding *fiqhī* issues are either ambiguous (*mujmal*), unconditional (*muṭlaq*) or general (*ʿāmm*), and therefore do not convey a clear concept when there is no associated evidence from the Sunna to interpret them.[67]

The Akhbārī position is, of course, not without nuance. Al-Baḥrānī claims that all late Akhbārīs are not unanimous in their denial of the authoritativeness of the Quran as a source for inferring rulings (*aḥkām*). While some believe that the door to understanding the Quran is categorically closed except for the Prophet and Imams, others believe that comprehension of the Quran is possible for all. Al-Baḥrānī himself accepts that the Quran can be regarded as a source, albeit within a limited and particular framework.[68] Al-Jazāʾirī insists that the mainstream Akhbārī view is that the exclusive authority of interpretation of the Quran is limited to the infallible Imams, leaving no room for any others to independently interpret the Qurʾan.[69] According to al-Jazāʾirī, Akhbārīs believe that the only source for determining the regulative and legal issues of *Sharīʿa* is the Sunna. The Quran is not a source, except in cases where the related verse has been interpreted by hadith; this is because they consider the Quran ambiguous (*mūjmal*), being addressed, in the first place, to the Prophet and then to his purified progeny. Al-Jazāʾirī himself, however, is among those Akhbārīs that believe that the Quran can be a source for legal issues. Interestingly, he too relies on al-Shaykh al-Ṭūsī's introduction to *al-Tibyān* in rejecting the dominant Akhbārī view on the ambiguity of the Qurʾan.[70]

None of the Akhbārī arguments seem convincing. The mission of the Quran is to communicate with people, not to give them puzzles and riddles. It would undermine the wisdom of God for Him to send a book and strongly enjoin people to contemplate upon it whilst leaving its practical teachings ambiguous. Based on earlier discussions and the assumption that the language of the Quran is normal and somehow ordinary, it is difficult to imagine that the legally relevant verses in the Quran are unclear. The authoritativeness of the apparent meaning of any text, when there is apparent meaning, is something essential. Many Uṣūlīs have taken this for granted. Mīrzā Abū al-Qāsim al-Qummī (d. 1815–16), a great Uṣūlī jurist, denies that there are any hadith that establish the Akhbārī claim regarding the non-authority of the apparent meaning of the

66 Yūsuf al-Baḥrānī, *al-Ḥadāʾiq al-Nāḍira* (Qum: Muʾassasat al-nashr al-islāmī, 1985), 1:27.

67 Ibid., 1:31.

68 Ibid., 1:27.

69 Niʿmat Allāh al-Jazāʾirī, *Manbaʿ al-ḥayāt wa ḥujjiyyat qawl al-mujtahid min al-amwāt* (Beirut: Muʾassasat al-ʿĀlamīyya, 1981), 41.

70 Ibid., 45.

Quran. No hadith, according to him, limits the authority of the interpretation of the Quran exclusively to the Imams.[71] On the other hand, he holds that the hadith suggesting that every doubtful hadith should be checked against the Quran are extensively-transmitted (*mutawātir*).[72]

Jaʿfar Kāshif al-Ghiṭā (d. 1812), a prominent Shīʿī jurist, assumes the authoritativeness of the apparent meaning of the Quran as being from among the self-evident and necessary teachings of Islam. He insists that whoever studies the legacy of the household of the Prophet would acknowledge that they argued with the People of the Book (Christians and Jews) and others through Quranic verses and this was also the manner and method of the jurists from the school of *Ahl al-Bayt*, generation after generation. Referring to some arguments raised by the Akhbārīs, he points out that the Akhbārīs themselves referred to Quranic verses in their own writings time and again, even when those verses had not been interpreted by one of the infallible Imams in the hadith literature. This implies, according to Kāshif al-Ghiṭā, that the Akhbārīs are not faithful in practice to that which they defend in theory. Accordingly, he argues that in practice there is consensus amongst all Shīʿī scholars on the authoritativeness of the apparent meaning of the Quran, not only in general but also with reference to legal issues.[73]

Aḥmad al-Narāqī (d. 1829) seemed to have attempted some sort of reconciliation between the Akhbārī position and the strong refutation of it by the likes of Mīrzā Qummī and Kāshif al-Ghiṭā. He claimed that the disagreement over the authoritativeness of the apparent meaning of the Quran in legal issues had no actual practical benefit when it came to legal reasoning. This was based on his belief that there is sufficient evidence from other sources, such as the hadith and scholarly consensus, that are capable of clarifying *Sharīʿa* precepts, leaving no need to refer to the Quran in legal reasoning.[74] Shaykh Anṣārī, the paradigmatic figure of modern Shīʿī *uṣūl al-fiqh*, rejects this idea outright, arguing that the jurist has great need for referring directly to the Quran across the entire scope of *Sharīʿa* regulations, including both the devotional acts (*ʿibādāt*) and, even more importantly, in the realm of interpersonal relations (*muʿāmalāt*).[75] In addition to what Anṣārī mentioned, this debate is a matter of methodology, and accordingly, would have an impact on the inference of

71 Mīrzā Abūl-Qāsim al-Qummī, *al-Qawānīn al-muḥkama fīl-uṣūl* (Beirut: Dār al-Murtaḍā, 1983), 2:317.

72 Ibid., 315.

73 Jaʿfar Kāshif al-Ghiṭā, *Kashf al-ghiṭā ʿan mubhamāt al-sharīʿa al-gharrāʾ* (Qum: Maktab al-iʿlām al-islāmī, 2001), 1:197.

74 Aḥmad al-Narāqī, *Manāhij al-aḥkām wal-uṣūl* (Tehran: Mīr Bāqir Press, 1809), 159.

75 Anṣārī, *Farāʾid al-uṣūl*, 1:155.

Sharīʿa precepts with regard to new legal issues – issues not covered by hadith nor subject to scholarly consensus. Moreover, as Anṣārī explains, if the plain meaning of the Quran has no authoritativeness because of ambiguity, then the same should be true in the case of the hadiths.[76]

Āyatullāh al-Burūjirdī affirmed and elaborated on the Uṣūlī premise that the authoritativeness of the apparent meaning of any text is something essential. He argued that even when it is said that the apparent meaning is authoritative because of common sense, or rational convention (*banāʾ al-ʿuqalā*), we do not mean to rely upon some *posteriori* argument (demonstration from effect to cause) or any *a priori* argument (demonstration from cause to effect) to prove its authoritativeness. In other words, common sense is not the middle term in a syllogistic argument; rather we are arguing to something axiomatic and self-evident.[77] According to this view, whenever there is apparent meaning, it is authoritative – irrespective of the type of source text; be it holy and divine in origin or otherwise.

Akhbārīs do acknowledge that there are reports in which the Imams sometimes inferred legally relevant issues from Quranic verses, yet they take these to imply that it is only the Imams who are able to do so.[78] However, the fact that the Imams are able to infer particular laws or points from the Quran does not imply in itself that others are prohibited from using the Quran as a source of inference in the very same way, be they legal or non-legal issues. This does not undermine the fact that the Quran, like many other texts, might have different layers of meaning and that the Imams might infer points that others are not able to, due to their level of purification, gnosis and divinely gifted knowledge.[79]

Despite the extensive theoretical Uṣūlī rejection of Akhbārī claims regarding the non-authoritativeness of the apparent meaning of the Quran, we can see that in practice Uṣūlī jurists often find it difficult to rely on the apparent meaning of the Quran when there is a specific interpretation of the verses in question available in hadith attributed to the Imams. For example, despite the fact that marriage to women of the People of the Book is apparently permitted

---

76 Ibid., 1:144.

77 al-Burūjirdī, *Nihāyat al-uṣūl*, 472.

78 al-Baḥrānī, *al-Ḥadāʾiq al-nāḍira*, 1:31.

79 This acknowledgment relates to another hermeneutical point relevant to the Akhbārīs' claim regarding the non-authoritativeness of the Quran; they firmly believe that the interpretation of the Quran is something gradative. According to al-Baḥrānī, al-Kāshānī (d. 1091/1680) in his exegesis *al-Ṣafī*, often tries to resolve apparent conflict between the related hadiths by resorting to the notion that people are at different levels in understanding the message of the Quran, a disparity that is reflected in apparent tensions internal to the hadith literature attributed to the Imams. See Baḥrānī, *al-Ḥadāʾiq al-nāḍira*, 1:35.

by the Quran (5:5) in a general and unqualified sense, a considerable number of Shīʿī jurists tend to limit this permissibility exclusively to temporary marriage due to some hadiths,[80] even though the apparent meaning of the verse does not seem consistent with such an interpretation. This reflects the station that Uṣūlī Shīʿī give to the Sunna as reported through hadith attributed to Prophet and the infallible Imams. Outside the context of legal theory, general works of Quranic exegeses dedicate extensive discussion to the role of hadith in the interpretation of the Quran, often construing them in a more rational and reasonable sense. Al-Ṭabāṭabāʾī for example, in many cases, takes it for granted that interpretative hadith from the Imam are often issued as examples of general concepts and should not necessarily be read as the exclusive interpretation of the verses, as is typical of the Uṣūlī method in legal theory. He uses different terms to describe hadith acting in this way, sometimes describing such hadith as a *jary* (implementation), sometimes *taṭbīq* (application), and sometimes an *inṭibāq* (imprint), all of which can be understood as describing the hadith as mentioning *an example* of a broader general Quranic concept.

I have to clarify, at the end of this discussion, that the majority of both Sunni and Shīʿī scholars of legal theory believe that the content of direct verbal commands and prohibitions in the Quran mentioned through phrases like: "O you who believe!", and: "O people"! are limited to the immediate addressees of the speech, i.e. the first generation who were alive when the Quran was first sent down.[81] However, holding such an opinion does not mean that the Quran is not a source for determining the obligations upon Muslims of every subsequent generation. The main concern in this debate was whether or not Muslims other than the first generation are allowed to rely upon the exoteric meaning of the Quran *without* trying to understand what the first generation understood from the outward sense of these Quranic verses. The concern is that there might have been some evidence accompanying those Quranic verses providing the first generation with a particular concept of their intended meaning that may not be obvious to others in the absence of that evidence. Therefore, subsequent generations of Muslims need to attempt to discover what the first generation understood from those Quranic verses and then generalize the duty, based on the accepted maxim that all believers share the same *Sharīʿa* duties

80 Muhammad Ḥasan al-Najafī, *Jawāhir al-kalām* (Beirut: Dār iḥyāʾ al-turāth al-ʿarabī, 1981), 30:27–43.

81 al-Qummī, *al-Qawānīn*, 1:517. For the opposite opinion, see Rūhollāh Mūsavī al-Khomeinī, *Manāhij al-wuṣūl ilā ʿilm al-uṣūl* (Qum: Muʾassasat tanẓīm wa nashr āthār al-Imām al-Khomeinī, 1994), 2:283–292.

(*qāʿidat al-ishtirāk*).[82] Accordingly this debate has no connection to the general discussion of authority or non-authority of the Quran in legal issues. It is, however, an important debate when it comes to methods of interpreting or inferring rulings from the Quran, for it recognises the importance of contextualism and impresses the idea that the Quran cannot be interpreted abstractly, without considering the circumstances in which it was revealed.

6 Some Notes on Challenges to the Uṣūlī Method

After outlining and defending the validity of Uṣūlī claims regarding the centrality of the Quran in legal reasoning, in this final section I wish to highlight some challenges, or point to some areas of concern, regarding the dominant method employed by Uṣūlī jurists in their reference to the Quran. Although not treated fully here, questions of how contemporary Shīʿī scholarship addresses such questions will be important in determining the future trajectory for the role of the Quran in legal reasoning.

Firstly, even though there are convincing proofs suggesting that the Quran ought to be a primary source for ongoing legal reasoning, it is quite clear that some Quranic verses were revealed in reference to particular cases and on specific occasions. In such cases, Uṣūlī scholars often believe that the import of the verse should still be considered as general and/or unconditional, and not restricted to the particularity of the case regarding which the verse was initially revealed. This might result, in many cases, in a type of unjustified and unintended generalization. For example, (5:1) states: "*O, you who believe! Fulfill all contracts.*" Too many legal rulings regarding contract law have been inferred from this abstract and general sentence. Consider the question of whether all contracts are deemed binding, or whether it is possible that some may be non-binding. Since the command to 'fulfill' in the verse applies to 'contracts' (*al-ʿuqūd*), a designation deemed general (*āmm*), and hence inclusive of every possible contract, jurists often infer that *all* conceivable contracts must be treated as binding. Similarly, when having a doubt about any qualifications to the parties of a contract or its considerations, such qualifications are deemed unnecessary due to the unqualified nature and absoluteness (*iṭlāq*) of the verse. This approach goes so far that one may claim that a large part of the

82 Although beyond the scope of this essay, this principle – when extended – may be useful in the context of debates on the universality of human rights. Developing the principle of common obligation to common rights may offer a basis to the assumption that all people are equal, until and unless there are reliable evidence for any inequality.

structure of contract law in some *fiqhī* approaches to the question have been shaped based on this single abstract Quranic verse. This verse, along with others like "*O you who believe! Do not use up your wealth between yourselves idly, unless it is for some business based on mutual consent among you.*" (4:29), have played a huge role in resolving many significant questions of contract law. For example, it is widely held that a proper contract does not need any literal offer and acceptance, because the verse is unconditional in this regard. However it may be argued that such verses did not set out to, were not in the context, nor in the state of expressing (*maqām al-bayān*) an entire system of contract law from A to Z, thus undermining the validity of employing the verses in this way.

A similar tension can be seen in reliance upon the Quran for issues of criminal law. One or two critical crimes in Islamic criminal law have been established, and a whole system of regulating crimes against security has been developed, on the basis of (5:33). Yet according to many scholars the verse was revealed regarding a particular case; when some hypocrite rebels tortured the Prophet's shepherd and some companions of the Prophet wanted to react toward them in a similar fashion.[83] It is seriously doubtful that the verse is expressed in a state of outlining a detailed designation for specific crimes, never mind being expressed in a manner that intended to establish a framework for fighting crimes against security as encountered in the contemporary era. In fact, due to the extent of ambiguity in the verse, scholars have been discussing for years whether the verse is talking about one crime or two crimes; and if the latter, what the relationship is between the two crimes. Accordingly, one may argue that this Quranic verse was not intended to frame the structure and details of regulating crimes against security, as perceived by traditional Uṣūlī jurists. Among the supporting evidence for this is the fact that many significant crimes have not been mentioned in the Quran at all, and almost all Quranic verses regarding crimes and punishments relate to specific cases that occurred during the lifetime of the Prophet. This may bring one to the conclusion that legally relevant verses in the Quran should not be seen as offering a detailed and precise system of law and that the tendency of Uṣūlī scholars to over-legalize the content of Quranic verses is problematic.

Secondly, and following on from the above, is that it is wrong to assume that the Quran has the characteristics of modern state legislation. Modern legislation has its own nature, often being very precise and comprehensive. Some Uṣūlīs seem to assume legally relevant Quranic verses are likewise very precise and comprehensive, akin to law in the modern age; while it is clear that at least some of the legally relevant Qur'anic verses cannot be described in

83 See al-Ṭūsī, *al-Tibyān*, 3:505.

this way.[84] The legally relevant Qur'anic verses, like any other type of Quranic verse, should be understood and construed in their own paradigm. The legislation in Quran and lawmaking in the parliaments belong to two different paradigms and therefore one cannot be equated with the other.

Thirdly, the Uṣūlīs' insistence that the language of the Quran is ordinary and normal may open the door for the untrained to develop his or her own personal understanding of the Quran, and accordingly, there should be standards for inferring from Quranic verses. Of course, it is often rightly insisted that to infer from the Quran and other sources some qualifications, in addition to familiarity with the Arabic language, are needed. To be able to understand the Quran, it is deemed necessary to be able to distinguish fully the abrogating verses from the abrogated, the univocal (*muḥkam*) from the equivocal (*mutashābih*), and many other such things. In fact, that the Akhbārīs take the Quran out of the hands of ordinary people is, somehow, positive. In the current context, the Islamic world is experiencing a vast array of hardline and *takfīrī* groups, like ISIS, who seem to reject any traditional Muslim sense of restricting the authority to interpret the legally relevant aspects of the Quran to suitably trained scholars. Instead they promote the idea that everybody is able to completely understand the Quran and interpret it. The Akhbārī approach emphasizes the impression that the Quran is not easily understood, and that it is widely misinterpreted. This is positive as far as it develops a sense of scientific precaution in one's engagement with the Quran and helps avoid simplicity in interpreting the Quran. We cannot forget that many legally relevant Quranic verses are very context-sensitive and accordingly it is hard to understand their core intent without a vast amount of knowledge of history, language and culture.

Acknowledgements

I have to thank many people including Dr. Julianna Swent for her sincere help regarding editorial points. Many thanks also to my daughter Fatemeh Nobahar for her hard and kind efforts on the transliteration.

Bibliography

al-ʿĀmilī, Muḥammad al-Ḥurr, *al-Fawā'id al-Ṭūsiyya*. Qum: Maktab al-Maḥallātī, 2002.

al-ʿĀmilī, Muḥammad al-Ḥurr, *Wasā'il al-Shīʿa ilā tafṣīl masā'il al-sharīʿa*. Tehran: Dār al-kutub al-islamiyya, 2007.

84 For an example, see Quran 5:33–34.

Anṣārī, Murtaḍā, *Farā'id al-uṣūl*. Qum: Majma' al-fikr al-islāmī, 2003.
al-Arājī Sattār Jabbār, Hammūd, *Ta'sīs al-A'imma li uṣūl manhaj fahm naṣṣ al-Qur'ānī*. Qum: Markaz al-Risāla, 2011.
Ardabīlī, 'Abd al-Karīm Mūsawī, *Dar Partow-e Vaḥy*. Qum: Daneshgāh-e Mofīd, 2009.
al-Astarabādī, Muḥammad Amīn, *al-Fawā'id al-Madaniyya*. Qum: Mu'assasat al-nashr al-islāmī, 2005.
Ayāzī, Muḥammad 'Alī, *Feqh pazhūhī-e Qur'ani*. Qum: Būstān-e Ketāb, 2007.
Bahmanpour, Mohammad Saeed, 'Book Reviews', *Journal of Shī'a Islamic Studies*. No. 2 (Spring 2010), Vol. III 231–233.
al-Baḥrānī, Yūsuf, *al-Ḥadā'iq al-Nāḍira*. Qum: Mu'assasat al-nashr al-islāmī, 1985.
Balāghi, Muḥammad Jawād, *Tafsīr ālā' al-Raḥmān*. Beirut: Dar iḥyā' al-turāth al-'arabī, 1989.
Beheshtī, Muḥammad Ḥusayn, *Ravesh-e bardāsht az Quran*. Tehran: Rowzaneh Publications, 2011.
al-Burūjirdī, Ḥusayn, *Nihāyat al-uṣūl*, dictated by Ḥusayn 'Alī Montaẓerī. Qum: Dār Tafakkur, first edition, 1995.
Fakhla'ī, Muḥammad Taqī, 'Jostārī dar tārīkh-e tafsīr-e āyāt al-aḥkām', *Majalleh-e Moṭāle'āte Eslāmī*. No. 49 & 50, (2000) 374–393.
al-Ḥillī, Ḥasan, *Kashf al-murād fī sharḥ tajrīd al-i'tiqād*. Qum: Mu'assasat al-nashr al-islāmī, 2012.
Ibn Sīnā, Ḥusayn ibn 'Abd Allāh, *al-Ishārāt wa al-tanbīhāt*. Qum: Daftar-e nashr-e ketāb, 1983.
Jāmi, Mohammad Hadi Moazzen, 'Barrasī-e Nazarīye-e Keyfiyat-e Nozool-e Quran', *Keyhān-e Andīsheh*. No. 37 (1991), 41–55.
Kohlberg, Etan and Amir-Moezzi, Mohammad Ali, *Revelation and Falsification: The Kitāb al-qirā'āt of Ahmad b. Muhammad al-Sayyārī*. Leiden: Brill, 2009.
al-Khomeinī, Rūhollāh Mūsavī, *Manāhij al-wuṣūl ilā 'ilm al-uṣūl*. Qum: Mu'assasat tanẓīm wa nashr āthār al-Imām al-Khomeinī, 1994.
al-Khū'ī, Abū al-Qāsim, *al-Bayān fī tafsīr al-Qur'ān*. Beirut: Dār al-Zahrā, 1975.
al-Kulaynī, Muḥammad ibn Ya'qūb, *al-Kāfī*. Tehran: Dār al-kutub al-islāmiyya, 2008.
al-Kūrānī, 'Alī, *Tadwīn al-Qur'ān*. Qum: Dār al-Qur'ān al-karīm, 1997.
al-Khurāsānī, Muḥammad Kāẓim, *Kifāyat al-usūl*. Qum: Mu'assasat al-nashr al-islāmī, 2006.
al-Ghiṭā, Ja'far Kāshif, *Kashf al-ghiṭā 'an mubhamāt al-sharī'a al-gharrā'*. Qum: Maktab al-i'lām al-islāmī, 200.
al-Ḥakīm, Muḥammad Taqī, *al-Uṣūl al-'āmma li al-fiqh al-muqāran*. Qum: Mu'assasat Āl al-Bayt, 1979.
al-Jazā'irī, Ni'mat Allāh, *Manba' al-ḥayāt wa ḥujjiyyat qawl al-mujtahid min al-amwāt*. Beirut: Mu'assasat al-'Ālamīyya, 1981.
Ma'rifat, Muḥammad Hādī, *al-Tamhīd fi 'ulūm al-Qur'an*. Qum: Mu'assasat al-Tamhīd, 2007.

Ma'rifat, Muḥammad Hādī, *Ṣīyanat al-Qur'ān min al-taḥrīf*. Qum: Mu'assasat al-Tamhīd, 2007.

Meibodī, Muḥammad Fākir, *Bāzpazhūhī-e āyāt-e feqhī-e Qur'ān*. Qum: Pazhūheshgāh-e farhang va andīsheh-e eslāmī, 2007.

Modarresī, Ḥossain, 'Early Debates on the Integrity of the Qur'an: A Brief Survey', *Studia Islamica*. No. 77 (1993), 5–39.

al-Mūsawī (Sharīf al-Murtaḍā), 'Alī ibn al-Ḥusayn, *Sharḥ jumal al-'ilm wal-'amal*. Qum: Dār al-uswa, 1994.

Al-Muẓaffar, Muḥammad Riḍā, *Uṣūl al-fiqh*. Qum: Mu'assasat al-nashr al-islāmī, 2002.

NajafĀbādī, Ni'matullāh Sālihī, 'Nazarīiyeīī dar Bārey-e Keyfīyat-e Nozool-e Quran', *Keyhān-e Andīsheh*. No. 32, (1990) 58–83.

al-Najafī, Muhammad Ḥasan, *Jawāhir al-kalām*. Beirut: Dār iḥyā' al-turāth al-'Arabī, 1981.

Nā'inī, Mīrzā Ḥusayn, *Fawā'id al-uṣūl*. Qum: Mu'assasat al-nashr al-islāmī, 1984.

al-Narāqī, Aḥmad, *Manāhij al-aḥkām wal-uṣūl*. Tehran: Mīr Bāqir Press, 1809.

al-Qummī, Mīrzā Abūl-Qāsim, *al-Qawānīn al-muḥkama fīl-uṣūl*. Beirut: Dār al-Murtaḍā, 1983.

al-Rāwandī, Quṭb al-Dīn, *Fiqh al-Qur'ān*. Qum: Maktabat Āyatullāh Mar'ashī Najafī, 1985.

al-Ṣadr, Muḥammad Bāqir, *Durūs fī 'ilm al-uṣūl*. Qum: Dār al-Ṣadr, 2010.

al-Sīstānī, 'Alī al-Ḥusaynī, *al-Rāfid fī 'ilm al-uṣūl*, transcribed by Munīr Qaṭīfī. Qum: Maktabat Āyatullāh Sīstānī, 1994.

Shahrābī, Muḥammad, *Maṣūnīyat-e Qur'ān az taḥrī*. Qum: Daftar-e tablīghāt-e islāmī, 1997.

al-Ṭabāṭabā'ī, Muḥammad Ḥusayn, *al-Mīzān fī tafsīr al-Qur'an*. Qum: Mu'assasat maṭbū'āt Ismā'īliyyān, 1973.

Tehrānī, Āqā Buzurg, *al-Dharī'a ilā taṣānīf al-shī'a*. Beirut: Dār al-Aḍwā', 1983.

Tehrānī, Abū al-Qāsim Kalāntarī, *Maṭāriḥ al-anẓār: Taqrīrāt al-Sheikh Murtaḍā Anṣārī*. Qum: Majma' al-fikr al-islāmī, 2007.

al-Tirmidhī, Muḥammad ibn 'Isā, *Jāmi' al-Tirmidhī*. Rīyāḍ: Dār al-Salām, 1999.

al-Ṭūsī, Abū Ja'far Muḥammad ibn al-Ḥasan, *Tafsīr al-Tibyān al-jām'i lil-'Ulūm al-Qur'ān*. Qum: Mu'assasat al-nashr al-islāmī, 2006.

Yazdī, Muḥammad, *Fiqh al-Qur'ān*. Qum: Ismā'ilīyyān, 2007.

CHAPTER 4

From Theory to Practice: The Role of the Subject in the Derivation of Rulings and Its Potential in Creating a System of Case Law for the Operation of Shīʿī Law

Imranali Panjwani

In this chapter, I will investigate how much attention Shīʿī legal theory (*uṣūl al-fiqh*) pays to the subject of the ruling (*mawḍūʿ al-ḥukm*) before a ruling is derived. The subject means the legally responsible person (*mukallaf*) as well as those factors that are relevant in the genesis and context of the subject which are more fact-oriented. My argument is that Shīʿī legal theory does not possess a methodological framework to recognise the subject of the ruling which would be beneficial for jurists when they derive a ruling in four areas. The first is to comprehend the human complexity of the legally responsible person in his/her intellectual, psychological, moral and biological dimensions; the second is to create a distinction between the person-oriented subject, which is the individual and the fact-oriented subject which relates to the world surrounding the individual; specifically, how he/she uses particular objects and the nature of these objects in themselves. Both dimensions help us consider the totality of factors affecting our understanding of the *sharīʿa* and its application of it; the third is to appreciate the changing quantitative and qualitative nature of both dimensions of the subject to facilitate relevant and adaptable Shīʿī rulings for contemporary issues and the fourth is to introduce the potential of the subject of the ruling in the operation of Shīʿī law as a whole.

The practice of rational people (*sīrat al-ʿuqalāʾ*) is a common source by which we can understand the subject of the ruling, its related facts and circumstances, but this source is general and new subjects of rulings can be complex in their own right. This complexity requires intricate mechanisms to elucidate what these new subjects actually are at a conceptual level. I intend to show that these mechanisms could be found within Shīʿī legal theory but they are under-explored and under-utilised. I have selected the relationship between the subject (*al-mawḍūʾ*) and the ruling (*al-ḥukm*) in Shīʿī legal theory and the notion of the practice of rational people as key entry points for this discussion, with reference to Shahīd Muḥammad Bāqir al-Ṣadr's (d. 1980) *Durūs fī*

© KONINKLIJKE BRILL NV, LEIDEN, 2020 | DOI:10.1163/9789004413948_006

'ilm al-uṣūl and Muḥammad Riḍā al-Muẓaffar's (d. 1964) *Uṣūl al-fiqh* – both being standard textbooks of jurisprudence in Shīʿī seminaries.

The final aspect of my chapter lays the ground for further research and attempts to broaden Shīʿī legal theory from a jurisprudence-oriented worldview to a law-oriented one. The subject of the ruling can act as a unifying mechanism to expand the scope of Shīʿī legal theory by considering its operation alongside English case law (*al-qānūn al-daʿwā al-injilīzīyya*) and international law (*al-qānūn al-duwalī*) (in addition to al-Ṣadr's own suggestions for jurisprudential reform within the context of a state[1]). Here, I argue that a Shīʿī case law system could be created that reforms the goal and operation of jurisprudence (*al-fiqh*) in a globalised world by introducing "evaluative law" and "jurisdictional law." Evaluative law reforms the solicitation of a legal opinion (*istiftā'*) by introducing a practical resolution mechanism for people's questions, enables people to participate in the derivation of rulings and reviews legal opinions periodically to see whether they are effective in resolving people's issues. It also holds jurists accountable for their management of the one-fifth tax (*khums*). Jurisdictional law reforms the system of jurisprudence itself by creating "regional jurisprudence" such as British Shīʿī fiqh, Iranian Shīʿī fiqh, Iraqi Shīʿī fiqh, etc. that focuses on the context-specific problems of Shīʿī Muslims. It also creates a case law system that could be recognised by a national legal system so that non-Muslim judges, lawyers and politicians are more aware of Muslim needs and problems like Islamophobia. Finally, jurisdictional law attempts to create Shīʿī International Law which unites Shīʿī Muslims around the world on common concerns and legal issues. These reforms could be applied to Sunni Muslims and other religious minorities as well.

Hence, terms such as 'ruling', which is not always enforceable (as in the case of recommended (*mustaḥabb*) and reprehensible (*makrūh*) rulings) in contrast to 'law', which is almost always enforceable in state political apparatus, have to be used with some fluidity, particularly in the final aspect of this chapter. As such, what I introduce at the end of my chapter are my thoughts on the relationship between Western law and Islamic law. Important work has been done investigating the historical relationship between so-called 'Islamic law' or 'Muhammadan law' and 'Western law' but not with a focus on case law.[2] Overall, three issues will be considered in this chapter:

---

1 For an overview of Ṣadr's ideas, see: Chibli Mallat, *The Renewal of Islamic Law: Muhammad Baqer as-Sadr, Najaf and the Shīʿī International* (Cambridge: Cambridge University Press, 2003).

2 See: George Makdisi, *The Rise of Humanism in Classical Islam and the Christian West with special reference to scholasticism* (Edinburgh University Press, 1990); Asaf A.A. Fyzee, *Cases in the Muhammadan Law of India, Pakistan and Bangladesh.* 2nd edition. (Oxford: Oxford

1) What is the subject of the ruling in Shīʿī legal theory?
2) Why is it important for the derivation of rulings?
3) What is its potential in expanding the goals of Shīʿī legal theory in a globalised world for the benefit of Shīʿī Muslims and to work alongside national and international legal systems?

1 Definitions

1.1 *Shīʿī Legal Theory*

Considering I am examining the interplay between Shīʿī legal theory, Western jurisprudence, law and case law some definitions are in order to see where all these disciplines meet together. As far as Shīʿī legal theory is concerned, Ṣadr problematises its definition by arguing that:

> The previous scholars from amongst them mention that its [Shīʿī legal theory] subject-matter is: 'the four sources (The Book [*al-kitāb*], Normative Practice [*al-sunna*], Consensus [*ijmāʿ*], Intellect [*al-ʿaql*]).' But the objection to that is that the [term] 'four sources' is not a comprehensive heading for its subject-matter's [Shīʿī legal theory] issues. For example, the issue of the prerequisites of the ruling's subject when it is said: does the ruling of the obligation of a thing necessitate the prohibition of its opposite by priority?; the issues of the authority of speculative evidences, which are many, such as the authority of an external issue from the four evidences like popular opinion (*shuhra*) and solitary report (*khabar al-wāḥid*); and issues to do with procedural principles …[3]

His statement shows that previously there was a debate amongst Shīʿī jurists as to what constituted the subject-matter of Shīʿī legal theory and some

---

University Press, 2005) and Asaf A.A. Fyzee, *Outlines of Muhammadan Law*. Edited by Tahir Mahmood. 5th edition. (Oxford: Oxford University Press, 2008). On how the two systems may work together, see: Mashood Baderin, *International Human Rights and Islamic Law* (Oxford: Oxford University Press, 2005); Chibli Mallat, *Introduction to Middle Eastern Law* (Oxford: Oxford University Press, 2007); Anver M. Emon, *Religious Pluralism and Islamic Law: Dhimmis and Others in the Empire of Law* (Oxford: Oxford University Press, 2012); Robin Griffith-Jones (ed.), *Islam and English Law – Rights, Responsibilities and the Place of Sharīʿa* (Cambridge: Cambridge University Press, 2013) and Hujjatullah Ibrāhīmīān et al., *Taʿamulāt Fiqhī dar hawzeh Qānūngozārī*, vol. 1 (Tehran: Kitābkhūne – Mūzeh va Markaz-e Isnād-e Majlis-e Shūrāī-e Islāmī, 2014).

3 Muḥammad Bāqir al-Ṣadr, *Durūs fī ʿilm al-uṣūl – al-Ḥalaqat al-thāniya* (Qum: Majmaʿ al-fikr al-islāmī, 1992), 19.

restricted it to the Qur'ān, Sunna, consensus and intellect. al-Ṣadr, however, objects to this, arguing that these four sources cannot cover all types of issues within Shīʿī legal theory such as the authority of speculative evidences (*al-adillat al-amāra*) and procedural principles (*al-uṣūl al-ʿamalīyya*).[4]

al-Ṣadr concludes his argument by stating that Shīʿī legal theory,

> ... does not need to be restricted to the four evidences. Indeed the subject-matter of the science of the principles [of jurisprudence] is everything that is anticipated to be an evidence and common element in the procedure of derivation of the religious law and the argumentation for it.[5]

His conclusion is important; it shows his belief in the capacity of Shīʿī legal theory to adapt to new jurisprudential questions because anything that is anticipated to be an evidence and common element in the procedure of the derivation of religious law can be considered as part of the subject-matter of Shīʿī legal theory.[6] It is for this reason that al-Ṣadr defines Shīʿī legal theory as, "the science of common elements in the procedure of derivation"[7] and a common element is the "commonness of the usefulness of a component in entering the derivation of a ruling in any instance amongst the instances which the jurist encounters ... like the imperative verbal form being apparent in obligation."[8] This means that a common element cannot be a specific component that has a self-contained subject-matter; rather it is a general principle that can be applied to specific issues. The example he gives is the apparentness of the imperative verbal form from which the meaning of obligation can be deduced, and so several obligations can be derived from the imperative verbal form such as the obligation of prayer and fasting.

al-Ṣadr's aforementioned comments give a firm foundation to begin discussion on incorporating a new common element such as a framework to understand the subject of the ruling. At least in theory, contemporary jurists emphasise the need to broaden the subject-matter of Shīʿī legal theory rather

---

4 *al-dalīl al-amāra* means an evidential indication that only results in a speculative ruling (as opposed to a certain or definitive ruling). A procedural principle (*al-asl al-ʿamalī*) outlines the practical standpoint in a performing a duty in the absence of *sharʿī* evidence.

5 *Ibid.*, 20.

6 al-Muẓaffar argues on similar grounds: Muḥammad Riḍā al-Muẓaffar., *Uṣūl al-fiqh* (Qum: Ismāʿīliyyān, 2010), 1:10–11.

7 Ṣadr, *al-Ḥalaqat al-thāniya*, 18; *al-Ḥalaqat al-thālitha* (Qum: Majma' al-fikr al-islāmī, 2011), 30. These common elements constitute the 'logic' (*mantiq*) i.e. the theoretical framework of *ʿilm al-fiqh*: al-Ṣadr, *Durūs fī ʿilm al-uṣūl – al-Ḥalaqat al-ūlā* (Qum: Intishārāt dār al-ʿilm,), 23 and *al-Ḥalaqat al-thāniya*, 21.

8 al-Ṣadr, *al-Ḥalaqat al-thāniya*, 18.

than restricting it to the four sources. This helps us to not only incorporate new methodological principles but also forge links with other disciplines that can assist in the derivation of religious rulings.

A rudimentary point by al-Ṣadr that can perhaps be overlooked when examining the purpose of religious rulings is that they aim to holistically organise the life of human beings and connect to all dimensions of their lives. He states:

> A Sharīʿ ruling is an instance of legislation issuing from God, the Exalted, with the purpose of organising the life of human beings. The revealed addresses (*al-khitābāt*) in the Qurʾan and the sunnah are not considered to be religious rulings in themselves, although they disclose and shed light on religious rulings. In light of this, it is incorrect to define a religious ruling with the well-known formula used by the earlier legal theorists: 'a legislative address concerning the actions of those held accountable by law (*al-mukallafūn*).' For the address merely discloses the ruling, the ruling itself is what is indicated by the address.
>
> In addition, the religious ruling is not always related to the actions of the accountable, for it is sometimes related to their persons or to other things connected to them. This is because the purpose of the religious rulings is to organise human life and just as this objective is achieved through an address related to the actions of the accountable, such as 'pray', 'fast' or 'do not drink alcohol', it is also achieved by addresses related to their persons or other things connected to their lives. Examples of the latter category are addresses such as those organising the matrimonial relationship by which, under specific conditions, a woman is considered a wife of a man, or the relationship involved in ownership, whereby a person is considered the owner of a property. These rulings are not related to the actions of the legally accountable" matrimony relates to their persons and ownership relates to their property. Thus it is better to change the popular form [of the definition] to what we said, namely: 'the religious ruling is the legislation issued from God, the Exalted, to organise human life, whether or not it is related to their [general] actions, to themselves or to other things related to their lives.'[9]

9 Muḥammad Bāqir al-Ṣadr, *Principles of Islamic Jurisprudence – according to Shīʿī Law*. Translated by Arif Abdulhussein (London: ICAS Press, 2003) 37 and in *al-Ḥalaqat al-thāniya*, Ṣadr states: "the religious ruling is an issued legislation from God, the most High, to order the life of human beings and direct it", 23. See also Muḥammad Bāqir al-Ṣadr, *al-Maʿālim al-Jadīdah lil-Usūl* (Beirut: Dār al-Taʿāruf Lil-Nashr, 1996), 99 and al-Faḍlī, ʿAbd al-Hādī. *Mabādī uṣūl al-fiqh* (Qum: Maṭbūāt al-dīnī, 1997), 7–8.

The fact that religious rulings are ultimately concerned with organising human life means they must take into account all relevant common elements, disciplines, systems and tools to achieve this aim (provided they do not conflict with the revealed word of God). The scope of Shīʿī legal theory, therefore, can be legitimately broadened to see how its principles function within the domain of law (*qānūn*). After all, if the religious rulings that are derived by jurists are to organise human life then the comprehension, organisation, functioning and implementation of these religious rulings are crucial for Shīʿī legal theory to fulfil its goal of understanding the law of God (*al-sharīʿa*). It is my submission that Shīʿī legal theory does not explore exactly how it should organise human affairs in the sense of the law yet this itself should be a juristic concern. We may therefore ask, is there a theory about the functioning of rules in society as opposed to their derivation? If the role of the jurist and institution of emulation (*taqlīd*) are discussed in relation to Shīʿī legal theory, then why can't considerations also be given to the way in which Shīʿī legal theory operates alongside other legal and social institutions?

The aforementioned questions can be answered by considering law and Shīʿī legal theory as two complimentary systems that must work alongside each other for human life to be successfully organised. My chapter, therefore, focuses on Shīʿī legal theory as only one component of law just as the executive, legislature, judiciary and enforcement are parts of law. Each part assists in the holistic function of the system of law for society to function effectively. It is here that Shīʿī legal theory, Western jurisprudence and law meet together since all are concerned with organising human affairs albeit with varying emphasis and different sources.

1.2 *Law and Jurisprudence*

The definitions of Western law and jurisprudence are, in some respects, similar to the concerns of Shīʿī legal theory. Law is defined as:

> The regime that orders human activities and relations through systematic application of the force of politically organised society, or through social pressure, backed by force, in such a society; the legal system <respect and obey the law>; 2. The aggregate of legislation, judicial precedents and accepted legal principles; the body of authoritative grounds of judicial and administrative action; esp. the body of rules, standard, and principles that the courts of a particular jurisdiction apply in deciding controversies brought before them <the law of the land>; 3. The set of rules or principles dealing with a specific area of a legal system <copyright law>; 4. The judicial and administrative process; legal action and proceedings <when

> settlement negotiations failed, they submitted their dispute to the law>; 5. A statute <Congress passed a law>. Abbr. L. 6 Common Law <law but not equity>. 7. The legal profession <she spent her entire career in law>.[10]

The definition above shows law is an enforceable notion usually backed by state apparatus but includes legal principles, judicial precedents, the legal profession and executive mechanisms. Shīʿī legal theory, which is the principles of jurisprudence, is not concerned with enforceability yet both are concerned with the derivation of laws that "order human activities." Western jurisprudence fulfils a similar role to Shīʿī legal theory in asking the fundamental questions as to what is the core nature of law, its sources, purpose, goals and means of legitimacy. As such, jurisprudence is defined as:

> Jurisprudence 1. Originally (in the 18th century), the study of the first principles of the law of nature, the civil law, and the law of nations – also termed jurisprudential naturalis. 2. More modernly, the study of the general or fundamental elements of a particular legal system, as opposed to its practical and concrete details. 3. The study of legal systems in general. 4. Judicial precedents considered collectively. 5. In German literature, the whole of legal knowledge. 6. A system, body, or division of law. 7. Case law.[11]

As one may observe, jurisprudence in the Western sense is significantly broader in character than Shīʿī legal theory which is more concerned with understanding the nature of God rather than the nature of human beings. This is why Western jurisprudence is usually studied in relation to a particular legal system and includes case law.

One may argue that Shīʿī legal theory is different to Western jurisprudence but as McCoubrey and White comment,

> jurisprudence is by its nature a trans-national subject, its concerns relate in various ways to most if not all legal systems. All states have systems of law and, despite the variety of forms, the problems and questions arising tend to be very similar in their general nature.[12]

---

10 Bryan A. Garner (ed), *Black's Law Dictionary* (9th ed) (Minnesota: West – Thomson Reuters, 2009), 962.

11 Ibid., 932.

12 Hilaire McCoubrey and Nigel D. White, *Textbook on Jurisprudence*. 3rd edition (Oxford: Oxford University Press, 1999), 9.

Moreover, the conception of law involves both practical and jurisprudential concerns as per Roscoe Pound's analysis:

> Some twenty years ago I pointed out two ideas running through definitions of law; one an imperative idea, an idea of a rule laid down by the lawmaking organ of a politically organised society, deriving its force from the authority of the sovereign; and the other a rational or ethical idea, an idea of a rule of right and justice deriving its authority from its intrinsic reasonableness or conformity to ideals of right and merely recognised, not made, by the sovereign.[13]

1.3 *Case Law*

So, what is case law? *The Essential Law Dictionary* defines it as "the body of law derived from examination of previously judged cases, including their treatment of a subject and interpretation of legislation."[14] *West's Encyclopaedia of American Law* states that case law means, "legal principles enunciated and embodied in judicial decisions that are derived from the application of particular areas of law to the facts of individual cases."[15] Finally, in Slapper and Kelly's *The English Legal System*: "case law, or common law, refers to the creation and refinement of law in the course of judicial decisions."[16] Interestingly, according to Black's Law Dictionary, case law is also known as jurisprudence and exists wherever there is law because it deals with practical problems of human society:

> The law to be found in the collection of reported cases that form all or part of the body of law within a given jurisdiction – also written case law; case-law. – Also termed decisional law; adjudicative law; jurisprudence; organic law.[17]

---

13 Roscoe Pound, "More about the Nature of Law" in *Legal Essays in Tribute to Orrin Kip McMurray* at 513. Cited in: Bryan A. Garner (ed), *Black's Law Dictionary* (9th ed) (Minnesota: West – Thomson Reuters, 2009), 932.

14 Blackwell: *The Essential Law Dictionary*, 70.

15 Jeffrey Lehmann and Shirelle Phelps, *West's Encyclopaedia of American Law*, 2nd Edition (Michigan: Thomson Gale, 2005), 36.

16 Gary Slapper and David Kelly, *The English Legal System: 2014–15* (Routledge: Abingdon, 2014), 129.

17 Bryan A. Garner (ed), *Black's Law Dictionary* (9th ed) (Minnesota: West – Thomson Reuters, 2009), 244.

And,

> Case law is in some form and to some extent found wherever there is law. A mere series of decisions of individual cases does not of course in itself constitute a system of law. But in any judicial system, rules of law arise sooner or later out of solution of practical problems, whether or not such formulations are desired, intended or consciously recognised. These generalisations contained in, or built upon, past decisions, when taken as a normative for future disputes, create a legal system.[18]

What we can reasonably conclude is that law, as a *conceptual* discipline, is more general than jurisprudence.[19] It includes questions about its enforceability and operation as well as its nature and legitimacy. My argument is that Shīʿī legal theory does not focus on the former aspect of religious law and law in general despite its admission that it attempts to organise the affairs of human beings and is connected to all spheres of human life. I believe that developing a framework to understand the subject of the ruling can be a unifying mechanism that satisfies the theoretical requirements within Shīʿī legal theory of recognising the realm of human fact and experience and then expanding this framework to consider the operation of derived religious rulings in human society through case law, which focuses on the subject of the law. This two-pronged approach is necessary to explain the implications of developing holistic framework for the subject of the ruling and avoiding a Eurocentric approach by looking at the resources within Shīʿī legal theory itself.

2 The Subject of the Ruling in Shīʿī Legal Theory

In Shīʿī legal theory and specifically according to Ṣadr, the subject of the ruling (*mawḍūʿ al-ḥukm*) means all the factors upon which the actualisation of the ruling rests on. For example, when God states, "… and pilgrimage to the House is a duty upon human beings for the sake of Allah for one who is capable to journey to it …",[20] the obligation of hajj is stipulated by God even if there isn't a current legally responsible person who can perform hajj. This is the stage of

18 Karl N. Llewellyn, "Case Law" in 3 Ency. Soc. Sci. 249 (1930). Cited in: Ibid.

19 The conceptual approach to law is discussed by Adams and Brownsword who argue, "conceptualisation involves sifting phenomena with a view to finding essences around which conceptual categories and classificatory frameworks may be developed." John N. Adams and Roger Brownsword, *Understanding Law* (London: Sweet and Maxwell, 1999), 1.

20 *The Qurʾān*, 3:97.

the stipulation of the ruling (*ja'l al-ḥukm*) where the application of the ruling is not a relevant factor. The ruling remains dormant until it can become actualised. It is here that the subject of the ruling becomes important – any ruling in the law of God (*al-sharīʿa*) only becomes actualised (*fiʿliyyat al-ḥukm*) when there exists for it a subject.[21] But what exactly is a ruling's subject?

Prima facie, al-Ṣadr and Shīʿī jurists in general regard the subject of the ruling to be the legally responsible person. Firstly, the legally responsible person must exist in order for the ruling in question to apply to him/her, and secondly, he/she must be in a position to understand and implement the ruling, which means, at a minimum, that he/she must possess maturity (*bulūgh*), capability (*qudra*) and sanity (*ʿaql*). If a legally responsible person is able to implement the ruling, he/she performs the referent (*mutaʿalliq*) which is the obligation of the act once the obligation has been directed to him/her. So the act of pilgrimage (i.e. the referent) exists by virtue of the obligation to perform the pilgrimage. Here the ruling or law is the obligatory (*wājib*) nature of the act and the referent or act to perform is the pilgrimage (hajj). In sum, the ruling depends on the actualisation of the subject – the presence of the legally responsible person who is able to implement that ruling.[22]

However, when we delve deeper we find that the subject of the ruling is not just the existence of the legally responsible person and his/her rational and biological characteristics but anything that helps in contributing to the subject of the ruling. This broader definition of the subject of the ruling is found firstly, in the distinction between the ruling and its preliminaries (*al-muqaddimāt*). The preliminaries are those factors upon which the existence of the obligatory act depends and is divided into two categories. The first category is preliminaries of the obligation (*muqaddimāt al-wujūb/al-wujūbiyya*) that constitute those preliminaries that are necessary to establish the subject of the obligation such as being mature and sane but also possessing the capability (*istiṭāʿa*) of performing an action, like acquiring financial means in the case of hajj. The second category is preliminaries of the obligatory (*muqaddimāt al-wājib/al-wujūdiyyah*) upon which the existence of the referent depends, such as ablution in the case of prayer. The former category, which is important for my discussion, is concerned with completing the subject of the ruling but this time, it expands the factors for this completion in relation to the legally responsible person. For example, whilst the legally responsible person is the subject of the ruling in the obligation to perform hajj, he/she must have the financial means and transportation to travel to hajj. Financial means and transportation,

---

21 al-Ṣadr, *al-Ḥalaqat al-ūlā*, 109–112, and al-Ṣadr, *al-Ḥalaqat al-thāniya*, 29–30.

22 *Ibid.* and al-Muẓaffar., *Uṣūl al-fiqh*, 1:80–81.

therefore, are considered as related issues to the legally responsible person and so by extension, the subject of the ruling is not only the legally responsible person but also other relevant factors that enable the legally responsible person to perform hajj.[23] Here we see a shift from factors that are closely related to the personal being of the legally responsible person, such as being mature and sane, to actions and/or preparatory factors related to the legally responsible person which are more to do with possession or usage of a thing rather than innate human characteristics. This gives us our first glimpse of the subject of the ruling being broadened to non-person factors.[24]

Secondly, the broadening of factors in relation to the subject is found in the distinction between action-orientating ruling (*al-ḥukm al-taklīfi*) and declaratory ruling (*al-ḥukm al-waḍʿī*). After stating that the purpose of religious rulings (*al-aḥkam al-sharʿiyya*), which emanate from God, is to order and direct the life of human beings, al-Ṣadr divides religious rulings into two categories – action-orientating rulings and declaratory rulings. Action-orientating rulings (*al-aḥkam al-taklīfī*) guide human beings' actions directly, are injunctive in nature and divided into the following sub-categories: obligatory (*wājib*), prohibited (*ḥaram*), recommended (*mustaḥabb*) and reprehensible (*makrūh*); there are many examples of these such as the prohibition of drinking wine and the obligation of prayer, which direct the legally responsible person to obey God.[25]

Declaratory rulings however, do not guide human beings' actions directly; rather they concern themselves with a cause (*sabab*), condition (*sharṭ*) or prevention (*mānīʿ*) of a *taklīfi* ruling in order facilitate its operation. This means that a declaratory ruling posits a specific condition which indirectly affects human conduct and the origination of the subject of the ruling.[26] Action-orientating rulings and declaratory rulings have a strong relationship with each other – for example, marriage is a declaratory ruling alongside which the obligation of the husband to financial maintain his wife (*al-nafaqa*) is imposed on the

23 A ruling that requires external conditions like financial means to be satisfied before the ruling is actualised is known as 'conditional ruling' (*al-ḥukm al-mashrūṭ*). al-Ṣadr, *al-Ḥalaqat al-thāniya*, 201–2. See also al-Muẓaffar, *Uṣūl al-fiqh*, 1:80 and 235.

24 al-Ṣadr, *al-Ḥalaqat al-ūlā*, 113–5 and al-Muẓaffar, *Uṣūl al-fiqh*, 1:234–235. Interestingly, the factor of capability for pilgrimage is defined broadly in current rulings in Shīʿī *fiqh* and includes person and non-person-oriented factors ranging from sufficient time to travel to Makkah, safe passage of travel and appropriate transportation, to possession of food, sound health and financial means. See for example: ʿAlī al-Husseini al-Sistānī, *al-Fiqh lil-mughtarabīn, 'Maʿna al-istiṭāʿa'*, http://www.sistani.org/arabic/book/17/956/ (accessed 31st December 2015).

25 al-Ṣadr, *al-Ḥalaqat al-thāniya*, 23.

26 al-Ṣadr, *al-Ḥalaqat al-thālitha*, 38.

husband once the act of marriage materialises;[27] stealing is a cause for cutting the hand in accordance with the verse, "as for the male and female thief, cut off their hands as a retribution for what they acquired – an exemplary punishment from Allah. And Allah is All-Mighty, All-Wise."[28] And, capability is a condition for the obligation of pilgrimage as per the verse, "... and pilgrimage to the House is a duty upon human beings for the sake of Allah for one who is capable to journey to it."[29]

Here, stealing and capability constitute particular circumstances in their own right which act as a cause and condition respectively for the materialisation of action-orientating rulings. If a person has stolen and one can identify that this actually constitutes stealing, then the law of cutting hands comes into force. Similarly, if one becomes capable through financial means of being able to perform hajj, then hajj becomes obligatory upon him/her. Therefore, declaratory rulings significantly broaden the concept of non-person factors in relation to the subject because we must first identify the action of the legally responsible person or circumstances surrounding the legally responsible person before a ruling can be issued. These non-person factors are wide-ranging, and are like social propositions which deal with various circumstances that the legally responsible person involves himself/herself in but need to be defined first to see how they affect a potential ruling. There may also be some causes and circumstances that are categorised under declaratory rulings but are not within the capacity of the legally responsible person or even society. For example, whilst a certain act or event that is affected by an action-orientating ruling may be within the ability of the subject such as not to steal, others may not be, such as the rising of the sun, which becomes a legal cause for the morning prayer but the subject cannot bring it about; the legally responsible person is not in control of when the sun rises.[30]

What is also important is that a circumstance, cause or prevention like stealing or capability are not defined (unless there is a clear evidence stemming from the Qur'ān and *Sunna*); they are specific circumstances that directly affect the actualisation of the subject but we ourselves must identify them. Only after identification and completion of the subject can a ruling materialise. al-Ṣadr explains this process by arguing that in the ruling of the prohibition of wine, the first step is to establish the subject of the ruling, known as *al-qaṭʿ*

27 al-Ṣadr, *al-Ḥalaqat al-thāniya*, 23.

28 *The Qur'ān*: 5:38.

29 *Ibid.*, 3:97.

30 For further discussion on the various subject-related qualifications externally imposed upon rulings and the way that they impact the responsibility of the *mukallaf* to bring them about, see: al-Ṣadr, *al-Ḥalaqat al-thāniya*, 205–212.

al-mawḍūʿī (certainty relating to the subject). In the first instance, we must be certain that the thing in question is actually wine (*maqṭūʿ al-khamr*) and then we must be certain of the ruling of prohibition in relation to wine (*maqṭūʾ al-ḥurma*). Taking these two elements together, certainty of the subject-matter (wine) and certainty of the ruling (prohibition), gives rise to methodological certainty (*al-qaṭʿ al-ṭarīqī*) from which the ruling materialises for the legally responsible person.[31] Here, al-Ṣadr does not just talk about the legally responsible person as the subject of the ruling but the object which he/she is apprehending (known as the subject-matter of law). This is another type of extension of the subject of the ruling to non-person factors and again, these factors are directly related to the legally responsible person's actions. al-Ṣadr's method of argumentation also positions the object or subject-matter as the basis of the ruling and therefore, in new cases of social interactions (*muʿāmalāt*) which are not covered by the Qur'ān and Sunna, the question remains as to how we understand what a particular object is before we consider the issuance of a particular ruling for it as well as the way in which it relates to other objects.[32]

It is interesting that non-person factors in relation to the subject, whilst more prominent under the category of declaratory rulings are also mentioned under the category of preliminaries of the obligation where for instance capability is both a declaratory ruling as well as a necessary preliminary in actualising the subject, the legally responsible person. There are also particular circumstances that the legally responsible person may be involved in or things such as a contract or piece of technology which he/she may use but these are not given any formal expression in themselves apart from how they affect action-orientating rulings. The problem that emerges in Shīʿī legal theory is that clearer distinctions need to be made between the following aspects: the existence of the legally responsible person as a subject, factors relating to his personal being that complete him/her as the subject of the ruling, contexts which act as circumstances, causes or preventions for the actualisation of the subject, and existing or new objects that need to be defined before a ruling can be issued.

At the very least, we can make a basic categorisation about the subject of the ruling in Shīʿī legal theory. The first is person-oriented i.e. the existence of the legally responsible person and his/her maturity, capability and sanity in order

---

31 *Ibid.*, 42–43. The distinction between *al-qaṭʿ al-ṭarīqī* and *al-qaṭʿ al-mawḍūʿī* was made significantly prior to al-Ṣadr by al-Shaykh al-Anṣārī in his *Farāid al-uṣūl.* See: Murtaḍā b. Muḥammad Amin al-Anṣārī, *Farāid al-uṣūl* Qum: Maṭbūʿāt al-dīnī, 2013), 1:4–7.

32 For the various categories of how a subject relates to another subject, see: al-Ṣadr, *al-Ḥalaqat al-thāniya*, 217–19.

to implement the ruling. The other is fact-oriented, such as the legally responsible person having the necessary financial resources to perform pilgrimage. Having financial resources and what they constitute are matter of fact. If the resources exist and the legally responsible person is mature, capable and sane, the obligation of hajj is actualised for him/her. Delineating these dimensions is crucial to understand the subject of the ruling in its totality thereby enabling rulings to be derived in a holistic and consistent manner.

3 A Lacuna in Shīʿī Legal Theory: Understanding the Subject of the Ruling

The aforementioned analysis shows that understanding the subject is crucial for the actualisation of the ruling and its correct application. However, I submit that a lacuna exists within Shīʿī legal theory concerning the recognition of subject of the ruling and the way in which our understanding of it has changed over time. "A lacuna is a 'missing rule', a rule which is *expected* but not found in the law"[33] but it has been argued that the meaning of lacuna is anything but clear.[34] Hence, a lacuna can be interpreted in several ways, from a missing piece of legislation for a particular case or a legal principle, norm and/or mechanism that results in a deficiency in the derivation and operation of law. My focus is on the latter – what mechanism exists in Shīʿī legal theory to recognise the subject of the ruling – both in a person-oriented and fact-oriented sense? For example, the rapid growth of internet technology has created the concept of virtual persons and new social tools by which people communicate with each other. These tools have changed our traditional forms of communication which puts pressure on the way in which Shīʿī jurisprudence defines the legally responsible person and his/her relationships. Today we must ask, is the virtual person the same as a real person in terms of the subject of the ruling and is it only related to a mere change in human custom or something more than that carrying moral implications? What criteria do we use to weigh psychological, biological, moral and rational faculties of the legally responsible person (including his/her existential issues) in the derivation of the law? When does a new object or subject-matter become a circumstance, cause or prevention for action-orientating rulings? The point of these questions is to illustrate that

33 Carlo Focarelli, *International Law as Social Construct: The Struggle for Global Justice* (Oxford: Oxford University Press, 2012), 257.

34 Hans Kelsen, *General Theory of Law and State* [1945] (New Brunswick and London: Transaction Publishers, 2007) 131–2.

there is no mechanism which exists in Shīʿī legal theory that pays attention to the subject of the ruling and its related circumstances. The subject is either assumed to be something which can be defined by the Qurʾān and Sunna, or if not, then it can be understood easily. Failing both of the above, we should rely on the custom (*ʿurf*) of society, the understanding of one jurist or even the legally responsible person in order to define it. In short, Shīʿī legal theory does not have a consistent methodological process to understand the subject of the ruling.

Investigating why historically there has been a lacuna in identifying the subject of the ruling in Shīʿī legal theory is important but falls outside the purpose this paper. However, the current theoretical source of this lacuna can be understood through al-Ṣadr's aforementioned categorisation of the subject being an 'external proposition' (*al-qaḍiyya al-khārijīyya*) despite it being crucial for the understanding and materialisation of God's rulings. It is so crucial that Ṣadr investigates various dimensions of the subject of the ruling that affect the legally responsible person's duty in bringing about God's rulings, their conditions and time frame. These result in the standard categorisation of obligations (*wujūbāt*) in Shīʿī legal theory such as timed and untimed obligations, defined and undefined obligations, etc.[35] Despite the important distinctions that Ṣadr makes about the subject of the ruling, they are geared towards understanding action-orientating rulings – not the subject of the ruling in itself i.e. not how to methodologically establish the quantitative and qualitative nature of conditions for an obligation that exist in reality. The subject of the ruling may be an external proposition but still requires a conceptual methodology to understand its complete nature.[36]

Similarly, in al-Muẓaffar's categorisation of maturity, capability, intellect and knowledge (*ʿilm*) as general conditions (*al-sharāʾiṭ al-ʿāmma*) for the discharge of an obligation, he explicitly states that knowledge does not constitute a condition within the obligation itself (unlike financial capability which is a specific condition for pilgrimage to materialise). Rather the possession of knowledge is generally applicable for responsibility (*taklīf*) and falls under the category of the discussion of authority (*mabāḥith al-ḥujja*) i.e. its value in verifying the authoritativeness of evidences for the derivation of God's rulings. Based on this categorisation of knowledge in Shīʿī legal theory, knowledge has methodological value in the realm of epistemology i.e. in the correlation (*mulāzima*) between rational and revelatory rulings but not in the realm of human fact and

35 For a summary of these obligations, see: ʿAbd al-Hādī al-Faḍlī, *Mabādī uṣūl al-fiqh* (Qum: Maṭbūʿāt al-dīnī, 1997), 10–13 and al-Muẓaffar., *Uṣūl al-fiqh*, 1:255.

36 See: al-Ṣadr, *al-Ḥalaqat al-thāniya*, 29, 129–30, 203–219.

experience and specifically, between the subject and the ruling. The lack of methodological attention given to internal and external conditions that form part of the subject of the ruling is seen in al-Muẓaffar's belief that the source of dispute and discussion lies more with the preliminaries of the obligatory, not the preliminaries of the obligation. Both al-Ṣadr and al-Muẓaffar, therefore, focus on the nature of primary real law (*al-wāqiʿ al-awwalī*), not secondary real law (*al-wāqiʿ al-thānawī*).[37]

Therefore, the expectation is not that all jurists should become experts in every scientific discipline, but rather, that they must have a consistent methodology to understand the subject of a ruling as a person with specific reference to intellectual, biological and moral characteristics, relevant circumstances and related objects or subject-matters. Even experts disagree amongst themselves as to how to define a particular technology, person or custom. Relying on custom is a very general, subjective and unclear standpoint especially when applying rulings to new, complex subjects.[38]

My submission is that it is necessary to create a methodological framework that helps us distinguish between the person-oriented and fact-oriented dimensions of a subject, its moral, social, psychological and contextual factors, and how the genesis of new subjects in society affect the way we think about the purpose and parameter of our existing jurisprudential laws. If it is accepted that such a framework is needed, how could it be incorporated in Shīʿī legal theory?

4 The Practice of Rational People as an Entry Point for Intellectual Tools

What is emphasised within Shīʿī legal theory is looking at custom (*ʿurf*) or specifically, the practice of rational people to help us understand new subjects, laws and behaviours of people. Maḥmoud al-Ḥashimī Shahrūdī, in explicating the thought of al-Ṣadr, emphasises the broadness of the practice of rational people as a speculative evidence in Shīʿī legal theory. He states,

> The reality is that the argumentation of the practice of rational people is not restricted to the particularities of jurisprudential issues or the chapter of speculative evidences. Rather, it is more general than that in

37 See: al-Muẓaffar, *Uṣūl al-fiqh*, 1:81, 225, 235 & 254.

38 See footnote 70 about the subjective nature of custom.

> jurisprudence – specifically in the chapters on social interactions, for example, in which laws stemming from rational people exist.[39]

Here, Shahrūdī argues that the practice of rational people is a source that is general in character, giving us different laws stemming from rational people. However, what is the practice of rational people and what implications does it have in helping us recognise the subject of the ruling? al-Ṣadr defines the practice of rational people as the practices, conventions, customs and thoughts of rational people, and locates it within the category of non-verbal religious evidence which is evidence that stems from an Infallible (*maʿṣūm*) i.e. Prophet Muḥammad or one of the Twelve Imāms for a legal ruling but does not belong to the domain of speech. This means that the performance of an action by an Infallible without any verbal expression indicates its permissibility (if it is an act of worship then it is regarded as recommended) and the omission of it means that it is not obligatory. Verbal religious evidence, however, is a statement (*qawl*) from the Infallible which includes abundant transmission of a report (*tawātur*), consensus and popular opinion, practice of the committed believers at the time of the Infallible (*sīrat al-mutasharriʿa*), and the trustworthy solitary report (*al-khabar al-wāḥid al-thiqa*). The link between all of these evidences is that they have the ability to yield verbal evidence from the Infallible. If they do not yield verbal evidence, then the sources in question cannot, prima facie, be relied upon to produce a binding ruling upon us.[40]

The practice of rational people does not belong to the category of verbal religious evidence since its subject-matter is the practice of rational human beings. Here, the Qurʾān or statement of an Infallible do not play a role in the formation of human beings' habits – habits such as the acceptance of the authority of apparent meaning (*ḥujjiyat al-ẓawāhir*), a trustworthy solitary report and possession as a proof of ownership of resources available for public use (*al-mubāhāt al-awwaliyya*).[41] All of these practices stem from human beings' own thoughts, and so prima facie, they do not yield any religious evidence we can rely on.[42] This is opposite to the practice of the committed believers at the time of the Infallible which is used as a means to discover verbal religious

39 Mahmoud Hāshimī Shāhrūdī, *Buḥūth fī ʿilm al-uṣūl*, 7 vols. (Al-Majmaʿ al-ʿīlmī li al-Shahid al-Ṣadr, 1985), 2:233.

40 al-Ṣadr, *al-Ḥalaqat al-ūlā*, 92–99; Shāhrūdī, *Buḥūth*, 2:234.

41 al-Ṣadr, *al-Ḥalaqat al-ūlā*, 99.

42 al-Muẓaffar similarly defines the practice of the rational people as: "what is intended from 'the *sīra*' – just as it is clear – is the continuous habits of human beings and their practical conventions in performing a thing or leaving a thing." al-Muẓaffar: *Uṣūl al-fiqh*, 2:139.

evidence since the practice of committed believers at the time of the Infallible may result from a verbal instruction from them which they implemented and practiced. We are therefore tracing the effect (practice of the committed believers) to its cause (verbal instruction of the Infallible).[43]

The practice of rational people, however, does not point to a particular verbal instruction from the Infallible. Where it carries legal probative force is if the rational practice in question is supported by a tacit endorsement (*taqrīr*) of the Infallible and we discover this endorsement, and ultimately the approval or signature of the Divine Legislator (*al-shāriʿ*) with certainty. So if the practice of relying upon the apparent meaning of a statement was done in the presence of an Infallible, and he did not say anything to the contrary, this silence signifies his tacit approval of the practice.[44] If the Infallible believed that practice to be incorrect, he would have disapproved of it. Had he not done so, he would be violating his own position as a representative of God with the duty to be just and disseminate the correct teachings of God. Non-prevention therefore indicates approval and acceptability of a particular practice.[45]

Human custom and specifically, the practice of rational people is an important evidence for jurists because from human practices, we can discern new intellectual tools and norms that help us in our understanding of religious texts. The question that arises, however, is: to what extent can we use these

---

43 Shāhrūdī argues that *sīrat al-mutasharriʿa* is like a proof originating from an effect (*al-burhān al-innī*) because in order to validate the authority of the *sīra*, we discover its cause (the verbal evidence of the *maʿṣūm*) through the effects of the verbal evidence, which is the practice of the committed believers at the time of the *maʿṣūm*. Therefore, the effects take precedence before their cause. In contrast, the practice of rational people is like a proof originating from a cause (*al-burhān al-limmī*) because in order to validate the authority of the *sīra*, we discover the cause first (the practice of rational people) and then substantiate the effects of that cause (the existence of the tacit endorsement by the *maʿṣūm*). Shāhrūdī, *Buḥūth*, 2:242.

44 al-Ṣadr, *al-Ḥalaqat al-thāniya*, 137–8; al-Ṣadr, *al-Ḥalaqat al-thālitha*, 367–9.

45 Similar reasoning is given by al-Muẓaffar, "The convention of rational people is not possible as an evidence except when it is discovered in the manner of certainty that the Holy Legislator is in agreement with it and His signature is in the way of the rational people because certainty decides on the authority of every proof", 2:140. Indeed, opinions in Shīʿī jurisprudence reflect a consensus on the subordinate nature of the practice of rational people. For example, the contemporary Iranian Shīʿī jurist, Muḥammad Ibrahīm Jannati states, "from the opinion of the Imāmiyya, an independent evidence for the validation and authority of human custom itself does not exist. Therefore, it cannot be any kind of independent evidence in front of the Book, Normative Practice, Consensus and Intellect. Rather its validation and authority rely upon the discovery of the signature of the Divine Legislator, which is a presumption entering in Normative Practice." Muḥammad Ibrahim Jannati, *Manābi-e-ijtihād az dīdgā-e-mazāhib-e-islāmī* (Tehran: Intishirāt-e-Kayhān, 1991), 408.

practices in interpreting the Qur'ān and Sunna? Are all laws and thoughts of rational people permissible in religious interpretation? If the subject of the ruling evolves or a new object arises in society that is not dealt with by religious texts, how do we correctly understand it in order to derive a ruling for it? It is here that the introduction of a methodological framework to understand the subject of the ruling becomes significant since we are dealing with methodological or "common elements" that are created by rational people and ultimately, custom. Therefore, we must assess the religious textual boundaries in admitting such a framework in Shīʿī legal theory.

5 The Current Evidential Boundaries of the Practice of Rational People in Creating Rulings and Modifying the Subject

Shahrūdī argues that the practice of rational people is an evidential tool which helps us review the subject of a religious ruling but does not have a role to play in the creation of a religious ruling which is reserved for the Qur'ān and Normative Practice, i.e. the practice of rational people cannot act as legislature but only as a modification for legislature. He states,

> The practice of rational people is that which reviews the subject of the religious ruling, does not legislate the ruling and only substantiates the ruling with the requirement of un-restrictedness (*iṭlāq*) of its evidence from the Book, Sunna or other than them.[46]

The practice of rational people therefore, has an intriguing and important position in modifying the subject of the ruling from the perspective of unrestricted evidence from the Qur'ān, Sunna or other than them.[47] It is a reviewer of the subject of the ruling, but in what way? Shahrūdī gives the following example of the husband's obligation to financially maintain his wife (*al-nafaqa*):

> Therefore, when the practice of rational people is required and known, regarding the financial maintenance of the wife in the current time-period – for example, in a manner that is more complete and perfect than

46 Shāhrudī, *Buḥūth*, 2:234.

47 This means unspecified *sharʿī* evidence where the subject of the law is stipulated generally through unrestricted (*iṭlāq*) words in the Qur'ān and Sunna. For example in the statement, 'respect the neighbour', 'neighbour' is left unqualified and has an unrestricted meaning indicating that one should respect all neighbours. al-Ṣadr, *al-Ḥalaqat al-ūlā*, 82.

> what was known in relation to it [the husband's obligation to financially maintain his wife] in previous years … as a result of differences in social, economic and intellectual circumstances, then the correctness of the model of how the husband financially maintains his wife broadens with what is [now] known in comparison to that [model] which was prior. This [current] level is necessary for it [the husband's obligation to financially maintain his wife] and the levels that were previously sufficient are [now] not sufficient. And this is according to the reality of the practice of rational people entering in the formation of the subject of the religious ruling, expanding or restricting it.[48]

Here, Shahrūdī argues that the custom of rational people is a general and permissible evidence for us, to examine how people understand a particular subject like the husband and his capacity to financially maintain his wife with particular reference to the prevailing custom of the time. If we want to investigate an existing or new subject then we must turn to the custom of rational people because from there we may obtain information about what the subject is in order to stipulate appropriate rules for it. Specifically, a case like the husband financially maintaining his wife can be looked at as a changing fact-oriented subject that is modified through rational custom over the passage of time. Different social circumstances will necessarily affect the way that people understand how husbands would financially maintain their wives is in our current century in comparison to previous ones. Whilst the legal obligation of the husband providing financial maintenance for his wife remains, what constitutes financial maintenance may change over time owing to new social and economic factors. This being the case, jurists are permitted to expand or restrict the scope of the fact-oriented subject before the law with due consideration of what people's capability and expectation of financially maintaining wives are in the present day. Whilst this changing custom is always weighed against textual religious evidence, jurists have no choice but to take the new understanding of a subject into consideration (which could also be based on non-textual evidence, known as *dalīl al-lubbī*) in the derivation of law since this is a social reality which any system of law must address.[49]

It appears from Shahrūdī's arguments that the practice of rational people can certainly modify the quantitative nature of the subject. Quantitative features are regarded to be measurable like material and economic factors, time

48 Op. Cit.

49 For discussion on the nature of *sīrat al-ʿuqalāʾ* as being a non-textual specifier for the subject of the law, see Shāhrudī, *Buḥūth*, 2:235 and al-Muẓaffar: *Uṣūl al-fiqh*, 1:133–36.

or place. However, it appears unclear to what extent the qualitative nature of the subject of a law can be modified. These are features regarded to be somewhat unmeasurable like moral and ethical features of a subject which have the potential to expand *uṣūlī* discussions in the areas of human dignity and potentiality, intellectual ability, mental capability, moral responsibility, psychological characteristics, biological make-up and more. For example, since 2008 in the United Kingdom, the British economy has seen a downward turn resulting in high unemployment and economic instability. This has forced couples to reassess the way in which they provide for each other meaning that at times both partners are required to work, or if the husband cannot find a job, the wife has to work. This role reversal, of course, is not just due to economic factors but the recognition of the dignity of a woman to work, her intellectual ability to do so and various socio-political movements like feminism. The reality is that now wives do provide for their husbands which results in the formation of a new custom. The effect of this change is not just quantitative – it affects the moral and social authority of wives over husbands in Islam. In such cases, can we modify the ethical nature of how husbands financially maintain their wives to the extent that now wives have a moral responsibility to financially maintain their husbands? If the above involves a violation in the practice of rational people in creating rulings of God, then we only have the option of lowering the financial threshold for husbands to maintain their wives. Indeed, how do we determine the appropriate intellectual domain of the issue – is the fact that wives maintain their husbands merely a matter of time and place or is it a moral and metaphysical matter pertaining to their human worth and intellectuality? Here, the point at which our changing understanding of a subject enters into the creation of the God's rulings itself requires further deliberation. Shīʿī legal theory is unclear in making a distinction between quantitative and qualitative factors, the amount of weight we place on both dimensions in determining the scope of the subject of the ruling and how this affects our understanding of the religious ruling itself.

Muḥammad Ibrahim Jannati has given a useful summary with examples of how Shīʿī' legal theory determines the extent by which the subject can influence a religious ruling in relation to custom:

> The Holy Legislator has permitted the identification and review of the minor propositions for subjects of universal rulings or reviewing them for the measurement of derivation or defining subjects of rulings like defining a poor person that is a subject for the welfare tax (zakat). This is because a poor person is someone who does not have the provisions and expenditures for his yearly livelihood and in defining the provisions of a

> year and its extent, custom ('urf) must be referred to. In this respect, differences in time, place and individuals from the perspective of custom emerge.
>
> And for example, expenditure in the way of God is also something that varies in accordance with different customs pertaining to time, place and culture. And for example, equality in marriage and its issues which at first sight, are ambiguous and so are other issues like that we cannot explain here. In these groups of cases, custom must be referred to.[50]

Jannati emphasises that minor propositions of the subject of the ruling such as time, place and culture can be determined by human beings to "expand or restrict" the scope of the ruling but never to create it. He does not comment on what exactly major propositions of rulings are but it appears such propositions would be determined by God and are ontological in nature because they act as the source and reality of the nature of subjects themselves. Perhaps these would encompass moral and metaphysical attributes that only God would know about in a human being and so to alter these attributes or ascribe new ones based on human custom may violate the sharīʿa. The problem, however, is that time, place and culture are inextricably linked to changing moral and social habits of human beings. They do relate to the ontological nature of religious rulings and that is why even the admission of "culture" as being a core part of custom is referred to by Jannati.

Therefore, the current scope of introducing a methodological framework to understand the subject of the ruling in Shīʿī legal theory is that such a framework cannot create religious rulings. However, it is permitted to review the subject of the ruling in relation to time, place and culture (despite the lack of clarity of the meaning of these dimensions). I submit that Shīʿī legal theory requires greater clarity even at this stage of reviewing the subject of the ruling by making a clearer distinction between person-oriented and fact-oriented subject which would help delineate personal characteristics involving biological make-up and intellectual capability with factual circumstances such as possession of money and economic circumstances of a society (just as in the case of *nafaqa*).

If the aforementioned distinction between the person-oriented and fact-oriented subject is developed, then at the least jurists would be able to consistently review the subject of the ruling. This methodological development would also fit in with the current epistemological paradigm within Shīʿī legal theory of the need to be certain about subjects before a religious ruling is

---

50 Jannati, *Manābi-e-ijtihād*, 408.

applicable to them. So as in the example of being certain that there is a legally responsible person who has definitely come into contact with wine, the ruling of the prohibition of wine would apply to him/her. As such, the realm of human fact and custom is not only observable but we can be certain about it. We can be certain that current economic circumstances dictate that a husband would need to provide a car or appropriate travel expenses to financially maintain his wife so that she can fulfil any errands.[51]

If the above development were to occur, we can then proceed to engage with the qualitative dimensions of the subject of the ruling such as moral and metaphysical questions pertaining to, for example, a woman's dignity. These are observable in society but we may not, at least according to the current epistemological paradigm of Shīʿī legal theory, be certain of how far we want to "expand or restrict" these attributes for human beings. If we would be permitted to expand these moral attributes, then we can develop a holistic framework of how religious rulings must consider the moral development of a subject of the ruling, not just changes in time, place and culture. Issues such as human worth, moral agency, psychological well-being and more can then be factored in the derivation of rulings. We would then be involving the subject of the ruling more in the creation of religious rulings themselves, whether in cases of acts of worship (*ʿibadāt*) or social transactions (*mu'amalāt*). The result of developing such a framework means there would be a greater emphasis within Shīʿī legal theory in understanding our human experience first before looking at the religious texts, a consistent procedure by which we can comprehend existing, new and changing subjects and possibly, a paradigm-shifting reversal in our process of jurisprudential reasoning and categorisation of sources of law which would now start from a non-verbal standpoint (our experience) rather than a verbal standpoint (religious scripture) – see Figure 4.1.

6 The Subject of the Ruling as a Bridge to Case Law

The subject of the ruling is in the domain of human experience and fact, as opposed to the realm of epistemology. Shīʿī jurists themselves have admitted that the subject as a human being changes as well as circumstances surrounding them such as financial, cultural, moral and social norms. This is why Shīʿī jurists accept that the subject of the ruling can be identified, recognised and/or reviewed. They consider both individual and social circumstances as important to review in how a ruling is applied such as in the case of the extent

51 See al-Muẓaffar, *Uṣūl al-fiqh*, 1:133; 2:140–1.

1) Discipline	2) Starting Point of Law	3) Methodological Connections	4) Conceptual Shifts in Legal Reasoning	5) Outcome
Shīʿī Legal Theory (*uṣūl al-fiqh*)	**Subject of the ruling** (*mawḍūʿ al-ḥukm*) → **Case Law** (*al-qānūn al-daʿwā*) The intellect (*al-ʿaql*) (Experiential & Evolutionary Process) →	Non-Verbal Evidences (*al-adillat ghayr al-lafẓiyya*) ↓ Practice of Rational People (*sīrat al-ʿuqalāʾ*) ↓ No Evidence (*la dalīl*) ↓ **Procedural Principles** (*al-uṣūl al-ʿamaliyya*) Verbal Evidences (*al-adillat al-lafẓiyya*) ↓ The Qurʾan Normative Practice (*al-sunna*) Solitary Report (*khabar al-wāḥid*) Practice of Committed Believers (*sīrat al-mutasharriʿa*) Consensus (*al-ijmāʿ*) Popular Opinion (*al-shuhra*)	**Non-Verbal to Verbal** (*ghayr lafẓīyya ilā lafẓīyya*) **Case to Concept** (*al-miṣdāq ilā al-mafhūm*) **A Posteriori to A Priori** (*al-baʿdī ilā al-badīhī*) **Context to Text** (*al-siyāq ilā al-naṣṣ*)	**Comprehensive Ruling** (*al-ḥukm al-shāmil*)

FIGURE 4.1 Implications of the subject of the ruling in Shīʿī legal theory

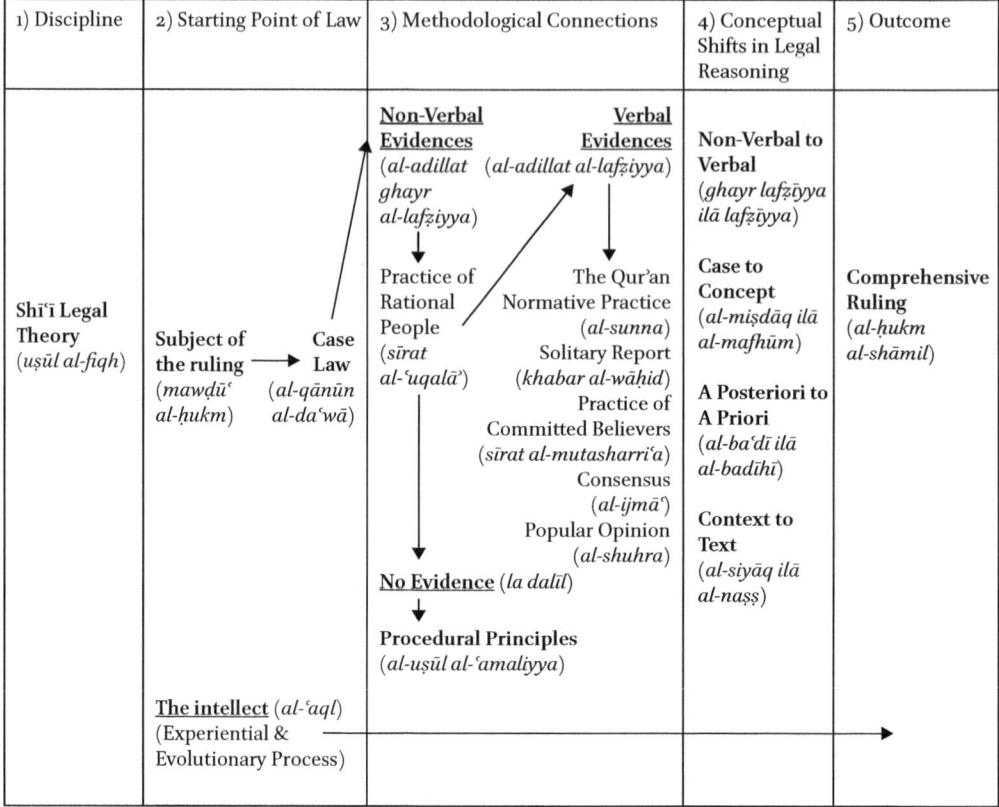

of financial maintenance a husband owes to his wife or identifying whether or not someone has the requisite capability for pilgrimage to be obligatory upon him/her. Even from this rather restrictive position in understanding the subject of the ruling, there is huge potential for it to act as a bridge between Shīʿī legal theory and law. This is because from a theoretical standpoint, we are deliberating about human experience and fact, which Shīʿī jurists recognise. This recognition helps us to consider ways in which the subject of the ruling has been examined in case law – the principal area of law that under both Shīʿī legal theory and English case law pays close attention to the subject of the ruling. The approach of Shīʿī legal theory and English case law towards the subject of the ruling is similar but with the key exception that English case law allows more scope for the subject of the ruling to create law, not merely to review it. An analysis of how English case law looks at the subject of the ruling helps us see the commonalities and links between Shīʿī legal theory and other legal systems in two ways. The first is in ways in which it can expand its understanding of the subject of the ruling and the second is in how the subject of ruling helps us to create rules that operate in relation *to and between* individuals for the effective "organisation of their affairs."

It is worthwhile noting that looking at another legal system to see how it examines the subject of the ruling and ultimately, derive relevant common elements from the practice of rational people is permitted under Shīʿī legal theory, as I have explained above. Case law is another rational method by which people resolve disputes, pay close attention to subjects before the law and has no apparent rejection by the Qurʾān or Sunna.[52] Just as a common element must be general in character helping a jurist to derive laws (like the trustworthy solitary report or the authority of apparent meaning), examining how judges analyse a subject constitutes another common element that provides a mechanism to recognise the subject of the ruling. We may even refer to an action of an Infallible himself or the practice of religious believers existing in an Infallible's time period which was verbally approved by him to justify using case law to help expand our understanding of the subject of the ruling.[53]

As stated earlier, case law is the body of law where judges examine the subject of the law in order to resolve a legal problem and create judicial precedent which can be relied upon in the future by a particular legal system. Case law consists of two elements. The first is legal and the second is jurisprudential. It is legal because case law is fundamentally "judges' law". Judges are vested with legitimate authority to interpret primary legislation and create legal principles to resolve disputes between two parties. Judges pay close attention to the subject of the law, i.e. the facts and dispute of the case as well as the intentions of both parties, and then apply the law to the facts. Each case is unique with a distinct set of facts and problems but may draw upon similar principles from previous cases to solve the dispute. Here, the body of case law is a source of law that relies on judicial precedent or *stare decisis* (let decided things stand). This is the doctrine of binding legal precedent, which as Slapper and Kelly explain,

> … lies at the heart of the English legal system. The doctrine refers to the fact that, within the hierarchical structure of the English courts, a decision of a higher court will be binding on a court lower than it in that hierarchy. In general terms, this means that when judges try cases, they will check to see if a similar situation has come before a court previously. If

52 al-Khūʾī argues that making a judgement on cases and disputes is both rationally and religiously obligatory and is not restricted to Islam – rather it can be found in other religions and countries as well. ʿAlā al-Dīn Baḥr al-ʿUlūm., *Kitāb al-Qaḍāʾ – Taqrīrān li-abḥāthi Āyatullāh al-ʿUdhamā al-Sayyid Abū al-Qāsim al-Mūsawī al-Khūʾī.* 6th Edition (Qum: Muʾassasat al-Rāfid lil-Maṭbūʿāt, 2010), 14, 16–17.

53 See al-Khūʾī's analysis of the way in which the Imams dealt with cases of property, contract and inheritance: Ibid., 165–251.

> the precedent was set by a court of equal or higher status to the court deciding the new case, then the judge in the present case should follow the rule of law established in the earlier case. Where the precedent is from a lower court in the hierarchy, the judge in the new case may not follow, but will certainly consider, it.[54]

Case law aims for legal consistency in producing law that can be applied to a wide range of facts but at the same time, has a dynamic quality in acknowledging that each case that comes before a court is unique and has the potential to refine or create new law. The refinement and creation of law is reflected in the judicial reasoning of a case which leads to the final legal judgement. This has two key components – the *ratio decidendi* (reason for deciding) and *obiter dicta* (things said by the way). The ratio decidendi is the most significant – it is that part of the judgement which is binding, "that is to say, the rule of law upon which the decision is founded."[55] Any judge that intends to refer to what was binding from a previous case must refer to the ratio decidendi of a case. Obiter dicta, on the other hand, constitute non-binding argumentation, which although it may have legal merit and be "respected according to the reputation of the judge, the eminence of the court and the circumstances in which it came to be pronounced",[56] does not hold any legal authority over a judge.

Therefore, the following components are significant in case law: the role and authority of judges to interpret and create law, the facts of the case, parties of the case, relevant evidences, witnesses and testimonies that contribute to a greater understanding of the facts and the way in which the law can be applied, the jurisdiction of the court to issue a law, stare decisis, ratio decidendi and obiter dicta. By considering all of these components, judges are able to resolve disputes between people, shape a legal system and periodically review the law to see if it is functioning effectively – specifically, whether it is actually addressing people's problems in society or not.

7 The Jurisprudential Nature of Case Law

The second element of case law is jurisprudential or theoretical in nature. Judges themselves must have a conception of the law and a methodology by which to examine the subject of the ruling before making a judgement. It is

54 *Ibid.*

55 Glanville Williams, *Learning the Law*. 15th edition (London: Sweet & Maxwell, 2013), 95.

56 *Ibid.*, 105.

here we see several commonalities with Shīʿī legal theory in the way judges and jurists understand the subject of the ruling. In English legal terminology, a 'subject' is defined as, "a topic; a person or thing that is being considered or discussed. (2) A citizen; a resident of a state or nation, excluding the monarch or ruler."[57] A subject, therefore, is wide-ranging and can include a particular topic or person; states are also regarded as subjects of international law.[58] Another related definition is the 'subject-matter' of law, which is more specific. This is defined as the "matter or topic presented for consideration or debate; the right or property that is the foundation of a dispute or lawsuit."[59] Both the subject and subject-matter are examined by judges to issue a comprehensive judgement in a case law. As an example of how case law looks at the subject of the ruling, I have included a summary of a well-known case in English company law (which is still a leading case), *Salomon v A Salomon and Co Ltd [1897] AC22*. The facts and judgements were as follows:

Aaron Salomon was a successful leather merchant who specialized in manufacturing leather boots. For many years he ran his business as a sole trader. By 1892, his sons had become interested in taking part in the business. Salomon decided to incorporate his business as a Limited company, Salomon & Co. Ltd. At the time, the legal requirement for incorporation was that at least seven persons subscribe as members of a company i.e. as shareholders. Mr. Salomon himself was managing director. Mr. Salomon owned 20,001 of the company's 20,007 shares – the remaining six were shared individually between the other six shareholders (wife, daughter and four sons). Mr. Salomon sold his business to the new corporation for almost £39,000, of which £10,000 was a debt to him. He was thus simultaneously the company's principal shareholder and its principal creditor. When the company went into liquidation, the liquidator argued that the debentures used by Mr. Salomon as security for the debt were invalid, on the grounds of fraud.

Judgement of the High Court: The judge, Vaughan Williams J, ruled against Mr. Salomon arguing that since Mr. Salomon had created the company solely to transfer his business to it, then the company and Salomon were one unit;

57 Amy Hackney Blackwell, *The Essential Law Dictionary* (Illinois: Sphinx Publishing, 2008), 475.

58 "The Court [International Court of Justice] may entertain two types of cases: legal disputes between States submitted to it by them (contentious cases) and requests for advisory opinions on legal questions referred to it by United Nations organs and specialized agencies (advisory proceedings)." "How the Court Works", *International Court of Justice*, accessed 3 August 2015, http://www.icj-cij.org/court/index.php?p1=1&p2=6.

59 Op. Cit.

the company was in reality his agent and he as principal was liable for debts to unsecured creditors.

Judgement of the Court of Appeal: The Court of Appeal also ruled against Mr. Salomon but on the grounds that Mr. Salomon had abused the privileges of incorporation and limited liability, which the Legislature had intended only to confer on "independent bona fide shareholders, who had a mind and will of their own and were not mere puppets."[60] The lord justices of appeal variously described the company as a myth and a fiction and said that the incorporation of the business by Mr. Salomon had been a mere scheme to enable him to carry on as before but with limited liability.

Judgement of the House of Lords (now known as the Supreme Court): The House of Lords unanimously overturned this decision, rejecting the arguments from agency and fraud. Salomon followed the required procedures to set the company; shares and debentures were issued. The House of Lords held that the company has been validly formed since the Act merely required 7 members holding at least one share each. There was no fraud as the company was a genuine creature of the Companies Act as there was compliance and it was in line with the requirements of the Registrar of Companies. The Company is at law a separate person. The 1862 Act created limited liability companies as legal persons separate and distinct from the shareholders. They held that there was nothing in the Act about whether the subscribers (i.e. the shareholders) should be independent of the majority shareholder.

It was held that: "Either the limited company was a legal entity or it was not. If it were, the business belonged to it and not to Mr. Salomon. If it was not, there was no person and nothing to be an agent [of] at all; and it is impossible to say at the same time that there is a company and there is not."[61] Hence the business belonged to the company and not to Salomon, and Salomon was its agent. The House of Lords further noted: "the company is at law a different person altogether from the [shareholders] …; and, though it may be that after incorporation the business is precisely the same as it was before, and the same persons are managers, and the same hands received the profits, the company is not in law the agent of the [shareholders] or trustee for them. Nor are the [shareholders], as members, liable in any shape or form, except to the extent and in the manner provided for by the Act."[62]

60 Salomon v A. Salomon and Co Ltd [1897] AC22, accessed 13 March 2019, https://www.trans-lex.org/310810.

61 Ibid., 31.

62 Ibid.

Salomon v A Salomon and Co Ltd demonstrates that deeply understanding the subject of the ruling is crucial for the appropriate judgement to be issued. The Salomon case shows four dimensions of the subject of the ruling were examined. The first is the individual or party in question i.e. the mental capacity of the individual, what is the individual claiming, what is the opposing party claiming and what can be deduced from an individual's actions that reveal their intentions. For example, the intentions of Mr. Salomon in setting up a company and whether or not he intended to defraud the creditors and his financial capability at the time. This is similar to Shīʿī legal theory defining the subject of the ruling as the individual, specifically the mukallaf and identifies his/her sanity, maturity, capability and knowledge at the time that a religious ruling is applicable to him/her.

The second dimension of a subject is the facts of the case i.e. what events occurred between the two parties in question, what notions or objects are we dealing with, whether we need experts to understand these facts, in what context these facts took place and how they connect to the appropriate legal issue. For example, the definition of a company and whether or not A Salomon and Co Ltd came under that definition and the financial circumstances of A Salomon and Co Ltd, the creditors and the UK economy at the time. This is similar to Shīʿī legal theory which regards preliminaries of the obligation and declaratory rulings as crucial for a religious law to be activated (like the existence of marriage for financial maintenance to be owed to the wife or for wine to be identified so that the ruling of prohibition takes effect). So in the Salomon case, the fundamental issue was whether A Salomon and Co Ltd was a company – if it was, then the relevant company legislation could be applied to validate its existence. If it wasn't, then judges would have to consider other laws or as we shall see below, create principles to fill any gap in the law.

The third dimension is how the subject of the ruling creates law or specifically, creates legal principles to fill a gap in current legislation. In the Salomon case, the key issue was how to identify a company when it was created by the same person. Mr. Salomon created A Salomon and Co Ltd so did that mean that they were one and the same entity or was there a difference between them? It was this question which the High Court and Court of Appeal grappled with. The House of Lords clarified this issue by coming up with the notion of artificial legal personality – that an entity could be recognised under law as possessing a valid existence, separate to real persons yet with similar legal powers such as the ability to enter into contracts, pay employees or be held liable for its own actions. Thus the modern entity of the company was born. The Salomon case showed that judges had a large scope to create legal notions that would shape and create the law even though their official position is to interpret it – akin to

Shīʿī legal theory which only admits that one can review the subject of the ruling in its application. The Salomon case shows English judges went further – they created a philosophical concept of artificial legal personality which in effect is the creation of a new moral and legal notion.

The fourth dimension is how the subject of the ruling jolts us to think about the purpose of law itself. The Salomon case showed that the Court of Appeal took a decidedly moral approach to the formation and goals of companies; companies should not be setup to defraud creditors by separating the real person from the company thereby avoiding liability for any debts which the company has. Jurisprudentially, this is very much a natural law position such as that of John Finnis who argued that human beings understand their individual aspirations and nature from an "internal" perspective and from there we can extrapolate understanding of good life and humanity in general.[63] Law therefore must try to achieve seven basic forms of good: life, knowledge, play, aesthetic experience, sociability or friendship, practical reasonableness and religion.[64]

The House of Lords, however, took a positivist position such as that of H.L.A. Hart who argued that as long as secondary rules validated primary rules giving them their authority (in particular, through the rule of recognition), then primary rules should be obeyed.[65] So in the Salomon case, the rules of incorporating a company were validly created by law-makers and upheld by legal officials such as judges and lawyers. As long as Mr. Salomon followed these rules to incorporate his company, he has not done anything wrong. Mr. Salomon followed all the procedures that company law legislation asked of him and the legislation did not say anything about whether or not one person can incorporate a company or the intentions of incorporation. Therefore, the House of Lords held that Mr. Salomon had followed the rules correctly. The outcome may have been different if the House of Lords adopted a more naturalist position which focused more on Mr. Salomon's responsibilities to the creditors – an issue which English company law still struggles with today. In Shīʿī legal theory, only the rudimentary notion of organising human affairs is expressed – deeper notions about what the law should accomplish and how examining the subjects of the ruling instigates us to think about our moral or amoral conception of law are not given due importance.

63 John Finnis, *Natural Law and Natural Rights*. 2nd edition (Oxford: Oxford University Press, 2011), 34.

64 Ibid., 81–95.

65 H.L.A. Hart, *The Concept of Law* (Oxford: Oxford University Press, 2012), 92.

The extensive nature of these dimensions shows that case law cannot just be categorised within the realm of law but falls under jurisprudence since it shapes the fundamental elements and purpose of a legal system. This is part of Dworkin's thesis who argues that especially in hard cases, judges formulate legal principles that are not enshrined in statute to produce a solution.[66]

In English case law, therefore, the subject of the ruling is understood in four ways – the first is the party or person itself (*person-oriented subject*); the second is the facts of the case (*fact-oriented subject*) – both in relation to the person such as the person possessing money and in itself such as how we conceive of money (the latter akin to the subject-matter of the law); the third is the usefulness of the subject of the ruling to help create legal principles or moral and social concepts (*creational-oriented subject*) and the fourth is how the subject helps us to think about the purpose of law itself (*purpose-oriented subject*). All four dimensions are relevant in the determination of the legal judgement since they clarify what happened, why and what legal implications should occur for the party in question. The distinction between person, fact, concept and purpose constitutes case law's theoretical methodology in analysing a subject in all of its social, contextual and moral complexities. According to Eisenberg, such a distinction would fall under the third component of common law legal reasoning called 'social propositions' which are,

> ... moral norms, policies, and empirical propositions (i.e., propositions that describe the way in which the world works, such as statements concerning individual behaviour and institutional design; statements that describe aspects of the present world, such as trade usages; or statements that describe historical events, such as how a trade usage developed)[67]

Case law refers to social propositions in identifying the subject of the law as shown in *Salomon v A Salomon and Co Ltd* and over time, develops legal principles to arrive at a deeper understanding of human experiences and conflicts. It is this methodological process that is relevant to Shīʿī legal theory in deepening

66 See: Ronald Dworkin, *Taking Rights Seriously* (Cambridge, Massachusetts: Harvard University Press, 1978).

67 Melvin A. Eisenberg, 'The Principles of Legal Reasoning in the Common Law' in Douglas E. Edlin (ed.), *Common Law Theory* (Cambridge: Cambridge University Press, 2007), 81–102 at 82. The four components of common law reasoning are: (1) courts should make law concerning private conduct in areas where the legislature has not acted, (2) the principles of legal reasoning turn on the interplay between doctrinal propositions and social propositions, (3) legal rules can be justified only by social propositions, (4) consistency in the common law depends on social propositions. Ibid., 81.

the way in which we examine the subject of the ruling which as I have mentioned is restricted to only reviewing it.

Whilst the normative practice (*sunna*) itself constitutes historical case law giving us a comparative model from which modern Shīʿī case law can be constructed, this requires an alternative enquiry rooted in historical investigation of the sunna as well as the inferential reason (*istidlāl*) used within books of jurisprudence which is not the purpose of this chapter. So if one were to compare how a judge interprets primary sources such as using linguistic devices to interpret the Company Act 2006 to a jurist who also uses linguistic devices to interpret verses of the Qurʾan then our discussion would be relevant in jurisprudence (*fiqh*) as the focus is on the inferential reason of both judges and jurists. Similarly, if we were to compare judicial procedures in English case law to, for example, the chapter of legal judgement (*kitāb al-qaḍāʾ*) then we would enter the domains of both jurisprudence and law. The focus in this chapter, however, is the methodological process prior to this (or lack of) in Shīʿī legal theory in understanding the subject of the ruling in our living reality.

The lack of theoretical focus on the subject of the ruling in Shīʿī legal theory is also present in the way jurists distinguish between the juristic opinion (*al-fatwa*) and legal judgement (*al-qaḍāʾ*). For example, Abū al-Qāsim al-Mūsawī al-Khūʾī (d. 1992) argues,

> … a juristic opinion is an expression about stating the ruling of God in relation to cases (*qaḍāyā*) whereby the ruling presupposes the existence of the subject without regard to its external, actual existence and non-existence – just like the affirmation of pilgrimage on the one who is capable and prayer on the one who is mature. Therefore, it [the juristic opinion] concerns a ruling of a conditional case which does not look at verifying the condition [in question] nor distinguishing between declaratory and action-orientating laws of God. As for the legal judgement, it is an expression about stating the ruling of an external and individual case or as it is said, the application of a ruling [of God] on an external subject – for example, this is an endowment (*waqf*) or that is a mosque (*masjid*).[68]

In both the juristic opinion and legal judgement, the subject of the ruling is looked at as a simple, external entity only requiring a kind of empirical verification. When a jurist issues a juristic opinion, his claim is that he does not need to examine a case of capability for hajj or maturity for prayer; it is up to

68 Baḥr al-ʿUlūm., *Kitāb al-Qaḍā*, 15–16.

the legally responsible person to verify the condition himself/herself in order for the juristic opinion to be applicable to him/her. Specifically, the jurist presupposes the existence of the subject of the ruling since his focus is on God's rulings – he does not intend to be an expert on human capability or maturity. However, there are, arguably, two problems with this approach. The first is that the jurist already possesses some personal, innate and/or experiential understanding of the subject of the ruling for him to make sense of God's rulings. His own understanding of the subject naturally affects his derivation of rulings yet this is without any principled mechanism. The second is that he must clarify what God means by capability when his followers ask him for clarification. It is at this point that the jurist enters the domain of the subject of the ruling and attempts to define it himself by looking at a variety of sources such as custom, experts, personal experiences and relevant theories.[69] The reality is that the jurist does not merely presuppose the existence of the subject of the ruling – he has already referred to external cases and operates on a working understanding of the subject, but we do not know how he has conceptually arrived at that understanding.[70] The legal judgement, in contrast, is less

---

69 A good example is al-Khūʾī's admission that there is no textual evidence for masculinity (*al-rajūla*) as a condition to be a judge and arguably, by implication, it is permissible for females to be judges. However, he ultimately decides that it is not appropriate for females to be judges because the role of women is only to veil and conceal themselves and perform household matters without entering into anything that would violate those matters. His reasoning is that according to his sense or taste of God, God would not be happy if a woman adopts such a forthright position. The problem here is that there is a lacuna or gap from the point that al-Khūʾī decided that there is no textual evidence for masculinity as a condition to be a judge to his decision that females should not hold the position of a judge. Within this gap, my submission is that he has already experienced a particular custom or conceived of the role of women (the subject of the ruling) and attributed this conception to God. Therefore, his juristic opinion becomes more subjective, is influenced by a particular culture and lacks a methodological framework as to how he determined the nature of the subject of the ruling – in this case, the intellectual and social attributes of a woman. See: Ibid., 33 and Abū al-Qāsim al-Mūsawī al-Khūʾī, *Al-Tanqīḥ fī Sharḥ al-ʿUrwat al-Wuthqa, vol. 1* (*taqlīd*)*, 18, accessed 23 March 2019,* https://www.al-khoei.us/books/?id=52.

70 In some respects, it is true as Mallat states that jurists do not generally deal with external cases as judges do. However, jurists do engage with external cases but in a tacit and personal manner, particularly when their followers ask them questions about real-life problems. Juristic opinions (*fatāwā*) are based on real-life cases but a juristic opinion is simplistic statement without any transparent inferential reason, contrary to cases which contain ratio decidendi and obiter dicta. Secondly, many narrations that jurists deal with in fiqh are historical cases that occurred in an Infallible's time-period. Therefore, fiqh is not completely casuistic, contrary to Mallat: "fiqh is case-law and its products are, to a variable extent, the result of the jurist's intellectual construct. With English common law

problematic since it is more concerned with verifying a particular object (such as whether a building is a mosque or not or whether this liquid is wine or not) after the conceptual processes behind the juristic opinion have been arrived at. It is then reasonable to bring in a range of experts to determine whether we are identifying a particular building as a mosque. There is still the issue of understanding the subject of the ruling but it is at the level of application. The core issue in distinguishing the juristic opinion from the legal judgement is not about whether or not the jurist verifies the subject of the ruling but rather the degree and nature of his verification.

8 From Theory to Practice: Broader Implications of Examining the Subject of the Ruling in Shīʿī Legal Theory

This section is purposefully broad to give an overview of how developing a methodological framework to understand the subject of the ruling can impact Shīʿī jurisprudence (*fiqh*) and national and international law (particularly for Muslims living in the West). Here, the nature and focus of case law in examining the subject of the ruling but more importantly, how it uses it to think about the purpose and operation of law becomes relevant. In other words, the 'legal' dimension of case law becomes significant to enable a transition in Shīʿī legal theory from jurisprudence to law. As I have argued, case law has a jurisprudential dimension which intimately connects it with Shīʿī legal theory but its legal dimension helps us to practically implement a methodological framework pertaining to the subject of the ruling in society. Here, the focus is not on understanding the subject of the ruling (which is the individual) but how the subject of the ruling lives in society, implements rulings and organises his/her affairs.[71]

---

it shares the inductive method by adducing a number of examples out of which some more general principles can be drawn. It does not posit, as in the continental European system of civil law (or Roman law in its late codified form), an overall principle or set of principles from which application derives. But fiqh is different from both in that it is eminently casuistic, and the cases it discusses are not necessarily based on precedents in real life." Mallat: *Introduction to Middle Eastern Law*, 47.

71 The approach of introducing models to bring the workings of Muslim jurisprudence and law closer together has also been employed by Mashood Baderin. For example, he suggests the doctrine of margin of appreciation should be adopted by Muslim states to interpret a particular human right in relation to their jurisprudence and culture. The doctrine holds that a gradual transition should occur in a state to implement human rights so that conflict between norms is reduced. For Muslim states with different moral and legal norms, this doctrine may be valuable to create harmony between Muslim jurisprudential

9 Evaluative Law

The first implication of the incorporation of case law in Shīʿī legal theory is that it has the ability to introduce what I would like to term as 'evaluative law' (*al-qānūn al-taqyīmī*). This is the process by which law assesses its jurisprudential concepts and rules in order to improve its system of law so that it can serve the needs of society better or specifically, subjects of rulings. Evaluative law comprises of three components: 'Resolution Mechanism' (*ālīyyat al-qarār*), 'People's Voice' (*ṣawt al-nās*) and 'Jurisprudential Review & Accountability' (*al-tanqīḥ al-fiqhī wa al-mas'ūlīyya*).

9.1 *Resolution Mechanism*

Resolution mechanism aims to replace the simplistic method of solicitation of a juristic opinion (*istiftā'*) in the system of imitation (*taqlīd*) with a sophisticated Shīʿī case law system. *Istiftā'* is the system by which the follower of a Shīʿī jurist (*muqallid*) sends jurisprudential questions to the office of the source of emulation (*marjaʿ*) and his representatives (*wukalā'*). In the West, the system of soliciting a juristic opinion is crucial as it is the only means by which a follower has contact with his/her jurist who usually resides in Iran or Iraq. The lack of communication, language barrier and geography makes it all the more difficult for a lucid and detailed conversation to take place between the follower and jurist. If the follower faces a difficult legal dilemma and needs an answer quickly, this puts further pressure on the system of soliciting a legal opinion.

In order to help solve the above problem, case law could replace the system of soliciting a juristic opinion through the creation of an internal case law system where people's questions and disputes are answered and adjudicated upon by local scholars akin to magistrates.[72] A court system could be set up in mosques or Muslim institutions to resolve people's problems with due consideration of their local context and create a system of accessible precedent, ratio decidendi and obiter dicta.

9.2 *People's Voice*

Resolution mechanism paves the way for 'people's voice' to be created in the derivation of juristic law. At present, Shīʿī jurisprudence is one-sided; it is the

norms and international ones – particularly in cases like apostasy, homosexuality and freedom of expression. See: Baderin, *International Human Rights and Islamic Law*, 232–35.

72 Principles already exist in Shīʿī jurisprudence under the chapter of judgement (*kitāb al-qaḍā'*) to manage disputes between two parties. See: Bāqir al-Irwānī, *Durūs tamhīdīyya fī al-fiqh al-istidlālī ʿala al-madhhab al-Jaʿfarī*. 3 vols. (Qum: Mu'assasat al-fiqh lil-ṭibāʿa wa al-nashr, 2005), 3:9–50.

jurist that derives the law in accordance with his legal reasoning. Whilst his followers contact and alert him to various problems, ultimately this contact is limited and does not take place in a regular and interactive arena in which both the jurist and his follower can challenge each other as to their expectations of jurisprudential laws. A case law system in which local scholars, for example, in the UK, have direct contact with followers of jurists can transform Shīʿī jurisprudence from being a passive legal system relying on the judgement of a jurist to a vibrant system where Shīʿī followers themselves critique Shīʿī laws in an open arena akin to a court hearing. Case law, therefore, allows a system in which people's views about Shīʿī laws can be recorded and considered in the derivation of law.[73]

9.3 *Jurisprudential Review & Accountability*

The final aspect of evaluative law is 'Jurisprudential Review & Accountability'. Presently, there is no way in which juristic opinions (*fatāwā*) can be reviewed to see whether they are actually resolving people's problems. It is assumed that a fatwa is issued by a Shīʿī jurist solves his follower's problem and can be implemented easily. This is a huge assumption since in a globalised world with different legal systems it is easy for juristic opinions to conflict with other laws. I propose that cases do not just have to be about an individual's legal issue but on reviewing the positive and negative effects of implementing legal opinions and any reform which needs to take place. This review process can be undertaken by skilled legal scholars who already live in that particular region. This is known as 'Jurisprudential Review.' Associated with this is 'Jurisprudential Accountability' which is the process of holding scholars accountable through case law for public misdeeds which adversely affect Shīʿī communities like the mishandling and misuse of the one-fifth savings tax (*khums*) – something I have unfortunately seen myself.[74]

73 The notion of 'people's voice' in the operation of *fiqh* leading to a devolution of authority from one *marjaʿ* to the *muqallidūn* radically departs from al-Ṣadr's idea that "the *marjaʿ* is the supreme representative of the state and the highest army commander." Mallat, *The Renewal of Islamic Law*, 74.

74 Moṭahhari also argues, "The way in which it [*khums*] is spent depends absolutely on the judgment of the person who has received the fund. Until now, it has not been customary to keep an exact account, including receipts and vouchers, of the expenditures. The use of the funds has depended on the *marjaʿ*'s fear of God, his piety, his good judgment, and his ability to avoid mistakes, as well as the opportunities available and his ability to implement projects he deems necessary ... The Shi'a clerics do not need to abide by the wishes of their governments, but they are forced to act in accordance with the popular style and opinion of the public and maintain the public's good will. Most of the corruption that exists among the Shi'a ulama is attributable to this." Mortaza Motahhari, "The Fundamental

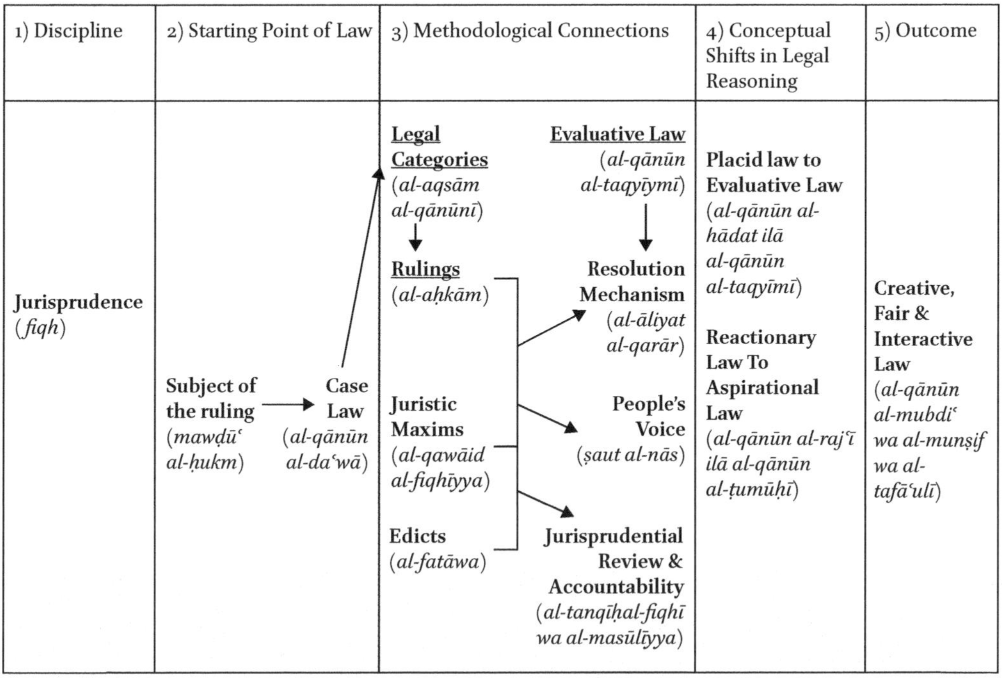

FIGURE 4.2 Implications of the subject of the ruling in Shīʿī jurisprudence

Together the three components of resolution mechanism, people's voice and jurisprudential review & accountability constitute evaluative law since through case law, the theory and operation of Shīʿī jurisprudence are regularly appraised with a view to establish procedural and substantive justice in Shīʿī communities around the world creating a kind of rule of law. Moreover, the aforementioned three components may reflect the division of the executive, legislature and judiciary in providing a checking and balancing mechanism in Shīʿī jurisprudence where no one legal authority should possess wielding power over people – see Figure 4.2.[75]

Problem in the Clerical Establishment" in Walbridge, Linda S (ed)., *The Most Learned of the Shīʿa: The Institution of the Marjaʿ Taqlid* (Oxford: Oxford University Press, 2001), 161–183 at 164.

75 In attempting to create a constitutional system of law for Iran after its revolution of 1979, al-Ṣadr also commented on the division between the executive, legislature and judiciary which could, theoretically, hold the *marjaʿiyya* accountable. Practically, however, the *marjaʿiyya* had supreme authority to override all three tiers. Mallat, *The Renewal of Islamic Law*, 71–72.

10 Jurisdictional Law

The second implication of the incorporation of case law in Shīʿī legal theory is that it has the capability of introducing what I would like to term as 'jurisdictional law' (*al-qānūn al-qaḍāʾī*). Jurisdictional law focuses on law as a substantively and procedurally diverse phenomenon that is generally incapable of being homogenous and universal; law needs jurisdictions and regional laws in order to solve people's problems effectively within their own contexts. The concept of jurisdictional law, however, does not exist in Shīʿī jurisprudence (even though jurists are independent of each other). A jurist assumes his legal opinions have a universal character and can be followed by all his followers around the world; but with multifarious legal, moral and social values across different regions in a globalised and pluralised world, how is Shīʿī jurisprudence meant to respond to a Shīʿī followers' unique problems? In order to answer this question, I would like to introduce three concepts under the heading of jurisdictional law in Shīʿī legal theory: 'Internal Jurisprudential Jurisdiction' (*al-sulṭat al-qaḍāʾ al-fiqhī al-dākhilī*), 'External Jurisprudential Jurisdiction' (*al-sulṭat al-qaḍāʾ al-fiqhī al-khārijī*) and 'Shīʿī International Law' (*al-qānūn al-duwalī al-shīʿī*).

10.1 *Internal Jurisprudential Jurisdiction*

The term 'Internal Jurisprudential Jurisdiction' means the ability of a legal system to create regional legal boundaries around the world acknowledging that regions face different problems to each other. This requires different regions to respect the principle of self-governance so that people's legal problems are addressed with due focus, efficiency and outside interference from other regions. The principle of respect for self-governance allows for the organic development of a legal system in a particular region but also fosters mutual respect between different regions since each region has its own legal jurisdiction with its own values, identity and laws. Mutual respect for each other's jurisdiction may still result in a shared legal identity but the result is the creation of regional boundaries within law that must be respected by all. In this vein, case law has the ability to create internal jurisdictions within Shīʿī jurisprudence which are localised to particular Shīʿī communities around the world. Each country where a substantial Shīʿī community resides could create its own set of case law and the goal is that over time specific laws develop for a particular region leading to its own, workable jurisprudential system in the future. The eventual goal is to create regional jurisprudence (*al-fiqh al-iqlīmī*) so that we can realistically talk of British Shīʿī jurisprudence, American Shīʿī jurisprudence, Iranian

Shīʿī jurisprudence, etc. within Shīʿī legal theory. Currently, only the jurisprudence of minorities (*fiqh al-aqalliyyāt*) is discussed by Muslim scholars.[76]

10.2 *External Jurisprudential Jurisdiction*

External jurisprudential jurisdiction is the process by which a working relationship is created between religious minorities who follow their own religious laws and the governing legal system whose laws are different. This relationship allows for legal conflicts between religious and secular law to be resolved, greater understanding over personal and public religious laws to be fostered and a powerful legal voice to be created for socio-political problems Muslims face such as Islamophobia and terrorism. Here, the creation of case law in Shīʿī communities is not just to resolve their own jurisprudential issues but to record problems they face on a national level. Cases compiled about such problems must try to mirror the judicial reasoning of national cases so that they are understood by judges who are not experts in Shīʿī jurisprudence. Over time, this case law could give Muslims greater legal credibility and evidentiary tools in courts to argue against laws which are discriminatory. Secondly, the creation of external jurisdiction also expands the scope of jurisprudence to deal with a broader range of legal issues that are not restricted to the Qurʾān, Sunna or even opinions of jurists – they are influenced by national issues that Shīʿī Muslims face. This diversifies chapters of Shīʿī jurisprudence leading to legal specialisms and division of labour – an issue raised by al-Ṣadr that has not yet materialised in the *marjaʿīyya*.[77]

The diversification of legal specialisms may be augmented by adding case law to Shīʿī seminary syllabuses. At present, seminary (*ḥawza*) students study core texts from Shīʿī jurisprudential heritage. Whilst this heritage must be respected, it cannot be considered as representing jurisprudence per se. Jurisprudence has many schools of thought both in the East and West and constitutes only one part of law. I propose that if case law from around the world is translated in requisite languages and added to Shīʿī jurisprudence syllabuses

76 See: Panjwani, Imranali: 'Book Review: Shari'a in the Modern Era: Muslim Minorities Jurisprudence by Iyad Zahalka', *American Journal of Islamic Social Sciences*, 34 (2017), 114–118.

77 al-Ṣadr suggested that the *marjaʿ* appoint a scholarly council composed of: "… one hundred spiritual intellectuals (muthaqqafīn ruḥiyyīn) and comprises a number of the best ʿulama of the hauza, a number of the best 'delegate ʿulamāʾ [wukalāʾ, i.e. ʿulamā charged with a specific mandate], and a number of the best Islamic orators (khutabāʾ), authors and thinkers (mufakkirīn). The council must include not less than ten mujtahids. The marjaʿiyya carries out its authority through this council." Mallat: *The Renewal of Islamic Law*, 75.

1) Discipline	2) Starting Point of Law	3) Methodological Connections	4) Conceptual Shifts in Legal Reasoning	5) Outcome
Hawza/ Madrasah Curriculum (*minhāj al-dirāsat al-madrasī*)	**Subject of the ruling** (*mawḍūʿ al-ḥukm*) → **Case Law** (*al-qānūn al-daʿwā*) ↑	**Current Sciences** (*al-ʿulūm al-ḥāliya*) ↓ **Principles of Jurisprudence** (*uṣūl al-fiqh*) → **Western & Eastern Jurisprudence** (*uṣūl al-fiqh al-gharbī wa al-sharqī*) ↑ **Additional Sciences** (*al-ʿulūm al-iẓāfiyya*) ↓ **Jurisprudence & Juristic Maxims** (*al-fiqh wa al-qawāʾid al-fiqhiyya*) → **Case Law** **Legal Opinions** (*fatāwā*) → **Practitioner Jurisprudence** (*al-fiqh al-mumāris*)	**Narrow Legal Education to Broad Legal Education** (*al-taʿlīm al-qānūnī al-ḍayyiq ilā al-taʿlīm al-qānūnī al-wāsiʿ*) **Theoretical Law To Procedural Law** (*al-qānūn al-naẓarī ilā al-qānūn al-ijrāīyya*)	**Diversification of Legal Training of Students** (*tanwīʿu al-tadrībī al-qānūnī al-ṭullāb*)

FIGURE 4.3 Implications of the subject of the ruling in the study of law

then students and jurists would gain an appreciation of different laws, problems, contexts and judicial reasoning beyond their own to solve global Shīʿī problems – see Figure 4.3.[78]

10.3 *Shīʿī International Law*

With the creation of internal and external jurisdictions within Shīʿī jurisprudence through case law, it may be possible to create Shīʿī international law which is a legal system that represents the laws and values of Shīʿī Muslims around the world. This system constantly aspires for a shared legal identity amongst Shīʿī Muslims that could work to fulfil their common interests and works towards the protection of their human rights. Case law is crucial to achieve this aim because if Shīʿī communities around the world compile cases about their own problems and then discover that some problems are faced by the majority of Shīʿa, they could work together to resolve them as well as create a powerful political and legal voice in the international community.

78 For al-Ṣadr's attitude towards the traditional *ḥawza* curriculum, see: *Ibid.*, 35–44.

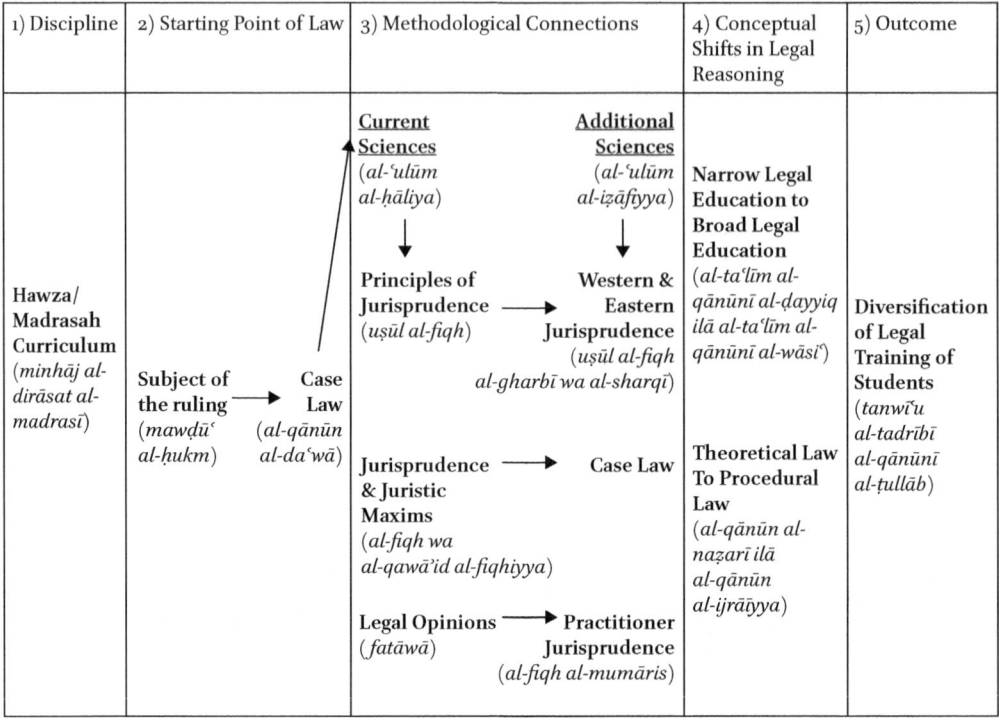

1) Discipline	2) Starting Point of Law	3) Methodological Connections	4) Conceptual Shifts in Legal Reasoning	5) Outcome
National Law & International Law (*al-qānūn al-waṭanī wa al-qānūn al-duwalī*)	**Subject of the ruling** (*mawḍūʿ al-ḥukm*) → **Case Law** (*al-qānūn al-daʿwā*) ↗	**Legal Systems** (*al-nuẓum al-qānūnī*) — **Jurisdictional Law** (*al-qānūn al-qaḍāʾī*) **Regional Jurisprudence** (*al-fiqh al-iqlīmī*) → **Internal Jurisprudential Jurisdiction** (*al-sulṭat al-qaḍā al-fiqhī al-dākhilī*) **National Law** (*al-qānūn al-waṭanī*) → **External Jurisprudential Jurisdiction** (*al-sulṭat al-qaḍā al-fiqhī al-khārijī*) **International Law** (*al-qānūn al-duwalī*) → **Shi'i International Law** (*al-qānūn al-duwalī al-shīʿī*)	**Jurists' Law to Institutional Law** (*qānūn al-fuqahāʾ ilā al-qānūn al-muʾassisī*) **Generalist Law to Specialist Law** (*al-qānūn al-ʿumūmī ilā al-qānūn al-ikhtiṣāṣī*)	**Expansion of Shīʿī National & International Legal Voice** (*tawsīʿu ṣawt al-qānūnī al-waṭanī wa al-duwalī al-shīʿī*)

FIGURE 4.4 Implications of the subject of the ruling in national & international law

Therefore, the three mechanisms of 'Internal Jurisprudential Jurisdiction', 'External Jurisprudential Jurisdiction' and 'Shīʿī International Law' could transform Shīʿī jurisprudence into a more adaptable legal system that focuses on particular regions and problems and ushers in the creation of Shīʿī legal institutions that are not led by one jurist but by specialist scholars dealing with issues of national and international concern to Shīʿī Muslims – see Figure 4.4. Both evaluative and jurisdictional law could usher in the creation of an additional discipline within Shīʿī sciences that focuses on the procedure of jurisprudence, not just its content. This may be termed as 'procedural law' (*al-qānūn al-ijrāīyya*) and enables Shīʿī rulings to function globally alongside other legal systems.[79]

79 See the work of Lon Fuller who argued that law should have a minimum criteria of law in the context of the morality of duty which orders society to function effectively i.e. the morality that makes law possible. This is a kind of morally procedural law: "the morality of aspiration ... is the morality of the Good, Life, of excellence, of the fullest realisation of human powers ... Where the morality of aspiration starts at the top of human achievement, the morality of duty starts at the bottom. It lays down basic rules without which

11 Conclusion

In conclusion, my submission is that developing a methodological framework to understand the subject of the ruling could fill what I see to be a lacuna in Shīʿī legal theory – the recognition and delineation of the subject in all its dimensions. The subject forms the basis of any ruling and sophisticated principles are required to understand it. The practice of rational people is the entry point for these principles since they are principles which rational people use that have not been rejected by the Divine Legislator. In the words of Ṣadr, these would constitute "common elements" in the derivation of God's ruling or perhaps the "logical rules" of the subject of the ruling. Paying more attention to the subject of the ruling may have the following implications in Shīʿī legal theory.

Firstly, a chapter devoted to a deeper methodology in understanding the subject of the ruling could be created – just as chapters on tools to understand language (*lugha*) exist in Shīʿī legal theory books. Four dimensions may constitute the foundation of this methodology: the first is the individual with all of his/her characteristics (*person-oriented subject*); the second is the facts of the case in relation to the individual (*fact-oriented subject*); the third is the usefulness of the subject of the ruling to help create legal principles or moral and social concepts (*creational-oriented subject*) and the fourth is how the subject helps us to think about the purpose of law itself (*purpose-oriented subject*). This methodology reverses the process of jurisprudential reasoning from a textual to a non-textual basis thereby grounding law in our immediate human reality and experience. Specifically, it would account for the subject of the ruling as an evolving entity capable of impacting the derivation of law.

Secondly, Shīʿī case law focusing on current dilemmas may be developed thereby helping us understand the subject of the ruling today and new objects arising in society. A range of legal principles can be derived from real cases along with a re-examination of the subject of the ruling in verses of the Qurʾan and narrations (*aḥadīth*). These principles can be applied to virtually all areas of Shīʿī jurisprudence making it a creative, evaluative and evolving legal system that is capable of adapting to and challenging national and international legal systems. Finally, a greater investigation into the subject of the ruling helps us define a metaphysical and mystical yardstick for Shīʿī legal theory which initiates a shift from a textualist understanding of law to an existentialist one since

an ordered society is impossible, or without which an ordered society directed toward certain specific goals must fail of its mark": Lon L. Fuller, *The Morality of Law* (New Haven, Conn: Yale University Press, 1969), 5–6.

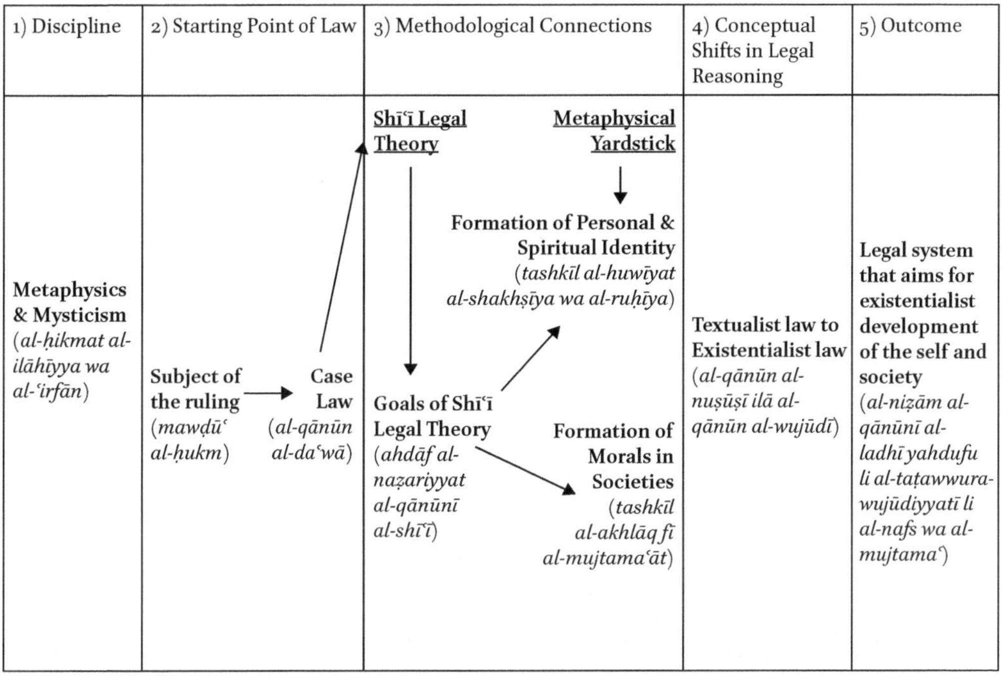

FIGURE 4.5 Implications of the subject of the ruling in metaphysics and mysticism

we, the subjects of rulings, are the primary experiencers of our own reality – see Figure 4.5. The effect of the aforementioned additions may produce a Shīʿī legal system that better appreciates human complexity and flourishing in the face of the Divine.

Acknowledgements

All praise belongs to God. This chapter, which builds from my research sabbatical at the Research Institute of Jāmiʿat al-Muṣṭafa in Mashhad, Iran would not have been possible without the help of the following people. The presence of the 8th Shīʿī Imām, ʿAlī b. Mūsa al-Riḍa and his sister, Lady Fāṭimah al-Maʿsūma was a source of great spiritual growth for me. Dr. Jafar Morvarid, Head of the Institute and his team were instrumental in organising my sabbatical. My teachers at Al-Mahdi Institute have always been encouraging to me – in particular, Shaykh Arif Abdulhussain, the Director of the Institute, as well as Dr. Mohammed Ghari Fatemi and Dr. Ali Fanaei. I would also like to thank Dr. Ali-Reza Bhojani for giving me Dr. Morvarid's contact details.

The sessions I had with Shaykh Ahmed Morvarid, Shaykh Ali Taliqani and Dr. Hossein Waleh were beneficial. Dr. Rahim Nobahar and his family were very hospitable to me during my visits to Iran. Shaykh Muhammad Kadhim Tawakkuli of Jāmiʿat al-Muṣṭafa Tamhīdīyyah who taught me Persian was an inspirational instructor as was my other teacher, Mohammed Sa'idi. The education I received in law at the University of Sheffield, University of Law and King's College London continually plays an instrumental role in my research. I would like to thank my dear father and mother for their support in my educational pursuits and beloved wife, Sabikah, for being a loving companion and looking after me and my dearest daughter, Maryam, during our time in Iran. May God grant His blessings and felicity to all the above – in this world and the next.

Bibliography

Adams, John N. and Brownsword, Roger. *Understanding Law*. London: Sweet and Maxwell, 1999.

al-Anṣārī, Murtaḍā b. Muḥammad Amīn. *Farāid al-uṣūl*. 2 vols. Qum: Maṭbūʿāt al-dīnī, 2013.

Baderin, Mashood. *International Human Rights and Islamic Law*. Oxford: Oxford University Press, 2005.

Baḥr al-ʿUlūm. *ʿAlā al-Dīn. Kitāb al-Qaḍā – Taqrīrān li-abḥāthi Ayatullah al-ʿUdhama al-Sayyid Abū al-Qāsim al-Mūsawī al-Khūʾī*. 6th Edition. Qum: Mu'assasat al-Rāfid lil-maṭbūʿāt, 2010.

Blackwell, Amy Hackney. *The Essential Law Dictionary*. Illinois: Sphinx Publishing, 2008.

Dworkin, Ronald. *Taking Rights Seriously*. Cambridge, Massachusetts: Harvard University Press, 1978.

Edlin, Douglas E. ed. *Common Law Theory*. Cambridge: Cambridge University Press, 2007.

Emon, Anver M. *Religious Pluralism and Islamic Law: Dhimmis and Others in the Empire of Law*. Oxford: Oxford University Press, 2012.

al-Faḍlī, ʿAbd al-Hādī. *Mabādī uṣūl al-fiqh*. Qum: Maṭbūāt al-dīnī, 1997.

Finnis, John. *Natural Law and Natural Rights*. 2nd edition. Oxford: Oxford University Press, 2011.

Focarelli, Carlo. *International Law as Social Construct: The Struggle for Global Justice*. Oxford: Oxford University Press, 2012.

Fuller, Lon L. *The Morality of Law*. New Haven, Conn: Yale University Press, 1969.

Fyzee, Asaf A.A. *Cases in the Muhammadan Law of India, Pakistan and Bangladesh*. Edited by Tahir Mahmood. 2nd Edition. Oxford: Oxford University Press, 2005.

Fyzee, Asaf A.A. *Outlines of Muhammadan Law*. Edited by Tahir Mahmood. 5th Edition. Oxford: Oxford University Press, 2008.

Garner, Bryan A. (ed). *Black's Law Dictionary*. 9th ed. Minnesota: West – Thomson Reuters, 2009.

Griffith-Jones, Robin ed. *Islam and English Law – Rights, Responsibilities and the Place of Shari'a*. Cambridge: Cambridge University Press, 2013.

Hart, H.L.A. *The Concept of Law*. Oxford: Oxford University Press, 2012.

Holmes Jr, Oliver Wendell. *The Common Law*. Cambridge, Massachusetts & London: The Belknap Press of Harvard University Press, 2009.

International Court of Justice. 'How the Court Works'. Accessed 23 March 2019. http://www.icj-cij.org/court/index.php?p1=1&p2=6.

Ibrāhīmīān, Hujjatullah et al. *Ta'amulāt fiqhī dar hawzeh qānūngozārī*. vol. 1. Tehran: Kitābkhūne – Mūzeh va markaz-e isnād-e majlis-e Shūrāī-i Islāmī, 2014.

al-Irwānī, Bāqir. *Durūs tamhīdīyya fī al-fiqh al-istidlālī ʿalā al-madhhab al-Jaʿfarī*. 3 vols. Qum: Muʾassasat al-fiqh lil-ṭibāʿa wa al-nashr, 2005.

Jannati, Muḥammad Ibrahim. *Manābi-e-ijtihād az dīdgā-e-mazāhib-e-islāmī*. Tehran: Intishirāt-e-Kayhān, 1991.

Kelsen, Hans. *General Theory of Law and State* [1945]. New Brunswick and London: Transaction Publishers, 2007.

al-Khūʾī, Abū al-Qāsim al-Mūsawī. *Al-Tanqīḥ fī Sharḥ al-ʿUrwat al-Wuthqa, vol. 1 (taqlīd), 187*. Accessed 23 March 2019. https://www.al-khoei.us/books/?id=52.

Lehmann, Jeffrey, and Phelps, Shirelle. *West's Encyclopaedia of American Law*. 2nd Edition. Michigan: Thomson Gale, 2005.

Makdisi, George. *The Rise of Humanism in Classical Islām and the Christian West with special reference to scholasticism*. Edinburgh University Press, 1990.

Mallat, Chibli. *The Renewal of Islamic Law: Muhammad Baqer as-Sadr, Najaf and the Shīʿī International*. Cambridge: Cambridge University Press, 2003.

Mallat, Chibli. *Introduction to Middle Eastern Law*. Oxford: Oxford University Press, 2007.

McCoubrey, Hilaire, and White, Nigel D. *Textbook on Jurisprudence*. 3rd edition. Oxford: Oxford University Press, 1999.

Mutahhari, Mortaza. "The Fundamental Problem in the Clerical Establishment". In Walbridge, Linda S. ed. *The Most Learned of the Shīʿa: The Institution of the Marjaʿ Taqlid*. 161–183. Oxford: Oxford University Press, 2001.

al-Muẓaffar, Muḥammad Riḍā. *Uṣūl al-fiqh*. 2 vols. Qum: Ismāʿīliyyān, 2010.

Panjwani, Imranali. 'Book Review: Shari'a in the Modern Era: Muslim Minorities Jurisprudence by Iyad Zahalka', *American Journal of Islamic Social Sciences*, 34 (2017), 114–118.

al-Ṣadr, Muḥammad Bāqir. *Durūs fī ʿilm al-uṣūl: al-Ḥalaqat al-ūlā*. Qum: Intishārāt Dār al-ʿilm, 2014.

al-Ṣadr, Muḥammad Bāqir. *Durūs fī 'ilm al-uṣūl: al-Ḥalaqat al-thāniya*. Qum: Majma' al-fikr al-islāmī, 1992.

al-Ṣadr, Muḥammad Bāqir. *Durūs fī 'ilm al-uṣūl: al-Ḥalaqat al-thālitha*. Qum: Majma' al-fikr al-islāmī, 2011.

al-Ṣadr, Muḥammad Bāqir. *Al-Ma'ālim al-Jadīdah lil-Usūl*. Beirut: Dār al-Ta'āruf Lil-Nashr, 1996.

al-Ṣadr, Muḥammad Bāqir. *Principles of Islamic Jurisprudence – according to Shī'ī Law*. Translated by Arif Abdulhussein. London: ICAS Press, 2003.

Salomon v A Salomon and Co Ltd [1897] AC22. Accessed 13 March 2018. https://www.trans-lex.org/310810.

Shāhrūdī, Maḥmūd al-Hāshimī. *Buḥūth fī 'ilm al-uṣūl*. 7 vols. Al-Majma' al-īlmī li al-Shaḥid al-Ṣadr, 1985.

al-Sistānī, 'Alī al-Husseini. *al-Fiqh lil-Mughtaribīn*. Accessed 23 March 2019. http://www.sistani.org/arabic/book/17/956/.

Slapper, Gary, and Kelly, David. *The English Legal System: 2014–15*. Routledge: Abingdon, 2014.

Turner, Chris. *Key Cases: Contract Law*. Abingdon: Hodder Education, 2011.

Williams, Glanville. *Learning the Law*. Fifteenth Edition. London: Sweet & Maxwell, 2013.

Zumout, Samia. *English/Arabic Legal Glossary*. The Superior Court of California – County of Sacramento, 2005.

CHAPTER 5

Strategic Juristic Omission and the Non-Muslim Blood Price: An Examination of Shīʿī Fiqh and Practice

Haider Ala Hamoudi

1 Introduction

This paper seeks to examine a problem that may arise with some frequency in modern Shīʿīsm.[1] Specifically, what is a jurist to do when a *fiqhī* rule of long-standing provenance proves inferior to the modern law of the state? I do not mean by "inferior" that the interpretive methodologies used to develop it are somehow less than sound, or that it is illiberal and therefore dissatisfying to Western audiences. Rather, I refer to a rule that – relative to existing, and legally controlling, state law – lies in considerable tension *not only* with the normative expectations of the relevant Shīʿī lay community that otherwise pledges fealty to the jurists, *but also* with the ethical precepts of the juristic community. Even the jurists, that is, do not actually prefer the application of their own rule in practice, though of course one would hardly expect them to say as much. If this is so, then surely the lay community could hardly be expected to support the *fiqhī* rule with any vigour. Yet how, under such circumstances, is formal loyalty to the rule of the jurist over the law of the state to be sensibly maintained in any state that recognizes some sort of distinction between the two?

This paper seeks to demonstrate that the jurists engage in a phenomenon I describe as *strategic juristic omission* in order to manage this gap. That is, rather than revisit or revise traditional rules that might seem inapt or even offensive to the lay devout, and stand in tension to their own ethical precepts, jurists merely reduce or often omit mention of such rules, with the result that few within the lay community are aware that the rules even exist. The matter seems to work well enough, in that it enables the jurists to avoid answering uncomfortable questions or advancing positions on *fiqh* that come near to contradicting ethical precepts and political commitments that they are

1 The only branch of Shīʿīsm that is relevant to this chapter is Twelver Shīʿīsm, and accordingly, for the sake of brevity, all references to Shīʿīsm are intended to be references to Twelver Shīʿīsm.

© KONINKLIJKE BRILL NV, LEIDEN, 2020 | DOI:10.1163/9789004413948_007

simultaneously propounding. However, it comes at some cost. Specifically, strategic juristic omission only works for as long as rules are unapplied. Thus it is, in a sense, an admission of failure in the *fiqh*. Moreover, it prevents the sensible re-evaluation of juristic rules in a manner that might render them more palatable in the modern era. This is dangerous, particularly in our times, when extremists seem all too willing to hijack Islam through the tendentious use of older texts.

Examples of strategic juristic abound. For example, traditionally, Shīʿī jurists describe marriage as being of three types – permanent marriage, temporary marriage, and the right of masters to the sexual enjoyment of their female slaves.[2] Grand Ayatollah al-Sīstānī (b. 1930), however, describes *two* types of marriage, permanent and temporary.[3] He thus does not lay out the rules respecting sex and female slaves, nor does he even explain why he has omitted them. That explanation only comes later, and in the most oblique of manners – in a footnote in an obscure passage concerning the right of a man to practice the birth control method of withdrawal when engaged in intercourse with his slave.[4] Other examples exist as well – it is rare to find a contemporary jurist suggest that it is recommended for a husband to imprison the wife in the home so that she only leaves when necessary, another traditional rule recounted as recently as the middle of the twentieth century by the late Muḥsin al-Ḥakīm (d. 1970).[5] A final, notable example[6] concerns female genital mutilation. Where earlier Shi'i texts clearly describe FGM as recommended at the age of sixteen,[7] reference to the practice is so reduced in al-Khūʾī's (d. 1992) account

2 *See, e.g.*, Abd al-Majīd al-Khūʾī, *Minhāj al-ṣāliḥīn* (Beirut: Dar al-Mujtaba, 1992) vol. 2, p. 258.

3 Alī al-Sīstānī, *Minhāj al-ṣāliḥīn*, (Beirut: Dar al-Mu'arrikh al-ʿArabī, 2008) 3:¶30.

4 *Id.* at 3:¶10 n. 1.

5 Muḥsin ibn Mahdī Ṭabāṭabāʾī al-Ḥakīm, *Mustamsik al-ʿurwat al-wuthqā* (Najaf: Matba'at al-Adab, 1971), 14:11.

6 These are not the only examples that exist – indeed, the phenomenon of strategic juristic omission abounds in any number of contexts, large and small. Hence, Muḥsin al-Ḥakīm recounts a famous report of the Sixth Imam that it is recommended for a father to hasten his daughter into marriage, because "it is to the happiness of a man that his daughter does not menstruate in his home." *Id.* As the idea of marrying a daughter and sending her off to live in a husband's home before her age of menstruation is not a common practice among most devout Shi'īs, it is unsurprising that most jurists do not recount these rules in their compendia either. Other examples relating to the insulting of the Prophet and the obligatory punishment for sorcery appear in footnote 10 *infra*. To reemphasize the point, the example of the blood price of the non-Muslim examined in the main text is intended as an illustration of a much broader phenomenon and not to highlight the peculiarities of one narrow rule.

7 Muḥammad Ḥasan al-Najafī, *Jawāhir al-kalām fi sharḥ sharāʾiʿ al-Islām*, edited by Abbas al-Quchani (Beirut: Dār iḥyāʾ al-turāth al-ʿArabī, 1981), 31:262–63 [hereinafter *Jawāhir*] ["As for females, [genital mutilation] is referred to as the curtailing of the maidens and it is

that a lay reader would know little more than that "curtailing" female slaves is recommended,[8] and al-Sīstānī omits mention of the matter altogether. Again, in each case, whether it is women leaving the home or the practice of FGM, the ethical precepts that contemporary jurists expound seem in tension with, if not directly contradictory to, deeply established rules of the *fiqh*, thereby causing them to rely on omission to manage the gap.

Nowhere is strategic juristic omission more apparent, and more obvious, than in the context of criminal law. There may be some justification for this as concerns the *ḥudūd*. After all, even in the classical *fiqh*, there is an expectation that the *ḥudūd* are to be applied relatively rarely in light of rather well known stringent evidentiary requirements.[9] To omit them, therefore, could be defended as an acknowledgment of that reality of rare enforcement rather than an attempt to conceal the rules through strategic removal of them from the contemporary *fiqh* manuals.

---

recommended [*mustaḥabb*] without disagreement.... The manifest opinion is that the time for them is seven years [after *bulūgh*]."

8 al-Khū'ī, *Minhāj al-ṣāliḥīn*, 2:1372.

9 The most obvious example of this involves fornication (*zinā*), where the evidentiary requirements are particularly difficult to meet. Grand Ayatollah al-Khū'ī, for example, notes the following:

"Fornication is not established by the testimony of two just male witnesses. Indeed, it requires four male witnesses, or three men and two women, or two men and four women, except stoning [as opposed to lashing] cannot be established by the latter, nor can any other [punishment for fornication] be established by the testimony of women alone, or by one man and six women, or by the swearing of an oath of one person. It is deemed that for testimony for fornication to be accepted, it must be directly observed, and if they witnessed it other than visually, then the witnessed person is not punished, but the witnesses are punished. Abdul Majīd al-Khū'ī, *Takmilat minhāj al-ṣāliḥīn* (Qum: Maktabat al-Sharqī lil Maʿlūmāt al-Dīnīyya, 1990) 142–43."

Even in the *ḥudūd*, however, strategic juristic omission appears to be at work in some contexts. A good example lies in the Shīʿī *ḥadd* of insulting the Prophet (*sabb al-nabī*). Not only must the offender be killed (perhaps a matter a jurist would have no trouble mentioning), but the person hearing the insult may kill him *without the need to seek permission from a judge in advance. See* al-Khū'ī, *Takmilat minhāj al-ṣāliḥīn*, 214. See also al-Najafī, *Jawāhir* at 41:432 (reporting a *khabar* from the Third Imam indicating that one who insults the Prophet "is killed as soon as possible, before the matter reaches the Imam"). Sanctioning extrajudicial killings of this sort, in particular following the rather horrific attack on Charlie Hebdo in France, is surely not a matter that the jurists of Najaf would wish to proclaim broadly. The other potential example of a *ḥadd* which jurists would naturally be reticent to publicize in our times is the imposition of capital punishment for sorcery. *See* al-Najafī, *Jawāhir*, 41:442. Whether or not rarely applied, the mere mention of it is likely to invite ridicule among critics and consternation among the more rationalist devout. In any event, the particular relationship of the *ḥudūd* to strategic juristic omission, while a valuable subject in its own right, is beyond the scope of this paper to discuss.

The approach seems less justified, however, as concerns the rules setting forth the punitive and compensatory consequences for intentional killings and physical injury. In the Islamic context, these are dealt by the infliction of retributive injury on an offender who kills or injures another (*qiṣāṣ*) or, in the alternative, through the receipt of blood money (*dīyya*).[10] In the absence of these rules, a society would have no choice but to develop alternative, secular ones in their place. After all, a society can hardly be indifferent to the commission of murder if it is to survive. And yet, both *qiṣāṣ* and *dīyya* are very much the subject of strategic juristic omission within Najaf, in a manner that contrasts sharply with their position on another major realm of private law; namely, the law of personal status.[11]

It is not immediately obvious why this is. Certainly it is true that the *qiṣāṣ* presume a right to claim the life of one who has killed intentionally in many instances.[12] However, this is not terribly controversial in Iraq, where the death penalty is widely practiced, even in cases where an offender does not kill someone.[13] The idea of compensation for a killing using values obtained from the *fiqh* is not a matter of controversy either – in fact tribes make frequent use of the *dīyya* in managing tribal resolutions for disputes arising out of a homicide.[14] Yet at the same time, there are aspects of the *qiṣāṣ* that do diverge,

10 Traditionally, jurists treat the *qiṣāṣ* and *dīyya* separately, in different sections, or "books." Volume 42 of the *Jawāhir* is thus devoted to the "Book of *Qiṣāṣ*" while volume 43 is the "Book of *Diya*", al-Najafī, *Jawāhir*, vols. 42–43. *See also* Imam Ruhollah Khomeini, *Taḥrīr al-wasīla* (Damascus: Embassy of the Islamic Republic of Iran in Syria, 1998), 463–502 (*Qiṣāṣ*); 503–530 (*Dīyya*); al-Khū'ī, *Takmilat minhāj al-ṣāliḥīn*, 59–94 (*Qiṣāṣ*); 95–139 (*Dīyya*).

11 Haider Ala Hamoudi, *Negotiating in Civil Conflict: Constitutional Construction and Imperfect Bargaining in Iraq* (Chicago: University of Chicago Press, 2014), (describing Shīʿī opposition to Personal Status Code not based on *fiqh*).

12 *See, e.g.*, Khomeini, *Taḥrīr al-wasīla*, 2:472 ("The free man is killed for a free man, and for a free woman, but only with the excess of the *dīyya*.")

13 In fact, the United States occupation authority, known as the Coalitional Provisional Authority, suspended the application of the death penalty in Iraq during the period of its tenure. *See* CPA Order 7, Section 3(1). Iraq's interim government reinstated it for certain crimes shortly after sovereignty was returned to it. Iraq Government Decree No. 3 of 2004. Since then, various laws and amendments include a death penalty where none existed before. Among them are the Antiterrorism Law, No. 7 of 2005, and the crime of kidnapping in the Penal Code (article 421).

14 Interview with Sheikh Mazen Falih Muhammad al-'Araiby, clan elder of the Muhammadawi tribe, in Sadr City, Iraq (April 25, 2013). In the spring of 2013, I spent a great deal of time in Iraq interviewing tribal leaders and observing tribal resolution processes with two professors from the Basra University College of Law, Wasfi al-Sharaa and Aqeel al-Dahhan. The information referenced in the main text in the context of this footnote was gathered while undertaking that fieldwork. Much of the result of this work appears in Haider Ala Hamoudi, Wasfi al-Sharaa and Aqeel al-Dahhan, "The Resolution of Disputes in State and

sharply, from the image that Najaf attempts to present of itself not only to Iraqis, but to the global community at large. The most obvious, and the subject of this paper, relates to the value of the *dīyya* for the *dhimmī*, the non-Muslim living under a covenant of protection in a Muslim land. Najaf has been broadly condemning acts of terrorism and violence directed at Iraq's non-Muslim communities for over a decade.[15] That it has done so, and that it has welcomed Iraq's non-Muslim internally displaced into the Holy City, is a source of some pride to Iraq's Shīʿī devout, and a matter extolled by them to the broader community. Yet, standing in some level of tension with this, Shīʿīsm's own rules respecting the *dīyya* owed for *dhimmī* lives wrongfully taken is extraordinarily low – far lower, in fact, than the value that probably would be ascribed by the very terrorists whom Najaf condemns for the unlawful killings.[16]

Strategic juristic omission works to narrow that divide. Iraqi law does not operate on the principle of the *dīyya*, so there are no stories that could be told of inadequate compensation being offered for the deaths of close relatives.[17] Given this considerable distance between law and *fiqh*, popular media could hardly be expected to know the substance of the *fiqh* rules across the Islamic schools. Moreover, the Sunni extremists who have targeted the Christian community have no interest in highlighting the rules of a sect that they consider to be heretical. As a result, the Shīʿī position on the *dhimmī*'s *dīyya* remains technically in place, but it is not a subject of discussion anywhere. In that sense, the endeavour has been a successful one, but it comes at significant cost, as described toward the end of this paper.

Beyond this Introduction, this paper is divided into three parts. Part 1 discusses the manner in which Najaf has stood stalwartly behind the non-Muslim communities currently targeted in contemporary Iraq. Part 2 then details the rules respecting *qiṣāṣ* generally in the Shīʿī fiqh, and the *dīyya* of the *dhimmī* in particular, to show some level of tension between the *fiqh* and the ethical precepts being advanced by the Najaf jurists, let alone the lay community. Part 3 details how these tensions are managed in this context through the use

Tribal Law in the South of Iraq: Toward a Cooperative Model of Pluralism". In *Negotiating State and Non-State Law: Challenges of Global and Local Pluralism* (Cambridge: Cambridge University Press, 2015).

15 This is discussed in detail in Part 1 *infra.*

16 This is discussed in detail in Part 2 *infra.*

17 Iraq's rules respecting compensation for injuries are set forth in Articles 202 through 217 of the Civil Code. These provisions (as elaborated upon by authoritative commentaries) cite the familiar civilian rule that a party is responsible for compensating an injured party for any moral or material harm caused, whether that harm was caused negligently or intentionally. The level of compensation is thus based not on a set schedule, as per the *dīyya*, but on the harm actually incurred. This is discussed in Part 3 *infra.*

of strategic juristic omission, and highlights some of the costs that emerge from this practice.

2 Iraq's Non-Muslims and the Najaf Elite

It was not long after the removal of the Saddam Hussein regime in Iraq that extremists initiated what first was referred to as resistance to the U.S. occupation. Some of their targeted violence was directed against U.S. soldiers, but much of it was not. In particular, those associated with "supporting" the occupation were targeted as well. This included not only members of the Iraq Governing Council[18] or other Iraqis of authority, but those at considerably lower levels.

Hence, for example, elements opposed to the U.S. occupation targeted and killed a number of Christian women as well as others working as cleaners for U.S. forces.[19] A large car bombing during Friday prayers in Najaf killed not only Shīʿī clerical leader (and Iraq Governing Council member) Muhammad Bāqir al-Ḥakīm, but it also killed dozens of others in attendance with no real connection to authority.[20]

Before long, these acts of violence were directed quite clearly at elements that had no demonstrable connection to any occupation, but instead were merely identitarian groups that were non-Muslim, or that were, in the eyes of those directing the violence, "rejectionist" Muslims, which was the term used by these elements to describe the Shīʿa.[21] Bombing of civilian areas in which the Shīʿa congregate, or at times they might be expected to congregate (the Arbaʿīn procession, for example, or anywhere on the day of Ashūra), were interspersed

18 The Iraq Governing Council was a body handpicked by the United States occupation authority to serve as its advisory council. Its members were clearly targeted by anti-US elements, and two were killed by attacks. "Suicide Attack Kills Head of Iraqi Governing Council", *Voice of America*, May 17, 2004.

19 "*Nine Killed in Iraq Violence*", *Birmingham Post* (UK), January 23, 2004.

20 Orly Halpern, "Bombing of Iraq Deepens Crisis; Top Shi'a Leader, more than 80 killed in bloodiest day since war ended", *Globe and Mail* (UK), August 30, 2003.

21 The slur "rejectionists" (*rāfiḍa*) to describe the Shīʿa has accompanied the history of Shi'ism from a very early period. Early Shi'īs used it as an honorific, as a description of those who "rejected" oppression and tyranny in favour of the Prophet Muhammad and Imam Ali, precisely as Pharaoh's magicians had rejected his authority in favour of Moses and Aaron. Etan Kohlberg, "The Term '*Rāfiḍa*' in Imāmī Shi'ī Usage," *Journal of the American Oriental Society* 677–79 (1979), 99. Contemporary Shi'īs, however, regard it as a Sunni slur. It was popularized in Iraq by Zarqāwī, who is described further in the main text. *See* V.G. Julie Rajan, *Al Qaeda's Global Crisis: The Islamic State, Takfir and the Genocide of Muslims* (London: Routledge, 2015), 122–23.

with attacks on Christian interests and Christian places of worship.[22] The idea of targeting these communities was made rather explicit by 2005 with the rise of Al Qaeda in Iraq and the articulation on the part of its leader, Abu Muṣ'ab al-Zarqāwī, of the need to stoke sectarian war.[23] Zarqāwī and his organization thus made it quite clear that they viewed both the Christian and Shīʿī populations as legitimate targets in their operations.

It was in this context somewhat predictable that the Shīʿī clerical elite would issue rather strong denunciations of the attacks against the Christian community.[24] First, of course, Shīʿī Islam takes no less a negative view of the targeted killing of civilians, Muslim or non-Muslim, than Sunni Islam does, meaning that such denunciations of such killings were completely compatible with the normative underpinnings of the Shīʿī *fiqh*. Moreover, there was natural sympathy, as both the Shīʿī and the Christian community found themselves under attack from the same terrorist groups advancing the same ideology, a narrow version of Sunni Islam rejected by the vast majority of Iraq's Sunnis and indeed most Sunnis across the world. Finally, it is important to note that the Shīʿa were quite clearly, for demographic reasons alone, destined to be the new power in Iraq, replacing Sunni dominated regimes that had ruled Iraq since its inception. That they planned to be tolerant, humane, and open to diversity was a message they strongly wished to deliver to the global community for obvious geopolitical reasons.

As such, Grand Ayatollah al-Sīstānī's criticisms of the attacks on Christian places of worship were not only unusually sharp, but they were also unusually public. While al-Sīstānī usually left his deputies to deliver the messages he wished to convey during Friday prayers, in the case of the attacks against Christians, he took the less common route of issuing memoranda, or *bayāns*, in his name. In such memoranda, he described the Christian community having the right to live peacefully in their home of Iraq, condemning absolutely attacks against that community, and calling upon the state to take action to prevent such attacks in the future.[25]

This support of the non-Muslim communities, and the opposition to attacks directed against it, increased considerably as the terrorist and extremist threats to Iraq proliferated. It reached its apex with the arrival of the Islamic State of Iraq and the Levant ("Dāʿish") on to Iraqi territory. The threats against the

22 For the variety of attacks against the Shīʿa during this period, *see Ibid.*, 122–23. As concerns attacks on Christians, *see* Steve Fainaru, *"Five Baghdad Churches Targeted by Bombers"*, *Washington Post*, October 17, 2004.

23 Rajan, *Al Qaeda's Global Crisis*, 122–23.

24 *"Iraq's Sistani Condemns Church Bombings"*, *Agence Free Press English Wire*, August 2, 2004.

25 *Ibid.*

non-Muslim communities posed by Dāʿish was considerably greater than any that preceded it. In fact, it was existential in nature. This is because it came to exercise effective control over territory as the Iraqi state started to unravel. In the territory that it controlled, in particular the city of Mosul and its environs, home to large numbers of Christians and a non-Muslim community known as the Yazīdīs, its treatment of the non-Muslim minorities proved to be appalling. Non-Muslim women, and primarily Yazīdīs, were abducted and sold into slave markets.[26] Christians had their possessions taken from them, and were told to pay a tax or die.[27] Finally, in the full view of the world, tens of thousands of Yazīdīs fled their villages and neighbourhoods to a nearby barren mountain where they faced almost certain starvation and ruin in the absence of an intervention coordinated by the global community and the Kurdish *pesh merga*.[28]

To the extent that Shīʿī leaders were predisposed to support non-Muslim communities before the rise of Dāʿish, they were doubly inspired to do so afterwards. The Dāʿish actions varied from highly opportunistic constructions of medieval Sunni rules to positions bearing no relationship at all to any recognizable version of Islamic law, classical or modern.[29] Thus, they were easy to condemn from a purely theological standpoint. Moreover, by the time of the rise of Dāʿish, the Shīʿī community was firmly in control of the apparatus of the state and in fact had largely sidelined the Sunni minority community.[30] By

26 "Yazidi Sex Slave Escapes ISIS, Tells Her Story", *Al Arabiya*, March 21, 2015.

27 Fazel Hawramy, "Iraqi Christians in Mosul Told by ISIS to Convert To Islam or Be Executed", *The Guardian* (UK), July 25, 2014.

28 Dominique Soquel, "A Sanctuary For Iraqi Yazidis – And A Plea For Obama's Intervention", *Christian Science Monitor*, August 12, 2014.

29 Some of the Dāʿish actions, such as the sexual enjoyment of female slaves, contain significant levels of pedigree across the various schools of Islamic law, Sunni and Shīʿī. *See, e.g.*, Kecia Ali, *Marriage and Slavery in Early Islam* (Harvard University Press: 2010), 39; Haider Ala Hamoudi, "Sex and the Shari'a: Defining Gender Norms and Sexual Deviancy in Shīʿī Islam," *Fordham International L.J.* 25, 27 n. 5 (2015), 39. Nevertheless, there is significant level of opportunism in Dāʿish depredations, as the taking of the Yazīdīs as slaves in the first place depends on the more tendentious positions that, first, Dāʿish is somehow engaged in a *jihād* in its military actions against states which declare Islam to be the religion of the state, and second, that the Yazīdīs are not entitled to *dhimmī* status. *See* John Kelsay, *Arguing the Just War in Islam* (Harvard University Press, 2007), 194–95 (pointing out the difficulty of justifying attacks against existing Muslim loci of power on the basis of the opinions of early Sunni classical jurists); Dabiq, *The Islamic State Online Magazine*, 4:14–16 (justifying the taking of Yazīdī slaves and denying them *dhimmī* status); William McCants, *The ISIS Apocalypse: The History, Strategy and Doomsday Vision of the Islamic State* (St. Martin's Press, 2015), 111–12. On the other hand, other actions, such as leaving civilians to starve on a mountain if they do not return to be enslaved or killed, are so divorced from traditional source material as to be nearly impossible to justify.

30 Scott Peterson, "Can Iraq Hold Together?", *Christian Science Monitor*, January 20, 2015.

leading an insurrection against the state of Iraq, Dāʿish was effectively fighting a Shīʿī state, and as such, it was no less sparing of the lives of Iraqi Shīʿī soldiers than it was those of non-Muslim minorities.[31] Again, the Shīʿa and the non-Muslim communities saw themselves as natural allies of one another as a result. Finally, the depredations of Dāʿish were almost designed to shock and offend a global community, thereby enabling the Najaf elite to demonstrate their ultimate humanity by showing some level of support for the non-Muslim minorities following the outrages conducted against them.

It was thus not a surprise that Najaf immediately issued statements strongly in condemnation of the attacks on Christian communities. The cities of Najaf and Karbala also took in large numbers of non-Muslim refugees, and began to provide them food and shelter pending their return.[32] The result of actions like these, as well as similar ones in favour of Sunni civilians likewise forced out of their homes either by Dāʿish or by civil conflict, earned Najaf generally, and Grand Ayatollah al-Sīstānī in particular, no shortage of well-deserved praise.

3 The Non-Muslim *Dīyya* and Shīʿī *Fiqh*

Al-Sīstānī's well-deserved reputation for ecumenicalism arising from these and other positions he has taken, whether borne out of contemporary political expediency, ideological commitment, or some combination of the two, does nevertheless stand in some tension to the Ja'fari *fiqh* as it concerns the non-Muslim *dīyya*. To demonstrate this, I refer to the rules set forth in perhaps the most influential of the juristic compendia of the modern era, that of Muḥammad Ḥasan al-Najafī (d. 1850), entitled *Jawāhir al kalām fī sharāʾiʿ al-Islām*.[33] That compendium is itself a commentary of an older, influential compendium of the 13th century (CE), known as the *Sharāʾiʿ al-Islām*, of Muḥaqqiq al-Ḥillī (d. 1277), perhaps the most influential of the Shīʿī jurists on the substantive rules of the *fiqh*.[34] (The original words of al-Ḥillī are set forth in the text of the *Jawāhir* in quotation marks, and I reflect this convention in the

31 Adam Lusher, "Iraq Crisis: The Footage That Shows ISIS Militants Taunting And Killing Shia Soldiers", *The Independent* (UK), June 17, 2014.

32 Rahat Husain, "Fleeing Christians Find Safe Haven at Shrine of Imam Ali", *Washington Times*, July 24, 2014.

33 *See* Abdulaziz Sachedina, *The Just Ruler in Shīʿite Islam: The Comprehensive Authority of the Jurist in Imamite Jurisprudence* (New York: Oxford University Press, 1988), 22 (describing the influence of the *Jawāhir*).

34 Ibid., 14.

passages quoted below.) It is also important to note that the rules do not differ significantly from jurist to jurist as to the matters discussed herein.

The standard *dīyya* for the free male Muslim for an intentional killing is set forth in the *Jawāhir* as follows:

> As for the value of the *dīyya*, the value of "the intentional *dīyya* is one hundred camels of the highest quality, two hundred cows, two hundred vestments, each garment is two shirts of the garments of Yemen, one thousand dinars, one thousand sheep, or twelve thousand dirhams" without debate in anything I can find from the *sunna*.[35]

For reasons that will be made clear shortly, the relevant measurement for the purposes of this paper is in the form of the silver *dirham*. As it weighed approximately three grams, this rendered the *dīyya* of a free Muslim man killed intentionally at 30,000 grams of silver, or US$16,526.[36]

As is the case among the Sunni schools, the family members of the victim may elect to receive this amount, or to demand retaliation from the perpetrator by demanding his or her death.[37] Also similarly to the Sunni schools, the *dīyya* for a free Muslim woman is one half of that of a man.[38] Importantly, however, and in some contrast to the rules of the Sunni schools, the family members of a free Muslim woman may demand the death of a free Muslim man who kills her, but only if they pay the difference in the *dīyya* between the two of them to the family of the perpetrator.[39]

By contrast, the value of the *dīyya* for the non-Muslim is extremely low, and there is no possibility of making up the difference and demanding the death of a Muslim for killing a non-Muslim.[40] The *Jawāhir* specifically notes that the value for a *dhimmī*[41] is 800 dirhams, the source material in support of the position is "overflowing with abundance"(*mustafīḍa ḥadd al-istifāda*) and

35 al-Najafī, *Jawāhir*, 43:4.

36 Calculated on the spot price of silver at 9 am on October 5, 2015. (Source: www.monex.com)

37 al-Najafī, *Jawāhir*, 42:7.

38 *Ibid.*, 43:32.

39 *Ibid.*, 43:82. *See also* Khomeini, *Taḥrīr al-wasīla*, 2:472.

40 al-Najafī, *Jawāhir*, 42:150.

41 Of course, the *fiqh* would not regard every non-Muslim as a *dhimmī*. However, as the focus of the paper concerns the discrepancy between Shīʿī fiqh on the one hand, and the political positions of the Shīʿī jurists as concerns *Iraqi* non-Muslims on the other, the relevant *dīyya* in that context would be that of the *dhimmī*. Hence, my focus is exclusively on the *dīyya* of the *dhimmī*, as opposed to, for example, the non-Muslim *mustaʾmin*, or even the *ḥarbi*.

therefore "deemed correct" (*muʿtabira*). This creates a stark discrepancy with the Sunni schools that the *Jawāhir* recognizes, because those schools attach a value for the *dhimmī* considerably higher, and specifically between one third of the *dīyya* to the full *dīyya* of a free Muslim man.[42] Finally, the *Jawāhir* adopts the position uniform across all schools and sects that a *dhimmī* woman's *dīyya* is half of that of a *dhimmī* man.[43]

Rendering the Shīʿī position even more extreme in contemporary circumstances is the fact that the value of silver is in our times far below its historic value. That is, the *Jawāhir* treats one thousand dinars of gold as equivalent to twelve thousand dirhams of silver in evaluating the *dīyya* generally. It moreover indicates that the currency in which the *dīyya* is paid for a Muslim life, whether it be camels, dinars, dirhams, garments, cows, or sheep, depends on the region where it is paid, and what might be traded in that region as an item of value.[44]

Yet the values of those listed items are not even close to equivalent in contemporary times, at least as concerns gold and silver. Thus, one thousand dinars of gold, (equivalent to 4.25 kilograms), would be worth in US currency today approximately $170,400, which is over ten times the amount of twelve thousand silver dirhams.[45] As few trade in silver as opposed to gold in modern times, the discrepancy might not seem particularly important when valuing the *dīyya* of a Muslim, as gold would be used in most instances. However, when valuing the *dīyya* of a non-Muslim, the discrepancy is quite important, because silver dirhams are the only measure given for that *dīyya*.

In other words, to translate the matter into contemporary currency, the current value of the *dīyya* for a male *dhimmī* is $1322. For a woman, it is $661. Moreover, the *dhimmī*'s family could not demand retribution, as the family of a Muslim woman could, merely by paying the difference in the *dīyya* between victim and offender to the family of the offender. By contrast, presuming for a moment that Dāʿish would perhaps apply the Ḥanbalī rules, as seems most likely, the value of the *dīyya* would be the same as that of a Muslim, which if measured in gold is several hundred thousands of dollars.[46]

42 al-Najafī, *Jawāhir*, 43:38.

43 *Ibid.*, 43:39.

44 *Ibid.*, 43:8–9 (quoting Shīʿī Islam's third Imam, Husayn bin Ali, to this effect).

45 Calculated on the spot price of gold at 9 am on October 5, 2015 (Source: www.monex.com).

46 *See, e.g.*, Ibn Qudāma, *Mughnī*, 8, no. 6833 (noting the blood price of the *dhimmī* as the same as that of a Muslim.). My purpose is not to slander the Ḥanbali *fiqh* by describing Dāʿish as adhering to it in any consistent fashion. Yet the influence on Ibn Taymiyya on groups such as Al Qaeda and Dāʿish is obvious, and he was of course Ḥanbali. *See* "As World Expresses Horror, IS Said To Show Immolation Video On Big Screens", *Radio Free Europe*, available at http://www.rferl.org/content/jordan-pilot-burned-video-isis-islamic-state/26829782.

The *fiqh*, it seems, is not following the practice. The clerical leadership that is emphasizing the importance of non-Muslim life, and issuing broad and serious condemnations against its taking, is the one whose rules value that life the least in setting the *dīyya*. By contrast, the group that appears to value non-Muslim life the least in practice claims to be adhering to a school of thought that measures that life at a much higher value in similar contexts. The tension is rather obvious.

Of course, in fairness to the Shīʿī clerical authorities, some limitations on the thesis need to be raised here. First, as an ethical matter, neither Shīʿī nor Sunni sources suggest that the payment of the *dīyya* expiates the grave, underlying sin of murder. That is, a person cannot kill other human beings, Muslim or non-Muslim, pay their *dīyya*, and by that action alone be deemed to be acting ethically. Moreover, even as a legal matter, it is plainly within the power of the state to impose the discretionary criminal penalties known as the *taʿzīr* to the extent that the state observed it in the public interest to do so.[47] Surely the occurrence of large numbers of killings directed at a non-Muslim community who are supposed to be living under the protection of the Muslim state would qualify as a serious threat to public interest.

I therefore *do not maintain*, to be clear, that Grand Ayatollah al-Sīstānī is acting inconsistently with Shīʿī *fiqh* in condemning the taking of non-Muslim life, and in calling for the state to put an end to it. To the contrary, stopping randomized murders is well within core principles of Islamic ethics and law. I do maintain, however, that there is some tension between, on the one hand, showing such laudable solicitude toward the protection of a vulnerable minority from the horrors of Dāʿish without, on the other hand, questioning rules concerning the compensation due for the taking of the individual lives of that minority at a level that puts them somewhere between .5% and 8% of the compensation due for an equivalent Muslim life. And I find that tension only increased when such rules are contrasted with those to which Dāʿish might purport to adhere in theory, even if it does not in fact.

---

html (pointing out ISIS use of Ibn Taymiyya fatwa to justify burning a Jordanian pilot alive). Thus, it is fair to assume that Dāʿish would generally privilege Ḥanbali interpretations over those of the other schools.

47 Iran does this in cases where there is no penalty imposed by virtue of *qisas*. Article 612 of its Penal Code reads as follows:

"Anyone who commits a murder and where there is no complainant, or there is a complainant but he has forgiven and withdrawn his application for *qisas*, or if *qisas* is not executed for any reason, if his act disrupts the public order and safety of the society or it is thought that it emboldens the offender or others [to commit murder again], the court shall sentence the offender to three to ten years' imprisonment."

4 Strategic Juristic Omission

The first section of this paper outlines some of the significant steps that the Shīʿī clerical leadership of Najaf has taken to protect the lives of the non-Muslim communities of Iraq from the violence perpetrated against them by extremists. The second section shows how this stands at some tension with core rules of Shīʿī fiqh, which sets the *dīyya* for the taking of a non-Muslim life at much lower levels than the Sunni schools do. Having exposed the problem, this final section will discuss how it is managed through the technique of strategic juristic omission, and the manner in which this presents dangers for the future of *fiqh*, notwithstanding its superficial appeal. Before doing so, however, I address potential alternatives that the Najaf jurists could have considered, and that in some cases have been received with some favour elsewhere.

One way to deal with the tensions described above would be to acknowledge them openly. This would involve an overt description of precisely what compensation is owed the families of the non-Muslims whose lives have been taken by Dāʿish, along with an explanation of the source material in defence of that conclusion. Such a description would of course indicate that the payment of these sums does not expiate the sin of the taking of the lives, and that the state can and should impose punishments in addition to restore public order.

Yet it is perfectly obvious that even with such qualifications, the pursuit of this option will lead to broad criticism of Najaf. The amounts that would be due to the families of the victims would be shockingly low, so low that they could not begin to actually approximate the actual losses those families incurred by virtue of the deaths. Moreover, such amounts would be far lower than that to which the families of the victims would be entitled under Iraqi law.

Current Iraqi law, as set forth in the Iraqi Civil Code, gives families of victims the right to recover for all material and moral harm that resulted from the death of the victim.[48] No reasonable person would argue that a young

48 Article 202 of the Civil Code imposes compensation for harmful acts. Article 205(1) indicates that the harm includes both moral and material harm, while subsection (2) of the same article extends the right of recovery to spouses and other relatives. In the words of Sanhuri, the drafter of the Iraqi Civil Code,

"The compensation level is measured by the direct harm. Compensation in whatever form it is – specific compensation or in substitution, monetary and nonmonetary, in installments or capital, is valued by the value of the direct harm which the wrong caused. This is regardless of whether the harm is material or moral, expected or not, present or future, so long as it is realized." Abdul Razzāq al-Sanhūrī, *al-Wāsiṭ fī sharḥ qānūn al-madanī al-jadīd*, (2000, 3rd edition), 1:1095.

Clearly, this is not the measure of the *fiqh*, and in particular as concerns the life of the *dhimmī*.

child suffers only $661 worth of harm from witnessing the death of the child's mother. The secular, Iraqi rules, transplanted from Western Civil Codes, seem to harmonize considerably better with al-Sīstānī's positions respecting the killing of Christians. Those same transplanted rules also harmonize better with the normative convictions of the vast majority of the Iraq's Shīʿa, given how eager the community has been to extol al-Sīstānī's humane treatment of Iraq's non-Muslims. Hence, the secular law seems to be offering the very result that the jurists and the community want. The juristic rules, quite simply, do not. This makes overtly propounding them troublesome in the extreme.

A second potential approach to managing the tension would be to reevaluate the rules. While it is true that the *Jawāhir* describes the source material as "plentiful", this would by no means prevent a later jurist from coming to a different conclusion respecting what the source material should be understood to mean. That sort of reevaluation is not unknown among more reformist minded Shīʿa, from Mohsen Kadivar to Abdulaziz Sachedina to Yusuf Saanei, all of whom have criticized traditional *fiqh* rules that clearly privilege Muslims over non-Muslims. All of them have called for a greater conception of religious equality from within the Islamic tradition, including in some cases over the valuation of the *dīyya* of the *dhimmī*.[49] Indeed, even Ayatollah Khamene'i has indicated that the *dīyya* of the Muslim and the permitted religious minorities in Iran should be equivalent, a conclusion which is now recognized in Iranian penal law.[50] (This is on the basis of a *fatwa* that Khamene'i issued in his capacity as Supreme Leader, in furtherance of the public interest, rather than as a reinterpretation of the *fiqh*).

By contrast, the process of reevaluating older rules has proven to be rare among traditionalists within Najaf, perhaps because it carries its own set of risks. Premier among these is a potential loss of authority.[51] That is, if jurists

49 *See, e.g.*, Mohsen Kadivar, "Human Rights and Intellectual Islam," in *New Directions of Islamic Thought*, eds. Kari Vogt, Lena Larsen and Christian Moe (London: I.B. Tauris, 2009), 47–73; Abdulaziz Sachedina, *The Islamic Roots of Democratic Pluralism* (New York: Oxford University Press, 2001) 64–66; Hamid Mavani, "Paradigm Shift in Twelver Shiʿī Legal Theory (*uṣūl al-fiqh*): Ayatullah Yusef Saanei," *Muslim World* 99:2009, 332–55 at 342–46.

50 Code of Criminal Laws of Iran (2013), art. 554.

51 Khamenei's seeming receptiveness to greater change within the jurisprudence, in particular as it concerns the equivalence of the *dīyya* of the Muslim to the *dhimmi*, may well be explained by the fact that as the leader of a state, any fears of diminished authority are significantly tempered by the power he is able to project. Moreover, as the leader of a state, he can proclaim that his actions are in the public interest rather than a necessary derivation of *fiqh*, and in this sense legitimize rules that stand independently of *fiqh*. Najaf jurists, by contrast, occupy no similar position and instead derive their authority on the

were to change historic rules in a manner that seemed to befit the times better, they would find it harder to argue that they are actually interpreting text rather than merely manipulating it to reach foreordained conclusions. Maintaining the same positions as jurists preceding them helps existing jurists establish a sense of legitimacy to the interpretive process that might otherwise be lacking. It is perhaps for this reason that the Najaf jurists are astonishingly conservative in their approaches to the *fiqh* and its potential evolution. Indeed, al-Sīstānī's general attitude toward such reforms is well revealed by his dismissive reactions to Sachedina's ideas of religious pluralism, and his effort to silence Sachedina precisely because of his espousal of such views.[52]

Of course, even if jurists do not always proclaim it, there is always some evolution over time, because some rules simply become unmanageable in modernity. For example, the *Jawāhir* describes a woman's voice as forbidden to hear ever, and describes the conclusion as necessary on the basis of the plentiful source material (*muqtaḍ al-mustafīḍ*).[53] Despite this, Najaf's modern jurists plainly and overwhelmingly do not agree, as they permit a woman's voice to be heard so long as it is not embellished.[54] However, such examples are exceptions that help to prove the rule that evolution, to the extent it occurs, is gradual – so gradual, in fact, as to be deliberately imperceptible.

Once the jurists can neither justify their rules, nor are they willing to change them significantly, they are left with one option, which is to ignore them when they prove inconvenient. Najaf jurists have thus proven extremely adept at what I describe herein as *strategic juristic omission* – or merely failing to mention those rules that are somewhat awkward and difficult to defend. This extends well beyond the subject of the *qiṣāṣ* and *dīyya*, but certainly it encompasses them. Hence, for example, Grand Ayatollah al-Sīstānī's compendium contains no reference to the *qiṣāṣ*, or the *dīyya*, at all. The same can be said of any number of Najaf's Grand Ayatollahs of the previous century, from Muḥsin al-Ḥakīm to Muḥammad Bāqir al-Ṣadr (d. 1980).

In fact, the only Najaf based Grand Ayatollah of note to issue rules relating to the *dīyya* in the twentieth century is Grand Ayatollah al-Khū'ī. Even he

---

basis of their role as the upholders of a proud jurisprudential tradition. They are therefore extremely loath to subject that tradition to rapid and significant shifts that could call their legitimacy into question.

52 Personal Account, Abdulaziz Sachedina, What Happened in Najaf?, http://islam.uga.edu/sachedina_silencing.html (last visited Feb. 26, 2019).

53 al-Najafī, *Jawāhir*, 29:97.

54 *See, e.g.*, al-Sīstānī, *Minhāj al-ṣāliḥīn* 3:29; Muḥsin al-Ḥakīm, *Mustamsik al-ʿurwat al-wuthqā*, 14:48–49; al-Khū'ī, *Minhāj al-ṣāliḥīn*, 2:1234; Muḥammad Saʿīd al-Ḥakīm, *Minhāj al-ṣāliḥīn* (Baghdad: Dar al-Kutub, 2008), 3:17.

does not do this in the context of a numbered volume in his juristic compendium, entitled *Minhāj al-ṣāliḥīn*. Rather, it appears separately in a book entitled "The Completion of *Minhāj al-ṣāliḥīn*." There, Khū'ī recites, very briefly, in two lines of text, the traditional rule that "the *dīyya* of the *dhimmi*, from among Christians, Jews, and Zoroastrians, is 800 *dirhams* and the *dīyya* of their women is half, but as for the rest of the unbelievers, there is neither *dīyya* nor *qiṣāṣ* for killing them." The rule is therefore barely noticeable, and indeed the entire volume is not normally included within the two-volume set of the compendium ordinarily sold on websites or in other locations. This is not to say that the volume is impossible to find, but it certainly is far more difficult to find than, say, Khū'ī's rules respecting ritual impurities, which appear in volume 1 and could be located online, or purchased in hard copy, with extreme ease.

The omission, on an issue that is in many ways an essential part of Islamic private law, is notable. In my own conversations in Najaf, the common explanation seems to be that payment of the *dīyya* is not relevant to ordinary devout believers, who live in legal systems which either do not recognize such matters or, if they do, have legal professionals who apply the rules in specialized tribunals, thereby obviating the need to explain them to lay audiences. This justification seems deeply inadequate for many reasons. In the first place, there are numerous Shīʿī rules set forth in various compendia that are not relevant to lay believers because they relate to conduct that the state does not countenance. The most obvious example lies in the rules concerning the marrying of and deriving sexual satisfaction from very young children.[55] The evident criminality of such religiously permissible conduct seems unimportant to the jurists, who recite rules relating to what kinds of sexual enjoyment a husband can receive from a prepubescent wife in detail. Secondly, payment of the *dīyya* remains relevant in the contemporary era in non-state tribunals. Iraqi tribes continue to negotiate compensation in cases of an inter-tribal killing, and they determine the value as against the price of one thousand sheep, one of the potential amounts referenced in the juristic compendia as the *dīyya* for a free Muslim man.[56] The valuation of the *dīyya* is therefore hardly entirely irrelevant, even in Iraq.

The omission, therefore, cannot possibly relate to a lack of relevance to lay believers. Rather, it seems a calculated attempt to avoid addressing

55 *See, e.g.* al-Sīstānī, *Minhāj al-ṣāliḥīn* 3:8 (deeming sexual acts with child wives under nine permissible so long as they do not include penetration).

56 Interview with Sheikh Mazen Falih Muhammad al-'Araiby, clan elder of the Muhammadawi tribe, in Sadr City, Iraq (April 25, 2013).

uncomfortable questions. And, at a superficial level, it works remarkably well. The position of the Shīʿī clerical elite vis a vis Iraq's non-Muslim population is widely touted by lay Shīʿa, broadly noted by global media sources, and any underlying tensions with *fiqh* are safely buried, with the secret, as it were, known only to those with the skills and energy to examine centuries-old texts in more detail.

Yet the approach has long term costs, all arising from the fact that the omissions and indirections are increasingly hard to maintain in the contemporary world. After all, it is one thing to exercise strategic omissions in a context in which few are literate, and knowledge of Islamic law in a particular location is limited to a village cleric. Masking uncomfortable aspects of doctrine would not be hard to do in such circumstances. It is much harder to achieve over the longer term, however, in our hyperconnected world, where much source material can be found through a Google search. Two significant problems are immediately apparent.

The first is that the omission is in effect an acknowledgement, albeit implicit, of a failure in the *fiqh*, and a certain insecurity in its conclusions. There are consequences to such an implicit admission. After all, a jurist cannot both insist that Islam provides a complete way of life, and that Islam lays out a manner by which a believer can organize his or her affairs absolutely, and at the same time seek to suppress rather fundamental rules respecting compensation for harm. At the very least, there would need to be some explanation of what parts of the *fiqh* deserve recognition, what parts do not, and why. Otherwise, the entire enterprise of rules-generation runs the risk of obsolescence, with the believer perhaps more comfortable ignoring rules respecting prayer or almsgiving once she knows that the jurist himself is ignoring other rules concerning payment of the *dīyya*.

The second is that the failure to openly and honestly reassess juristic rules, and instead to ignore them when inconvenient, leaves the door open to radical and extremist movements to exploit the ignored rules and claim to adopt them. Hence, for example, if Muslim scholars are willing to review the historic *fiqh* rules on slavery, deem them morally offensive, and, in fact, declare such rules to be a betrayal of the traditions of the Prophet and the commands of God as set forth in the Qur'an, then any group who wished to revitalize those rules would stand against the weight of modern scholars on the point. However, if Muslim scholars instead were to merely ignore those historic rules relating to slavery, and pretend they never existed, or somehow were more limited and temporally constrained than they claimed to be, then it is all the harder to refute the extremist, when he metaphorically dusts off the historic book that is already being cited by mainstream scholars for other purposes and insists that the rules on the sexual enjoyment of female slaves deserve recognition as well.

Applied to the present context, the fact is that any Shīʿī, devout layperson who insisted that he owed no more than about $700 for killing a non-Muslim woman *would be right* as a matter of *fiqh* according to the traditional jurists of Najaf. The fact that an Iraqi judge applying the Civil Code will not care, and that the jurist is happy to pretend that the juristic rules do not exist, may work in the short term. However, it leaves the entire system dangerously vulnerable to elements who might find interest in reversing al-Sīstānī's tendencies towards humane treatment of non-Muslims. In more stable societies, perhaps the vulnerability can be overlooked. In the context of the weak states that dominate the Middle East, the problem becomes an existential one.

5 Conclusion

This paper has tried to show the manner in which Shīʿī jurists often take contemporary political positions that are quite popular with lay communities, but that lie in some tension with historic rules of Shīʿī *fiqh.* I have made particular reference to one specific rule – that concerning the value of the *dīyya* for a non-Muslim life. In the context of so doing, I have attempted to demonstrate that jurists often seek to manage the tension between their rules and their political positions through strategic juristic omission, or, to put it more simply, merely ignoring inconvenient or embarrassing rules. This method may work for a time, even as it may have worked historically. However, once the underlying truths are exposed, it carries two significant, long-term consequences. First, it makes a mockery of any claim by the jurist that Islamic rules require absolute adherence. After all, if rules might be ignored when they are inconvenient to the political positions maintained by a jurist, why might they not be similarly ignored when inconvenient for the lay believer? Second, strategic juristic omission renders extremist positions all the more plausible. When the jurist fails to categorically reject earlier derivations of sacred text, the extremist seeking to defend his outrages is in a position to point to such texts, long ignored but never refuted, as all the justification he needs. This leaves the entire community in an even more difficult position as it seeks to describe the outrages then committed as "un-Islamic." In these times, that is a dangerous proposition indeed.

Acknowledgements

The author would like to thank Arif Abdul Hussain, Ali Reza Bhojani, Michael Bohlander, Laurens de Rooij, Abdulaziz Sachedina, and all of the participants at the Joint Symposium sponsored by the Centre of Islam, Law and Modernity of Durham University and the Al-Mahdi Institute for their generous comments and support. Any errors or omissions are the responsibility of the author alone.

Bibliography

Ali, Kecia, *Marriage and Slavery in Early Islam*. Harvard University Press: 2010.

al-Ḥakīm, Muḥsin ibn Mahdī Ṭabāṭabā'ī, *Mustamsik al-ʿurwat al-wuthqā*. Najaf, Matba'at al-Adab, 1971.

al-Ḥakīm, Muḥammad Saʿīd, *Minhāj al-ṣāliḥīn*. Baghdad: Dar al-Kutub, 2008.

Hamoudi, Haider Ala, *Negotiating in Civil Conflict: Constitutional Construction and Imperfect Bargaining in Iraq*. Chicago: University of Chicago Press, 2014.

Hamoudi, Haider Ala, "Sex and the Shari'a: Defining Gender Norms and Sexual Deviancy in Shīʿī Islam", *Fordham International L.J.* 39 (2015), 25–99.

Hamoudi, Haider Ala, Wasfi al-Sharaa and Aqeel al-Dahhan, "The Resolution of Disputes in State and Tribal Law in the South of Iraq: Toward a Cooperative Model of Pluralism." In *Negotiating State and Non-State Law: Challenges of Global and Local Pluralism*. Cambridge: Cambridge University Press, 2015.

Kadivar, Mohsen, "Human Rights and Intellectual Islam," in *New Directions of Islamic Thought*, ed. Kari Vogt, Lena Larsen and Christian Moe. London: I.B. Tauris, 2009.

Khomeini, Imam Ruhollah, *Taḥrīr al-wasīla*. Damascus: Embassy of the Islamic Republic of Iran in Syria, 1998.

al-Khū'ī, Abdul Majīd, *Takmilat minhāj al-ṣāliḥīn*. Qum: Maktabat al-Sharqī lil Maʿlūmāt al-Dīnīyya, 1990.

al-Khū'ī, Abdul Majīd, *Minhāj al-ṣāliḥīn*. Beirut: Dar al-Mujtaba, 1992.

Kelsay, John, *Arguing the Just War in Islam*. Harvard University Press, 2007.

Kohlberg, Etan, "The Term '*Rāfiḍa*' in Imāmī Shi'ī Usage," *Journal of the American Oriental Society* 677–79 (1979).

Mavani, Hamid, "Paradigm Shift in Twelver Shiʿī Legal Theory (uṣūl al-fiqh): Ayatullah Yusef Saanei," *Muslim World* 99 (2009), 332–55.

McCants, William, *The ISIS Apocalypse: The History, Strategy and Doomsday Vision of the Islamic State*. St. Martin's Press, 2015.

Rajan, V.G. Julie, *Al Qaeda's Global Crisis: The Islamic State, Takfir and the Genocide of Muslims*. London: Routledge, 2015.

Sachedina, Abdulaziz, *The Just Ruler in Shīʿite Islam: The Comprehensive Authority of the Jurist in Imamite Jurisprudence*. New York: Oxford University Press, 1988.

Sachedina, Abdulaziz, *The Islamic Roots of Democratic Pluralism*. New York: Oxford University Press, 2001.

al-Sīstānī, Alī, *Minhāj al-ṣāliḥīn*. Beirut: Dar al-Muʾarrikh al-ʿArabī, 2008.

al-Najafī, Muḥammad Ḥasan, *Jawāhir al-kalām fi sharḥ sharāʾiʿ al-Islām*, edited by Abbas al-Quchani. Beirut: Dār iḥyāʾ al-turāth al-ʿArabī, 1981.

CHAPTER 6

Towards the Hermeneutics of a Justice-Oriented Reading of *Sharīʿa*

Ali-Reza Bhojani

This study explores and proposes hermeneutical features or 'common elements' regulating the reconciliation of apparent conflicts between scripture-dependent and non-scripture-dependent judgments of morality in the inference of *Sharīʿa* precepts, within a justice-oriented (*ʿAdliyya*) reading of *Sharīʿa*. The distinctive feature of such a reading is its role for non-scriptural judgments of morality alongside the scriptural sources of the Quran and Sunna. This allows non-scripture-dependent judgments of morality to be a substantive condition in the validity of any scripturally inferred precept that is attributed to a just and moral God. The justice-oriented reading of *Sharīʿa* in Shīʿī jurisprudence is grounded in the fundamental moral rationalism of Imāmī Shīʿī theology. The space in modern Shīʿī *uṣūl al-fiqh* (legal theory) for human judgments of morality to act as an independent source of *Sharīʿa* precepts in this way has, however, been undercut by assumptions that deem certainty (*qaṭʿ*) to be the exclusive grounding for the authoritativeness (*ḥujjiyya*) of *Sharīʿa* sources. The increasing untenability of this position, referred to in this study, demands that non-scripture-dependent judgments of morality be considered relevant to the inference of *Sharīʿa* precepts that are attributed to a moral and just God, even if these judgments are conjectural (*ẓannī*). After outlining the theoretical resources and challenges to the emergence of an *ʿAdliyya* reading of *Sharīʿa* in Shīʿī thought, this study aims to explore the identification and development of principles at the level of *uṣūl al-fiqh* that can assist in the process of reconciling apparent conflicts between scriptural and non-scriptural indicators to *Sharīʿa* precepts; even if they are conjectural. Illustrated with reference to possible conflicts regarding the testimony of women, apostasy and female circumcision, a three-stage hermeneutic is suggested, where conflicting evidence is either contextualised, reread or entirely discounted from the inferential process.

Part 1 of this study introduces the fundamental moral rationalism in Shīʿī thought and the scope that this offers for an *ʿAdliyya* reading of *Sharīʿa*. Part 2 discusses the role of *uṣūl al-fiqh* in the development of an *ʿAdliyya* hermeneutic within the context of ongoing debates over the purpose and function of the

© KONINKLIJKE BRILL NV, LEIDEN, 2020 | DOI:10.1163/9789004413948_008

discipline. Part 3 outlines the major theoretical obstacle in modern Shīʿī *uṣūl al-fiqh* that is responsible for the redundancy of independent moral reasoning in the actual process of *Sharīʿa* inference and how this obstacle can be overcome. After assuming the potential authority of conjectural sources of *Sharīʿa* inference, Part 4 indicates the need to further clarify philosophical issues important to establishing a criterion for identifying what type of conjectural judgments of non-scriptural morality are actually relevant. Finally, a three-stage hermeneutic to regulate the reconciliation of apparent conflicts between scriptural and non-scriptural evidence is proposed in Part 5. In conflict with a relevant non-scriptural judgment, the step-by-step approach suggests a preference for contextualization of the scriptural evidence over rereading the authorial intent, and prefers rereading the authorial intent before discounting any evidence. The basis of this hierarchy will be supported by reference to accepted principles of modern Shīʿī *uṣūl al-fiqh* that maintain the authority of apparent meaning and prefer reconciliation over the discounting of any evidence.

Part 1: Moral Rationalism and an *ʿAdliyya* Reading of *Sharīʿa*

The term *ʿAdliyya*, literally meaning 'the people of justice', is predominantly associated with classical Muʿtazilī and Shīʿī theologians. This essay employs the term, in an adjectival way, to denote the sense of justice associated with these schools. In its technical sense it is a term used self-referentially to describe those who built a range of theological positions upon their attribution of a humanly discernible conception of justice to a God who is held to be just in His essence, His actions and His regulative instructions. This hallmark conception of God's justice was premised on a belief that basic moral values are independent of God's legislative commands and can be understood by humans without the aid of scriptural revelation. There are two particularly prominent justifications offered by classical Shīʿī theologians for this moral rationalism. The first is an argument by way of a claimed universality of basic moral judgments; since people who deny revealed religion, either outright or through a rejection of prophecy, still come to agree with the proponents of scriptural traditions about the validity of some basic moral propositions, knowledge of these propositions must be discernible without scripture.[1] The second justification is more particular to the Muslim audience and a little more sophisticated in its construction. The argument states that without accepting the possibility

1 Ḥasan ibn Yūsuf ibn Muṭahhar al-ʿAllāma al-Ḥillī, *Kashf al-murād fī tajrīd al-iʿtiqād* (Beirut: Dār al-Amira, 2006), 59.

of non-scriptural moral knowledge, we would have no reason to trust in the validity of the moral knowledge imparted by scripture, as we would have no way of establishing that God would not lie in those scriptures.[2] All Muslims believe in the integrity and reliability of the moral knowledge imparted by scripture; therefore, some moral knowledge must necessarily be accessible by non-scriptural means. These two central arguments are often presented in various forms or accompanied by further independent justifications and are almost always prefaced by a simple claim that the validity of basic moral propositions is self-evident.[3]

The theological context that gave rise to the development of these ideas was linked to a rejection of an ethical voluntarism that held moral values to be indiscriminately stipulated, or defined, by God's command.[4] For the proponents of such theories, moral knowledge can only be attained through scripture (*sharʿ*) or authoritative transmission (*samʿ*). The *ʿAdliyya* arguments against this position only deny the exclusivity of scripture and authoritative transmission as the only sources of moral knowledge. Accordingly, the typical *ʿAdliyya* doctrine that 'the praiseworthy and blameworthy are rationally discernible (*al-ḥusn wa al-qubḥ ʿaqliyyān*)' in itself should not be read as ascribing the capability of understanding moral values to any particular notion of rationality; it simply reflects the belief that some moral values can be understood by humans without reference to scripture. The importance of understanding precisely what type of human judgments may attain proper moral knowledge was not ignored, and as will be seen in Part 4; it is a question that continues to stir debate amongst proponents of an *ʿAdliyya* moral rationalism.

The principle of the intelligibility of the praiseworthy and blameworthy plays a fundamental role in the formulation of the Shīʿī theological doctrine that is self-styled as *ʿAdliyya*. It is the premise that allows Shīʿī theologians to argue for a range of fundamental positions including their belief that all responsible people have a rational duty to come to know God, that God's acts must be free from futility, and that the giving of religious responsibility (*taklīf*) to humankind and the sending of prophets were necessary. When the moral rationalism upon which these positions are based plays a substantive and

2 Ibid.

3 For further details and analysis of a variety of such justifications, see Ali-Reza Bhojani, *Moral Rationalism and Sharīʿa: Independent rationality in modern Shīʿī uṣūl al-fiqh* (London: Routledge, 2015), 52–79.

4 For a review of the history and development of this theory and how it may have evolved in light of the *ʿAdliyya* critique against it, see Mariam al-Attar, "The Ethics and Metaphysics of Divine Command Theory" in *The Routledge Companion to Islamic Philosophy*, ed. Richard C. Taylor and Luis Xavier Lopez-Farjeat (London: Routledge, 2015), 315–325.

significant role in the actual inference of *Sharīʿa* precepts, it is a reading of the *Sharīʿa* that may be described as *ʿAdliyya*, or justice-oriented. The pivotal role of moral rationalism in Shīʿī theological thought has led the dominant trend in modern Shīʿī *uṣūl al-fiqh* to acknowledge that non-scripture-dependent moral judgments can act as an independent source of *Sharīʿa* precepts through the category of rational indicator (*al-dalīl al-ʿaqlī*) that is referred to as independent rationality (*al-mustaqillāt al-ʿaqliyya*). However, despite this theoretical space, independent rationality plays little or no role in the actual inference of *Sharīʿa* precepts at the level of *fiqh* in modern Shīʿī thought.[5]

An *ʿAdliyya* reading of *Sharīʿa* seeks to resolve the theoretical inconsistency between a fundamental moral rationalism in theology and the apparent redundancy of non-scriptural moral considerations in the process of juristic inference. It assumes that the indication of scriptural texts cannot be understood or accepted without considering any apparently conflicting non-scriptural moral indicators such that no immoral inference from *Sharīʿa* sources be attributed to a moral and just God. Rational, or non-scripture-dependent, morality must be a substantive condition in the validity of the interpretation of texts attempting to infer God's regulative precepts. Cases of apparent conflict between scriptural indicators and relevant non-scriptural moral judgments require reconciliation – this process of reconciliation may be described as an *ʿAdliyya* hermeneutic.

Part 2: *Uṣūl al-fiqh* and Its Role in the Development of an *ʿAdliyya* Hermeneutic

A shift towards an *ʿAdliyya* reading of *Sharīʿa*, implicitly or explicitly, can be seen in a wide range of emerging and contemporary expressions or critiques of *Sharīʿa*.[6] These efforts are notable within the context of responses to certain normative questions. Prominent examples of fields of normative enquiry that

5 For example, see Muḥammad Bāqir al-Ṣadr's explicit denial of any impact for independent rationality in his own juristic inferences; *Durūs fī ʿilm al-uṣūl* (Qum: Markaz al-abḥāth wa al-dirāsāt al-takhaṣṣuṣiyya lil Imām al-Shahīd al-Ṣadr, 2003), 2:203; *al-Fatāwa al-wāḍiḥa* (Beirut: Dār al-taʿāruf lil-matbūʿāt, 1983), 98 and Hossein Modarressi Ṭabāṭabāʾī, *An Introduction to Shīʿī Law: A Bibliographical Study* (London: Ithaca Press, 1984), 4.

6 For the shift towards an *ʿAdliyya* moral rationalism at the root of modernist *maqāṣidī* discourse, see David Johnston, "A Turn in the Epistemology and Hermeneutics of Twentieth Century *Uṣūl al-Fiqh*", *Islamic Law and Society* 11 (2003), 233–282; for its influence on later Ashʿarī thinking, see al-Attar, "The Ethics and Metaphysics of Divine Command Theory", 322–323.

have given rise to challenging the validity of inferred scriptural precepts can be seen in the treatment of issues relating to Islam and gender, human rights and international law, and Islamic finance.[7] However, the development of general principles that can regulate such interpretive challenges, irrespective of their particular normative context, seems considerably underdeveloped. I consider the discussion of such general principles to be within the remit of *uṣūl al-fiqh*, a discipline whose nature and function has not been uncontested.

The theoretical discipline of *uṣūl al-fiqh* (usually rendered legal theory) emerged out of concerns for consistency in the process of inferring – or justifying – *Sharīʿa* precepts in the applied discipline of *fiqh* (juristic inference). This drive for consistency and coherence in *uṣūl al-fiqh*, defined as "the study of the common elements in the actual process of inference of *Sharīʿa* precepts from their sources",[8] has been noted to be the result of both pragmatic and theological considerations.[9] Debates on the actual nature and extent of the function of *uṣūl al-fiqh* as being either predominantly prescriptive or justificatory are ongoing within accounts of the discipline in Islamic legal studies.[10] A prescriptive role for *uṣūl al-fiqh* may be described as its function in outlining or regulating how normative expressions of *Sharīʿa* ought to be derived. This sense is captured particularly well by Muhammad Bāqir al-Ṣadr's (d. 1400/1980) depiction of *uṣūl al-fiqh* as the logic of juristic inference (*manṭiq al-fiqh*).[11] A justificatory role for the discipline may be understood as its ability to outline how pre-existing normative positions can be legitimized as valid expressions of *Sharīʿa* and divine intent, thereby arguably reducing the role of *uṣūl al-fiqh* to a type of 'theory talk'.[12]

The strength of the arguments challenging insider accounts of the portrayal of the relationship between *uṣūl al-fiqh* and *fiqh* as being the 'logic of juristic inference' do not, however, undermine its contemporary relevance. In a

7 For example, see Adis Duderija, "Towards a Scriptural Hermeneutics of Islamic Feminism", *Journal of Feminist Studies in Religion* 31 (2015), 45–64; Abdullahi A. An-Na'im, *Towards an Islamic Reformation: Civil Liberties, Human Rights, and International Law* (New York: Syracuse University Press, 1990) and Haider Ala Hamoudi, "Jurisprudential Schizophrenia: On Form and Function in Islamic Finance", *Chicago Journal of International Law* 7 (2007), 605–622.

8 al-Ṣadr, *Durūs*, 1:46.

9 Robert Gleave, "Deriving Rules of Law" in *The Ashgate Research Companion to Islamic Law*, ed. Rudolph Peters and Peri Bearman (Farnham: Ashgate, 2014), 57.

10 For a brief, yet lucid, survey on the debates in Islamic legal studies regarding the function of *uṣūl al-fiqh* and its relation to *fiqh*, see Gleave, "Deriving Rules of Law", 65.

11 al-Ṣadr, *Durūs*, 1:50.

12 Sherman A. Jackson, "Fiction and Formalism: Towards a Functional Analysis of *Uṣūl al-Fiqh*" in *Studies in Islamic Legal Theory*, ed. Bernard G. Weiss (Leiden: Brill, 2002), 178–179.

context where Muslims are responding to unprecedented degrees of change, it seems that the importance of *uṣūl al-fiqh* is heightened, even if its function is predominantly justificatory. *Uṣūl al-fiqh* offers an established language for theorizing, refining and even legitimizing emergent, often eclectic, normative Muslim responses to the conditions of contemporary societies. It can offer a greater theoretical rigour and authority to fresh expressions of *Sharīʿa* that are subject to the very pragmatic and theological demands for consistency that gave rise to the discipline in the first place. Accordingly, it is through the language of *uṣūl al-fiqh* that issues surrounding the development of a rigorous and theoretically consistent *ʿAdliyya* hermeneutic are developed in this study.

Part 3: The Major Obstacle to the Relevance of Non-Scripture-Dependent Judgments in Modern Shīʿī *uṣūl al-fiqh*

The major theoretical obstacle in the Uṣūlī school of modern Shīʿī *uṣūl al-fiqh* preventing non-scripture-dependent judgments of morality from playing a substantive role in the process of juristic inference relates to the criteria for the authoritativeness (*ḥujjiyya*) of *Sharīʿa* sources. The theological premise regarding the intelligibility of the praiseworthy and blameworthy is not rejected. However, two conditions must be met for non-scripture-dependent judgments of morality to become a substantive tool in the juristic arsenal of one attempting to actually infer *Sharīʿa* precepts. First, there must be a correlation (*mulāzama*) between the non-scripture-dependent judgments of morality and the judgment of the Divine Legislator. Second, assuming the existence of such a correlation, the knowledge of *Sharīʿa* precepts attained by way of this correlation must be considered authoritative (*ḥujja*). Although there are extensive debates regarding what type of non-scriptural judgments may correlate to the judgment of the Divine Lawgiver and how the mechanics of this correlation can be conceived of, the very existence of a correlation – in principle – is seen as a distinctive feature of the Uṣūlī school.[13] Various accounts of the particularities of this correlation, and its mechanics, are linked to different conceptions of the nature of moral propositions amongst Uṣūlī scholars. Accordingly, the common obstacle to the impact of non-scripture-dependent moral judgments, however conceived, relates to whether or not the resultant knowledge of *Sharīʿa* precepts can be deemed authoritative or not.

13 See Bhojani, *Moral Rationalism and Sharīʿa*, 80–116.

The current dominant framework of Shīʿī legal theory, as set out by Shaykh Murtaḍā al-Anṣārī (d. 1281/1864),[14] considers certainty (*qatʿ*) to be the ultimate criterion for the authoritativeness of any source of *Sharīʿa* precepts. Within this system, for an indicator to a *Sharīʿa* precept to be considered authoritative, in the sense that it confers either accountability or excusability before God, it must either directly yield certainty or be grounded in a certain validation from the Divine Legislator. If the indicator is not certainty-bearing (*qatʿī*) in itself, and is only conjectural (*ẓannī*), then its authority depends upon establishing a certain validation from God for the permissibility of its employment. Uṣūlī scholars find no certain validation for conjectural judgments of rational morality and thus, independent judgments of morality are only considered authoritative if they bear certainty in and of themselves.

Uṣūlī scholars accept that the judgment of the Divine Legislator correlates with the certain and definitive non-scripture-dependent moral judgments that 'justice is praiseworthy' and 'oppression is blameworthy'. However, these authoritative independent rational indicators are too basic to have any relevance to *fiqh*. When it comes to inferences from these basic rational moral propositions, the required level of certainty is more elusive, and any potentially relevant non-scripture-dependent moral judgments are, more often than not, deemed to be merely conjectural and thus un-authoritative.

To highlight the problem, we can restate some of the fundamentals of the Shīʿī moral rationalism. The judgments 'justice is praiseworthy' and 'oppression is blameworthy' are examples of what is described by modern Uṣūlī scholars as instances of essential praiseworthiness and blameworthiness.[15] What is intended here is not a philosophical sense of essential, but rather the implication that these are basic and categorical judgments of rational morality such that whenever there is justice, it is deemed praiseworthy and whenever there is oppression, it is deemed blameworthy. However, inferences from these basic moral propositions lose their definitive nature and are hence not considered to be authoritative at the level of *fiqh*. If only conjectural, the non-scripture-dependent judgment that a woman's unequal right to divorce (despite possibly being beaten and raped in her marriage) is an instance of oppression, cannot be considered authoritative in its correlation to the judgment of the Divine Legislator. Accordingly, within such a framework, it is deemed irrelevant to the inference of the *Sharīʿa* position on divorce. The tension arising from the rejection of conjectural non-scripture-dependent judgments of morality is of

---

14 The influence of al-Anṣārī's formulation of *uṣūl al-fiqh*, is so great that he has been described as founding a new 'school'; see Tabātabāʾī, *Introduction to Shiʿi Law*, 57–58.

15 Muḥammad Riḍā al-Muẓaffar, *Uṣūl al-fiqh* (Qum: Intishārāt Ismāʿīlīyyān, 2000), 1:199–201.

course compounded by the epistemic discrimination that accepts conjectural scriptural sources as authoritative, albeit due to a claim that there is certain evidence for their authority.

Arguing for new instances of certainty in non-scripture-dependent judgments of morality is one avenue of overcoming the theoretical inconsistency between the fundamental theological moral rationalism in Shīʿī thought and the redundancy of independent rationality in Shīʿī *fiqh*. This strategy can be seen in the significant, and arguably path breaking work, of Mohsen Kadivar. Kadivar argues that it is a certain judgment, in his terminology of conventional rationality (*al-ʿaql al-ʿurfī*), that egalitarian equality between men and women is an instance of justness.[16] Whether or not such a claim solves the previously mentioned tension requires clarification of exactly what is intended by 'egalitarian equality' and whether or not conventional rationality can have certainty in what are instances of egalitarian equality. Kadivar has further clarified his position in a more recent work where he positions legal equality as an undoubted feature of egalitarian justice in contrast with the proportional equality of traditional deserts-based justice.[17] Accordingly, in the context of debates on gender equality, he argues that scriptural evidence implying legal discrimination against women are "situational and not absolute premises, that is, they refer to a specific time and place" and that "the arguments for egalitarian justice and fundamental equality are strong enough to lead to their provisional abrogation".[18]

In Part 5 of this article, a similar notion will be endorsed arguing that valid non-scripture-dependent judgments of morality may disclose the temporal or contextual specification of apparently conflicting scriptural evidence. However, I argue that this is only one of three possible paths in an *ʿAdliyya* hermeneutic, maintaining that conflicting scriptural evidence may need to have its authorial intent reread entirely or that both conflicting evidences may need to be dropped from consideration altogether. My departure from Kadivar is, however, not limited to what I call the mechanics of reconciliation for it seems that he has not addressed the fundamental epistemic obstacle to the relevance of non-scripture-dependent judgments in modern Shīʿī *uṣūl al-fiqh*. Kadivar's approach seems to continue within the epistemic framework of

16 "From Traditional Islam to Islam as an End in Itself", *Die Welt des Islams* 51 (2011), 478–483 and Yasuyuki Matsunaga, "Human Rights and New Jurisprudence in Mohsen Kadivar's Advocacy of 'New-Thinker' Islam", *Die Welt des Islams* 51 (2011), 358–381.

17 See 'Revisiting Women's Rights in Islam: "Egalitarian Justice" in Lieu of "Deserts-based Justice"' in *Gender and Equality in Muslim Family Law*, ed. Z. Mir-Hosseini, K. Voght, L. Larsen and C. Moe (London: I.B. Tauris, 2013), 213–235.

18 Ibid., 229.

al-Anṣārī, adopting his ideas about the nature and grounding of authority in certainty – an approach that seems increasingly untenable on both pragmatic and philosophical grounds. Here I advocate the potential relevance of non-scriptural judgments of morality even if they are not definitive.

It is an accepted premise of Uṣūlī scholars that there is insufficient certainty-bearing evidence to offer detailed knowledge of *Sharīʿa* precepts. Scholars from within the school of al-Anṣārī thus set out justifications claiming that particular conjectural forms of evidence, such as the isolated report (*khabar al-wāḥid*), have definitively certain validation from the Divine Legislator allowing them to be treated as authoritative means to inferring *Sharīʿa* precepts. Elsewhere, I have argued for the absence of any definitive and unqualified validation for specific sources of conjectural knowledge, and demonstrated the scope within the Uṣūlī tradition for an acceptance of the authority of conjectural knowledge irrespective of its source.[19] The precedent for such an approach, as set out in the theory of *insidād bāb al-ʿilmī* advocated by Ibn Zayn al-Dīn (d. 1011/1601) and Mīrzā al-Qummī (d. 1231/1815–16), is a pragmatic argument for the unqualified authority of conjectural sources due to phenomenological obstacles to certainty in the context of our distance from the period of revelation.[20] Furthermore, the actual philosophical possibility of the Uṣūlī notion of certainty and its relation to authoritativeness has now also been problematized as detailed in the work of Hashim Bata.[21] On both pragmatic and philosophical grounds, it seems that the epistemic framework for authoritativeness (*ḥujjiyya*) adopted within the school of al-Anṣārī is increasingly difficult to justify, leading to the necessity of acknowledging the potential authority of conjectural knowledge irrespective of its source: scriptural or non-scriptural. Further discussion on the epistemic groundings for the authority of *Sharīʿa* evidence is beyond the scope of this study. However, what is clear is that a shift towards accepting the authority of conjectural knowledge, irrespective of its source, ought to allow non-scripture-dependent judgments of morality to play a substantive role at the level of *fiqh* such that independent judgments of morality cannot be ignored in the inference of *Sharīʿa* precepts attributed to a moral and just God.[22]

19 Bhojani, *Moral Rationalism and Sharīʿa*, 152–156.

20 Ḥasan Ibn Zayn al-Dīn, *Maʿālim al-dīn fī al-uṣūl*, (Qum: n.p. n.d.), 192; Mīrzā Abū al-Qāsim al-Qummī, *al-Qawānin al-muḥkama fi al-uṣūl* (Beirut: Dār al-Murtaḍā, 2009), 2:420–429.

21 See Chapter 3 of this volume and, *Towards the utility of a wider range of evidence in the derivation of Sharīʿa precepts: paradigm shift in contemporary Usūlī epistemology*. Diss. University of Warwick, 2013.

22 Despite making arguments for the unqualified authority of conjecture, neither Ibn Zayn al-Dīn nor Mīrzā al-Qummī explored the implications of their position on the potential role of conjectural judgments of morality in the manner argued for here. Mīrzā al-Qummī

The concern here is to discuss principles at the level of *uṣūl al-fiqh* that may help regulate the reconciliation of apparent conflicts between scriptural and non-scriptural evidence, assuming that judgments of rational morality cannot be ignored in the process of *Sharīʿa* inference within an *ʿAdliyya* framework, even if these judgments are not certain. Before moving to a discussion of possible principles capable of regulating what I term an *ʿAdliyya* hermeneutic, it must be noted that there are some unresolved questions regarding exactly what type of non-scripture-dependent judgments are relevant to the inference of *Sharīʿa* in the first place.

Part 4: Identifying Relevant Non-Scripture-Dependent Judgments of Morality: a Meta-*uṣūlī* Question

This study sets out to explore principles, at the level of *uṣūl al-fiqh*, for reconciling apparent conflicts between conjectural indications of both scriptural and non-scripture-dependent judgements in the process of *Sharīʿa* inference. However, before doing so, the need for clarifying further philosophical issues important in establishing the criteria for identifying what type of conjectural judgments of non-scripture-dependent morality are actually relevant to *Sharīʿa* inference cannot be entirely ignored. The intent here is only to highlight the relevance of these issues as requiring clarification for those in pursuit of a theoretically consistent and coherent *ʿAdliyya* reading of *Sharīʿa*. This will serve to demonstrate how the development of rigorous principles of *uṣūl al-fiqh* demand equal rigour in the philosophical presuppositions upon which these principles stand.

The *ʿAdliyya* justification for a moral rationalism, as cited above, argues against the notion that moral value can only be understood through scripture without identifying exactly what broader human means allow for the non-scripture-dependent understanding of value. This space has allowed extensive debate and discussion amongst proponents of the intelligibility of the praiseworthy and blameworthy regarding the nature of moral propositions and the grounds upon which humans make judgments of praiseworthiness and blameworthiness. The extent of such debates, even when only considering the Imāmī

---

does dedicate considerable discussion to reason as an independent source of *Sharīʿa* precepts, arguing strongly for the independent authority of *ʿaql*. Yet when it comes to independent non-scriptural judgments of morality his focus is in on defending definitive instances of such judgements. This is presumably framed against an Akhbārī rejection of any non-scriptural sources, even when they are definitive. See *al-Qawānīn al-muḥkama fī al-uṣūl al-mutqana* (Qum: Iḥyāʾ al-kutub al-Islāmiyya, 2010) 3:8–39.

Shīʿa reception, is my basis for describing the principle as a moral rationalism rather than an 'objectivism'.[23] This designation allows for the stark differences regarding moral ontology that have arisen amongst Shīʿī scholars, despite their concurrence that the praiseworthiness and blameworthiness of an action can be intelligible without reliance on scripture.

There are two major theories amongst modern Shīʿī Uṣūlī scholars about the nature of propositions regarding judgments of praiseworthiness and blameworthiness. The first suggests that propositions regarding the praiseworthiness or blameworthiness of an action are statements about ontological facts, described as *yaqīnīyyāt*. The validity of these propositions, whether they are true or false, depends upon the correspondence of the proposition with that which exists in the realm of fact (*nafs al-amr*). Although these facts are considered intelligible, other than assenting to the intuitive nature of basic moral propositions, proponents of this theory seem to resist outlining any other detailed features of the nature of what constitutes these ontologically occurring facts of morality.[24] This limits the extent to which principles may be developed to establish a criterion for a valid conjecture regarding these moral facts.[25] It also seems to imply that personal claims to the discovery of these facts, based on a particular individual's own foundationalist moral theory, does not need to rely on any form of inter-subjectivity as a check on the validity of a claim to his or her discovery.[26]

The second major theory, notably advocated by Muḥammad Ḥusayn al-Iṣfahānī (d. 1365/1945)[27] and popularized by his student Muḥammad Riḍā al-Muẓaffar (d. 1384/1964),[28] is based on a reading of Ibn Sīnā's view of the nature of moral propositions. al-Iṣfahānī holds that propositions regarding the praiseworthiness or blameworthiness of an action fall under the category of propositions described as *mashhūrāt* or *maqbūlāt khāṣṣa*. Such propositions are contrasted with *yaqiniyyāt* as having no ontological grounds other than the

23 George Hourani characterised Muʿtazilī ethics as a 'rationalistic objectivism' in his important study, *Islamic Rationalism* (Oxford: Clarendon Press, 1971).

24 For example, see al-Ṣadr, *Durūs*, 2:306–308.

25 The absence of such criteria seems central to al-Ṣadr's pessimism regarding the actual occurrence of correlations between human judgments of theoretical rationality and judgments of the Divine Legislator; see *Durūs*, 2:305–306.

26 See Nāṣir Makārim Shīrāzī for criticism of those who suggest that anything other than an individual *mujtahid*'s certainty is the basis for determining relevant judgments of non-scripture-dependent morality, *Anwār al-uṣūl* (Qum: Madrasat al-Imām Amīr al-Mu'minīn, 1994) 2:512.

27 Muḥammad Ḥusayn al-Iṣfahānī, *Nihāyat al-dirāya fī sharḥ al-kifāya* (Beirut: Mu'assasat Ahl al-Bayt li iḥyā' al-turāth, 2009), 3:29–31.

28 Muẓaffar, *Uṣūl al-fiqh*, 1:188–192.

concurrence of opinion that gives rise to them. Accordingly, this view of the nature of moral propositions may be described as a form of conventional morality. For al-Iṣfahānī, judgments of conventional morality may be termed rational, with potential correspondence to the judgment of the Divine Legislator, when these judgments are based on considerations of 'general utility, social order and the preservation of humankind'.[29] al-Muẓaffar further refines this through a detailed analysis of the possible causes of judgments of practical rationality with a view to identifying exactly what type of grounds give rise to a relevant concurrence of rational beings regarding the praiseworthiness or blameworthiness of an action.[30] al-Muẓaffar agrees with his teacher al-Iṣfahānī, in that these judgments have no ontological basis beyond the concurrence of opinion that gives rise to them. For him, such judgements of conventional morality are deemed rational, with potential correspondence to the opinion of the Divine Legislator, when they arise from universal judgments regarding the perfection (*kamāl*) and imperfection (*naqṣ*) of a thing, in addition to when they relate to universal judgements of social utility (*maṣlaḥa naw'iyya*) or social detriment (*mafsada naw'iyya*).[31] The theory of the nature of morality advocated by al-Muẓaffar allows for the possibility that the actuality (*wāqi'*) of moral values, and not just their understanding, can change with the changing opinion of the rational community. It is a theory that reduces the ontology of moral values to their epistemology, and thus demands at least some level of inter-subjectivity as a criterion to the validity of any conjectural non-scripture-dependent judgment of morality.[32]

From this brief account of the two major theories amongst modern Shī'ī scholars on the nature of moral propositions, it should be clear that any criterion for identifying relevant conjectural non-scripture-dependent judgments of morality depends upon one's conception of the nature of morality and its grounds. Outlining and justifying a particular conception of the nature of morality is, however, a question firmly within the remit of moral philosophy and accordingly can be described as meta-*uṣūlī*. Debates on such questions in modern Shī'ī thought seemed to have had little practical relevance when it

29 Iṣfahānī, *Nihāyat al-dirāya*, 3:29–30.

30 Muẓaffar, *Uṣūl al-fiqh*, 1:195–199.

31 Ibid., 199.

32 Kadivar follows Muẓaffar in his conception of the nature of moral propositions without drawing out the implications of the theory for developing an inter-subjective approach to the disclosure of such propositions. Instead, he maintains that the discovery of valid judgments of non-scripture-dependent morality is the prerogative of an individual specialist *mujtahid*, aware of the conditions of time and place; 'Revisiting Women's Rights in Islam: "Egalitarian Justice" in Lieu of "Deserts-based Justice"', 231.

comes to the inference of *Sharīʿa* precepts. Grounding authority in certainty meant that irrespective of one's conception of the nature of morality, independent rational judgments had no significant impact on the actual inference of *Sharīʿa* precepts. A shift to accepting the potential authority of conjectural non-scripture-dependent judgments of morality would give renewed impetus to the relevance of such meta-*uṣūlī* questions due to a real impact at the level of *Sharīʿa* inference. However, further deliberations here on questions of moral philosophy would be beyond the scope of a chapter whose focus is to advance conversation on the coherence of an *ʿAdliyya* reading of the *Sharīʿa* through principles at the level of *uṣūl–fiqh*. What is firmly within the remit of *uṣūl al-fiqh* is to discuss how scriptural evidence might be reconciled with apparently conflicting non-scriptural evidence, having assumed that relevant conjectural non-scripture-dependent judgments of morality can be identified, and that these judgments are potentially valid at the level of *Sharīʿa* inference.

Part 5: A Three-Step *ʿAdliyya* Hermeneutic: Contextualize, Reread and Discount

An *ʿAdliyya*, or justice-oriented reading of *Sharīʿa*, rejects the attribution to God of any inferred scriptural precept that conflicts with valid non-scripture-dependent judgments of morality. Immoral precepts cannot be attributed to a moral God. This offers a theoretical framework to check the attribution of apparently unjust inferences from scripture to a God who is held to be just, in a sense discernible to humankind. For these essentially theological resources to have impact at the level of juristic inference, there is a need for principles to regulate the reconciliation of apparent conflicts between scripture-dependent and non-scripture-dependent judgments of morality. After assuming that potentially valid conjectural non-scripture-dependent judgments of morality can be identified, I suggest a three-stage process here for reconciling these judgments with apparently conflicting scriptural texts. In order of priority, conflicting texts should be either contextualized, have their authorial intent reread or be discounted entirely from the inferential process along with the conjectural non-scriptural evidence. This process may be referred to as an *ʿAdliyya* hermeneutic. The suggested preference for contextualizing apparently conflicting texts before rereading their authorial intent, and rereading their authorial intent before discounting the evidence, is based on established principles that prefer reconciliation where possible and maintain that the apparent meaning of a scriptural indicator is authoritative where there is no evidence to the contrary.

As common elements in the actual inferential process of *Sharīʿa* precepts, discussion of the basis and mechanisms of this hermeneutical process falls within the remit of *uṣūl al-fiqh*. In line with my adoption of *uṣūl al-fiqh* as a theoretical discipline that acts as a site for contestation and deliberation in pursuit of regulating consistency and coherence within the actual process of inferring or justifying *Sharīʿa* precepts, the suggested mechanism is by no means intended to be final or complete. Instead, the suggestions here are intended as a platform from which further deliberations regarding an *ʿAdliyya* reading of *Sharīʿa* may emerge; a reading of *Sharīʿa* committed to the principle that valid human judgments of morality can be a substantive condition for the validity of scripturally inferred precepts attributed to a moral and just God. In outlining the basis for this three-stage approach to regulating apparent conflicts between scriptural and non-scriptural evidence, reference will be made to possible cases that may fall under the scope of each step in the hermeneutic. References to these cases are intended only to illustrate what is expected in the hermeneutical process itself and, therefore, they are simply framed as plausible applications. The actual application of such a mechanism to any particular case demands an exhaustive engagement with the specifics of both the scripture-dependent as well as the non-scripture-dependent evidence relevant to that particular case, an exercise within the remit of *fiqh*, and thus a task that falls beyond the scope of this study.

Modern Shīʿī *uṣūl al-fiqh* undertakes extensive discussion of principles and common elements involved in the process of identifying and resolving apparent or actual conflicts between *Sharīʿa* indicators. The three-stage *ʿAdliyya* hermeneutic that I suggest here for reconciling conflicts between scriptural and non-scriptural evidence takes these existing discussions within *uṣūl al-fiqh* as its starting point. The class of conflicts discussed in *uṣul al-fiqh* that are relevant to our concern are those conflicts referred to as *taʿāruḍ*. *Taʿāruḍ* is said to occur when two potentially authoritative evidences have some mutual contradiction in their indication.[33] This contradiction implies that each indicator either partially, or entirely, falsifies the indication of the other; accordingly, *taʿāruḍ* may be considered as a conflict at the level of legislation.[34] Amongst the otherwise exhaustive approaches used in modern Shīʿī *uṣūl al-fiqh* towards the different categories of this class of conflict, the question of reconciling conflicts between conjectural non-scriptural and conjectural scriptural evidence

---

33 See al-Ṣadr, *Durūs*, 2:529 and al-Muẓaffar, *Uṣūl al-fiqh*, 2:168.

34 This is in contrast to the class of conflicts occurring at the level of implementation referred to within discussions of *al-tazāhum*. For details of the distinction between these two types of conflicts, see al-Muẓaffar, *Uṣūl al-fiqh*, 2:171.

is not engaged with. Within a system that grounds authority in certainty, "if a non-scripture-dependent indicator (*dalīl ʿaqlī*) is not certain (*qaṭʿī*), then it has no authority in itself to be able to conflict with the authority of another indicator".[35] Nevertheless, the general typology and principles developed within discussions of conflicts at the level of legislation (*taʿāruḍ*) remain relevant to our concern, having assumed that potentially valid conjectural non-scripture-dependent judgments of morality can be identified.

A conflict at the level of legislation is said to occur when each indicator is deemed potentially authoritative,[36] when there is some mutual falsification between the two indicators and when no designated preferential factor distinguishes one indicator over the other. In such circumstances, it is argued that the primary principle for dealing with an actual conflict of this type is to discount both pieces of evidence from consideration (*tasāquṭ*).[37] However, if the indication of the mutually falsifying indicators can be reconciled in a manner acceptable to conventional understanding (*ʿurf*), this is deemed preferable to discounting.[38] When ordinary people accept the modification of the apparent meaning of either or both indicators in light of the entirety of the evidence, in a manner that alleviates the conflict, it is this modified understanding that should be considered sound. In the context of conflicts between conjectural scriptural and non-scriptural evidence, the indication of the non-scripture-dependent evidence cannot be modified. A non-scripture-dependent judgment of morality amounts to a regulation (*ḥukm*) in and of itself and is accordingly classified as *al-dalīl al-lubbī*. This is in contrast to scriptural evidence that conveys something from which a regulation is then inferred. The inference of a regulation from a conjectural scriptural indicator is based on how it is understood in light of the linguistic principles (*al-uṣūl al-lafẓiyya*) that form the central pivot of the hermeneutical theory in *uṣūl al-fiqh*. Arguably, the most important linguistic principle employed in modern Shīʿī *uṣūl al-fiqh* is the primacy of apparent meaning (*aṣālat al-ẓuhūr*). The dynamics of the theory of apparent meaning in modern Shīʿī *uṣūl al-fiqh* allow for the modification of scriptural indication in cases of conflict, and accordingly open up the first two movements in the proposed three-step *ʿAdliyya* hermeneutic; before discounting any evidence,

35 al-Ṣadr, *Durūs*, 1:442.

36 I use the term 'potentially' authoritative throughout and not actually authoritative, as it is claimed impossible for there to be active conjecture (*al-ẓann al-fiʿlī*) regarding the authority of both evidences at the same time, see al-Muẓaffar, *Uṣūl al-fiqh*, 2:169.

37 See al-Muẓaffar, *Uṣūl al-fiqh*, 2:180–182 and al-Ṣadr, *Durūs*, 2:448–451.

38 This is referred to as 'conventional reconciliation' (*al-jamʿ al-ʿurfī*), see al-Ṣadr, *Durūs*, 1:445 and al-Muẓaffar, *Uṣūl al-fiqh*, 2:182–188.

attempts should be made to contextualize or reread the authorial intent of the scriptural evidence.

The principle of apparent meaning holds that when the indication of a text is not explicit,[39] the apparent meaning is considered to be the intended meaning and is deemed authoritative. The apparent meaning is the foremost conception occurring in the mind as a result of an expression. In the absence of any associated factors (*qarāʾin*), scriptural or non-scriptural, this foremost occurring meaning is assumed to be that which is closest to the linguistic or literal indication of the expression. However, the presence of associated factors, linguistic or otherwise, can shape the foremost conception occurring in the mind into something other than the closest linguistic meaning. In such cases, it is this apparent meaning, as shaped by the associated factors, that is deemed authoritative. In effect, there are two elements at work here. First, the principle itself; that one can assume that a speaker intends what he seems to be saying – even if he is not absolutely explicit in doing so. And second, the authoritative nature of the principle; that God allows us to rely on apparent meaning in the inference of *Sharīʿa* precepts from scriptural evidence – even though there is a possibility that the authorial intent may have actually been something other than that which is apparently understood.

There are various justifications offered in modern Shīʿī *uṣūl al-fiqh* for the authority of apparent meaning. These include the claim that understanding communication based on apparent meaning is a convention of ordinary rational people (*banāʾ al-ʿuqalāʾ*), or the established practice of religiously observant people (*sīrat al-mutasharriʿa*). The justification from rational convention claims that since the Divine Legislator is a rational being, He must necessarily partake in the convention of ordinary rational beings that relies on apparent meaning. Had He wished to be understood in any other way, it would be upon Him to inform us of this alternative mode of comprehension.[40] The argument by way of the practice of religiously observant people argues that the companions of the Prophet and the Imams had an established practice of relying on the apparent meaning of the Qurʾan and the Sunna. Since the Prophet and the Imams witnessed this established practice without objecting to it, tacit

39 The indication of a text is deemed explicit (*naṣṣ*) when it has only one possible meaning. The indication is deemed apparent (*ẓāhir*) when one meaning is deemed the most plausible amongst more than one possible meaning. The text is deemed ambiguous (*mujmal*) when it has more than one possible meaning and none of these is more apparent than any other. According to this distinction, if there is scope even for a mere suspicion regarding an alternative meaning of to an otherwise clear text, it cannot be described as explicit.

40 See al-Muẓaffar, *Uṣūl al-fiqh*, 2:120.

approval can be assumed, and acting in accordance with apparent meaning can be considered as ratified by the Divine Legislator.[41]

There seems to be no reason to give up the principle of the primacy of apparent meaning in the context of reconciling apparent conflicts between scriptural and non-scriptural evidence. The intended meaning of the scriptural evidence should be assumed to be arising from the linguistic meaning of the expression so long as there is no evidence or associated factors acting as an obstacle to this apparent meaning. Where associated factors, which may include non-scripture-dependent judgments, alter the foremost conception occurring in the mind, it is this modified conception that is actually deemed apparent, and hence the intended meaning of the expression. Based on these dynamics of apparent meaning and the preference for reconciliation of conflicts before the discounting of evidence, I outline my suggested three-stage *ʿAdliyya* hermeneutic for resolving conflicts between conjectural scriptural and non-scriptural evidence. On the occurrence of such conflicts, attempts should be made to first contextualize the scriptural evidence; where this is not possible, attempts should be made to reread its authorial intent in a manner consistent with the non-scriptural evidence and only if this is unsuccessful should both forms of evidence be discounted. The three stages of the *ʿAdliyya* hermeneutic are illustrated and further outlined below.

Step One: Contextualisation of Scriptural Indication

In the case of conflicts between conjectural scriptural and non-scriptural evidence, the apparent meaning of the scriptural indicator should be assumed to be the linguistic meaning of the expression insofar as there is no evidence to the contrary. Accepting that the linguistic meaning is intended, insofar as it does not conflict with other indicators, maintains the fundamental premise of the primacy of apparent meaning; we assume that the speaker intends what he seems to be saying. Accordingly, if the scriptural evidence that conflicts with non-scriptural evidence can be contextualized as being intended only within particular circumstances, this would be preferable to rereading its authorial intent as being something other than the closest linguistic meaning, or subsequently moving to discount the conflicting evidence. To contextualize the indication of scriptural evidence in this way, there would need to be sufficient justification to explain how the scriptural indication, as understood through its apparent meaning, may not have always been immoral. Subject

41 See al-Ṣadr, *Durūs*. 1:107.

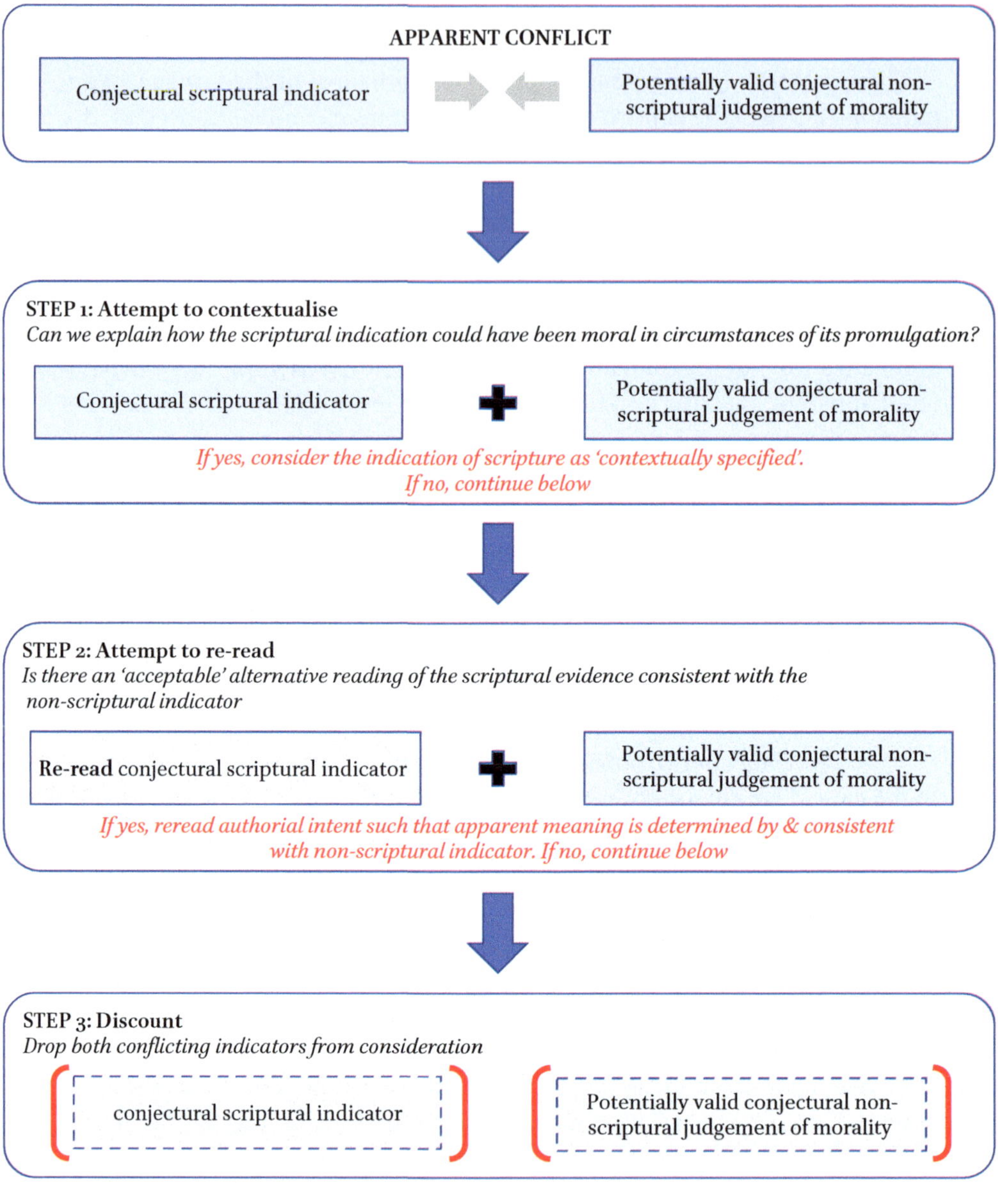

APPARENT CONFLICT
Conjectural scriptural indicator
Potentially valid conjectural non-scriptural judgement of morality
STEP 1: Attempt to contextualise
Can we explain how the scriptural indication could have been moral in circumstances of its promulgation?
Conjectural scriptural indicator
Potentially valid conjectural non-scriptural judgement of morality
If yes, consider the indication of scripture as 'contextually specified'.
If no, continue below
STEP 2: Attempt to re-read
Is there an 'acceptable' alternative reading of the scriptural evidence consistent with the non-scriptural indicator
Re-read conjectural scriptural indicator
Potentially valid conjectural non-scriptural judgement of morality
If yes, reread authorial intent such that apparent meaning is determined by & consistent with non-scriptural indicator. If no, continue below
STEP 3: Discount
Drop both conflicting indicators from consideration
conjectural scriptural indicator
Potentially valid conjectural non-scriptural judgement of morality

FIGURE 6.1 A three-step *ʿAdliyya* hermeneutic

to these reasons being strong enough, the authorial intent of the scriptural evidence does not need to be reread entirely or rejected. It can be maintained that the Divine Legislator intended that indication in its particular context, but that it has now been temporally or contextually specified in light of the non-scriptural evidence.[42] Where circumstances occurring at the time of revelation are present, or re-occur, the ruling inferred from the apparent meaning of the linguistic indication would be considered active and authoritative.

A possible application of this first movement within the proposed *'Adliyya* hermeneutic may be seen with moral challenges to inferred *Sharī'a* regulations that deem female testimony as being of unequal worth to male testimony. A conflict arises from a possible conjectural non-scripture-dependent judgment stating that 'when all things are equal, it is immoral to consider the testimony of women as less than men', and textual evidence suggesting that a woman's testimony is worth less than the testimony of a man.[43] Accepting the validity of the non-scriptural moral judgment does not necessarily imply the need to discount the scriptural evidence, or reread its authorial intent. Rather, if there is sufficient justification to explain how the linguistic indication may not have been immoral within the particular circumstances of revelation, the indication can be maintained, whilst its ruling can be deemed contextually specified in light of any current conflicting moral judgment. If requiring two female witnesses during the context of revelation can be understood as a requirement to ensure justice in light of the general societal unfamiliarity women may have had with the subject matter regulated through the scriptural evidence, the immediate address may not have been immoral.[44] Of course, in most contemporary societies women have no general societal impediment to understanding commercial transactions and may often be more qualified and experienced than a male counterpart. Within such changed circumstances, the ruling of the scriptural evidence may be considered contextually specified in light of the conflicting non-scriptural evidence, but the linguistic indication of the scriptural evidence is maintained as the apparent and intended meaning for the circumstances of revelation.

---

42 This is akin to what Kadivar refers to as 'provisional abrogation'. See "Revisiting Women's Rights", 229.

43 See Quran 2:282 and al-Ḥurr al-'Āmilī, *Wasā'il al-shī'a ilā taḥṣīl masā'il al-sharī'a* (Qum: Mu'assasat Āl al-Bayt, 1992), 27:350–366.

44 For further discussion of the space and precedent for such a reading, see S.H. Nasr, C.K. Dagli, M.M. Dakake, J. Lumbard and M. Rustom (eds.) *The Study Quran: A New Translation and Commentary* (New York: Harper One, 2015), 122–123.

Step Two: Rereading the Authorial Intent

Where there is insufficient justification to explain how a scriptural indicator may have been moral at the time of revelation, despite a current conflict with a non-scripture-dependent judgment, contextualization is not possible and thus movement to the second step in the proposed *'Adliyya* hermeneutic is required. This second step demands that attempts be made to reread the authorial intent of the scriptural evidence in light of the apparently conflicting non-scripture-dependent evidence. The non-scriptural evidence here acts as an associated factor (*qarīna*) that may modify the apparent meaning of the scriptural indicator away from its linguistic meaning. Should a conventionally acceptable reading emerge in light of the entirety of the evidence, in a manner that alleviates the conflict, this understanding would be identified as the apparent and intended meaning of the scriptural evidence.

A possible instance illustrating the application of this second stage of the *'Adliyya* hermeneutic may be seen in approaches to reconciling texts that have been read to suggest that apostasy (*irtidād*) from Islam should be punished with death, in light of a possible conjectural non-scripture-dependent judgment holding that 'to restrict freedom of conscience in matters of belief, with the threat of death, is immoral'.[45] The lack of reasons to explain how a linguistic indication for the scriptural evidence, which suggests a death penalty be applied purely for a choice of conscience, could *ever* have been moral means that step-one contextualization is not possible and efforts must be made to reread the authorial intent. A plausible alternative indication of these texts, as shaped by the non-scriptural judgment acting as an associated factor modifying the apparent meaning, is that the intended meaning actually referred to an act of treason, or socio-political rebellion, and not simply an act of conscience. If such a reading is not inconsistent with any other contextual elements and associated factors, it can be identified as the apparent meaning and assumed that this was always the intention of the Divine Legislator. In light of the non-scriptural evidence, the texts may be reread as prescribing the death penalty for particular acts of treason or socio-political rebellion and not simply apostasy as an act of conscience evoking one to leave the fold of Islamic belief.

---

45 For texts dealing with apostasy, see 'Āmilī, *Wasā'il al-shī'a*, 28:323–330. For an example of how these texts have been employed to infer that the apostate ought to receive the death penalty, see Ja'far ibn Ḥasan al-Muḥaqqiq al-Ḥillī, *Sharā'i al-Islām fī masā'il al-ḥalāl wa al-ḥarām* (Qum: Mu'assasat al-ma'ārif al-islāmiyya, 1995), 4:188–191 and Abū al-Qāsim al-Khū'ī, *Mabānī takmilat al-minhāj* (Najaf: Matba'at al-Ādāb, n.d.), 1:325–328.

Step Three: Discounting Evidence

In light of the principle that reconciliation of apparent conflicts is preferable to the discounting of evidence, attempts must be made to first contextualize and then reread scriptural evidence in light of a conflict with valid non-scripture-dependent evidence. The third step of discounting evidence is only resorted to if and when the first two steps of the *'Adliyya* hermeneutic prove to be unsuccessful. In cases of conflict, where there is no plausible justification to explain how the apparent meaning of the scriptural evidence could have been moral in the circumstances of revelation, and no plausible rereading of the authorial intent emerges, then both the scriptural and non-scriptural evidence need to be discounted from the inferential process such that neither is determinative of the ruling for the question at hand. In the absence of other overarching evidence, the jurist would then refer to the appropriate procedural principle (*aṣl 'amalī*) to establish the practical stance for the case at hand.[46]

A possible instance of conflict that may be deemed to reach this third step in the *'Adliyya* hermeneutic may arise from texts that have been referred to as a basis for considering female circumcision to be a recommended act.[47] An apparent conflict between scriptural and non-scriptural evidence arises with texts describing the act of circumcising females (*khatn al-jawāriḥ*) as 'honourable' (*mukarrama*)[48] and a conjectural non-scripture-dependent judgment that 'subjecting a child to female circumcision is immoral'. There seems to be no plausible reasons or justifications to explain how the linguistic indication of such texts cannot be subjected to the moral argument against them, even at the time of their promulgation. Accordingly, the apparent indication of the texts cannot be contextually abrogated. Attempts to reread these texts do not readily suggest any apparent meaning that may be considered as the intended meaning in a manner that resolves the conflict with the non-scripture-dependent judgment. If attempts to reconcile both indicators are deemed unsuccessful in this manner, the hermeneutic strategy would demand that both indicators, scriptural and non-scriptural, be dropped entirely from consideration, thereby

46 The procedural principles (*al-uṣūl al-'amaliyya*) are referred to in modern Shī'ī *fiqh* in situations where evidence capable of disclosing the actual ruling is inconclusive or unavailable. The principles usually listed are; exemption (*barā'a*), caution (*iḥtiyāṭ*), continuity (*istiṣḥāb*) or choice (*takhyīr*). These principles are not deemed reality-securing evidence (*al-adillat al-muḥriza*), instead they are simply intended to offer practical solutions to situations of doubt. See al-Ṣadr, *Durūs*, Vols. 129–155 and Ja'far Subḥānī, *al-Mūjiz fī uṣūl al-fiqh* (Qum: Maktabat al-Tawḥīd, 2008), 176–217.

47 See Muḥammad Ḥasan al-Najafī, *Jawāhir al-kalām fi sharḥ sharā'i' al-Islām* (Beirut: Mu'assasat al-Murtaḍā al-'Ālamiyya, 1996), 11:169.

48 See 'Āmilī, *Wasā'il al-shī'a*, 21:441–442.

allowing the outright rejection of the authority of any texts encouraging the act of female circumcision.

Conclusion

An *ʿAdliyya*, or justice-oriented reading of *Sharīʿa*, rejects the attribution of immoral or unjust human inferences of *Sharīʿa* precepts to a moral and just God. This is based on the acceptance of humans having the ability to understand at least some basic moral values, independent of scriptural revelation, and that the sense of justice ascribed to God is accordingly understandable by humankind. This theological premise about the nature of God and His regulative instructions gives space for an *ʿAdliyya* hermeneutic in Shīʿī jurisprudence. An *ʿAdliyya* hermeneutic seeks to resolve tensions that may arise between apparently immoral conjectural texts and non-scripture-dependent judgments of morality such that no immoral precept is attributed to a moral God. Despite the prominence of such thinking across a wide range of modern and contemporary Muslim approaches to reading the *Sharīʿa*, it seems that a theoretically consistent approach has yet to emerge. The dominant trend in modern Shīʿī thought, despite its explicit adoption of an *ʿAdliyya* theology and declaring a resultant space for independent rationality within its juristic arsenal, renders independent judgments of morality irrelevant to the actual inference of *Sharīʿa* precepts.

Treating *uṣūl al-fiqh* as a discourse of contestation and deliberation in pursuit of regulating consistency and coherence in inferring and/or justifying *Sharīʿa* precepts allows it to be employed as a tool to understand both the obstacles and means to develop a rigorous *ʿAdliyya* hermeneutic. Modern Shīʿī *uṣūl al-fiqh*, within the school of Anṣārī, grounds the authority of *Sharīʿa* indicators in certainty. Either the evidence must be certainty-bearing in itself or, if conjectural, it should be deemed to have certain validation for its authority. Pragmatic and philosophical reasons are increasingly demonstrating the untenability of this position, allowing for an acceptance of the potential validity of conjectural evidence, irrespective of its source. Accepting such an epistemic shift opens up the possibility of non-scripture-dependent judgments of morality playing a substantive role in the inference of *Sharīʿa* precepts.

Accepting such a shift opens up a range of previously purely theoretical questions that are pivotal to the actual inference of *Sharīʿa* precepts within an *ʿAdliyya* framework. Significant to these is the need for the clarification of philosophical and epistemological debates relating to the identification of what constitutes a relevant non-scripture-dependent judgment of morality and what is the nature of these potentially relevant moral judgments in the first place. Adopting either one of the two prevalent and contrasting theories about the nature of morality in modern Shīʿī thought, where morality may be seen as either factual or conventional, would undoubtedly have a significant impact on issues of legal theory. For instance, the conventional theory of morality seems to imply that any non-scripture-dependent judgment of morality must have at least some degree of inter-subjectivity for it to be deemed as relevant. This is not necessarily the case with the competing theory, where the fallible claim of an individual *mujtahid* to having discovered a moral precept may be sufficient for it to be considered potentially authoritative. Despite the relevance, at their core, these questions are dependent on moral philosophy and, accordingly, they need to be dealt with in a context of philosophy. Therefore, the successful development of a theoretically consistent and rigorous *ʿAdliyya* reading of *Sharīʿa*, not only depends upon new trajectories in legal theory; but also demands rigorous engagement in the philosophical and epistemological assumptions employed in such theory.

Irrespective of one's assumptions about the nature of morality, once potentially relevant judgments of non-scriptural morality have been identified, study of the process or general principles involved in reconciling these judgments with any apparent conflicting scriptural evidence *does* fall within the core remit of *uṣūl al-fiqh*. Despite not having been previously applied to cases involving conjectural non-scripture-dependent judgments of morality, *uṣūl al-fiqh* offers an established language for theorizing the development of a rigorous and consistent approach to dealing with such conflicts occurring at the level of legislation. When conflicts between conjectural scriptural and non-scriptural evidence are seen in light of the principle of reconciliation being preferable to the discounting of evidence and the primacy of apparent meaning, a three-step *ʿAdliyya* hermeneutic seems to emerge. This suggests that when faced with potentially valid non-scriptural moral evidence, attempts should be made to first contextualize the conflicting text; and, if unsuccessful, attempts should then be made to reread its authorial intent in light of the non-scriptural evidence, and only failing these two steps should both conjectural sources be discounted from the inferential process.

Bibliography

al-ʿĀmilī, al-Ḥurr, *Wasāʾil al-shīʿa ilā taḥṣīl masāʾil al-sharīʿa*. Qum: Muʾassasat Āl al-Bayt, 1992.

al-Attar, Mariam, "The Ethics and Metaphysics of Divine Command Theory" in *The Routledge Companion to Islamic Philosophy*, ed. Richard C. Taylor and Luis Xavier Lopez-Farjeat. London: Routledge, 2015.

An-Na'im, Abdullahi A., *Towards an Islamic Reformation: Civil Liberties, Human Rights, and International Law*. New York: Syracuse University Press, 1990.

Bata, Hashim, *Towards the utility of a wider range of evidence in the derivation of Sharīʿa precepts: paradigm shift in contemporary Usūlī epistemology*. Diss. University of Warwick, 2013.

Bhojani, Ali-Reza, *Moral Rationalism and Sharīʿa: Independent rationality in modern Shīʿī uṣūl al-fiqh*. London: Routledge, 2015.

Duderija, Adis, "Towards a Scriptural Hermeneutics of Islamic Feminism", *Journal of Feminist Studies in Religion* 31 (2015), 45–64.

Gleave, Robert, "Deriving Rules of Law" in *The Ashgate Research Companion to Islamic Law*, ed. Rudolph Peters and Peri Bearman. Farnham: Ashgate, 2014.

Hamoudi, Haider Ala, "Jurisprudential Schizophrenia: On Form and Function in Islamic Finance", *Chicago Journal of International Law* 7 (2007), 605–622.

al-Ḥillī, Ḥasan ibn Yūsuf ibn Muṭahhar al-ʿAllāma, *Kashf al-murād fī tajrīd al-iʿtiqād*. Beirut: Dār al-Amira, 2006.

al-Ḥillī, Jaʿfar ibn Ḥasan al-Muḥaqqiq, *Sharāʾiʿ al-Islām fī masāʾil al-ḥalāl wa al-ḥarām*. Qum: Mu'assasat al-maʿārif al-islāmiyya, 1995.

Hourani, George, *Islamic Rationalism*. Oxford: Clarendon Press, 1971.

Ibn Zayn al-Dīn, Ḥasan, *Maʿālim al-dīn fī al-uṣūl*. Qum: n.p. n.d.

al-Iṣfahānī, Muḥammad Ḥusayn, *Nihāyat al-dirāya fī sharḥ al-kifāya*. Beirut: Mu'assasat Ahl al-Bayt li iḥyā' al-turāth, 2009.

Jackson, Sherman A., "Fiction and Formalism: Towards a Functional Analysis of Uṣūl al-Fiqh" in *Studies in Islamic Legal Theory*, ed. Bernard G. Weiss. Leiden: Brill, 2002.

Johnston, David, "A Turn in the Epistemology and Hermeneutics of Twentieth Century Uṣūl al-Fiqh", *Islamic Law and Society* 11 (2003), 233–282.

Kadivar, Mohsen, "From Traditional Islam to Islam as an End in Itself", *Die Welt des Islams* 51 (2011), 478–483.

Kadivar, Mohsen, 'Revisiting Women's Rights in Islam: "Egalitarian Justice" in Lieu of "Deserts-based Justice"' in *Gender and Equality in Muslim Family Law*, ed. Z. Mir-Hosseini, K. Voght, L. Larsen and C. Moe. London: I.B. Tauris, 2013.

al-Khū'ī, Abū al-Qāsim, *Mabānī takmilat al-minhāj*. Najaf: Matbaʿat al-Ādāb, n.d.

Matsunaga, Yasuyuki, "Human Rights and New Jurisprudence in Mohsen Kadivar's Advocacy of 'New-Thinker' Islam", *Die Welt des Islams* 51 (2011), 358–381.

al-Muẓaffar, Muḥammad Riḍā, *Uṣūl al-fiqh*. Qum: Intishārāt Ismāʿīlīyyān, 2000.

al-Najafī, Muḥammad Ḥasan, *Jawāhir al-kalām fī sharḥ sharāʾiʿ al-Islām*. Beirut: Mu'assasat al-Murtaḍā al-ʿĀlamiyya, 1996.

Nasr, S.H., C.K. Dagli, M.M. Dakake, J. Lumbard and M. Rustom (eds.), *The Study Quran: A New Translation and Commentary*. New York: Harper One, 2015.

al-Qummī, Mīrzā Abū al-Qāsim, *al-Qawānin al-muḥkama fī al-uṣūl*. Beirut: Dār al-Murtaḍā, 2009.

al-Qummī, Mīrzā Abū al-Qāsim, *al-Qawānīn al-muḥkama fī al-uṣūl al-mutqana*. Qum: Iḥyāʾ al-kutub al-Islāmiyya, 2010.

al-Ṣadr, Muḥammad Bāqir, *al-Fatāwa al-wāḍiḥa*. Beirut: Dār al-taʿāruf lil-matbūʿāt, 1983.

al-Ṣadr, Muḥammad Bāqir, *Durūs fī ʿilm al-uṣūl*. Qum: Markaz al-abḥāth wa al-dirāsāt al-takhaṣṣuṣiyya lil Imām al-Shahīd al-Ṣadr, 2003.

Shīrāzī, Nāṣir Makārim, *Anwār al-uṣūl*. Qum: Madrasat al-Imām Amīr al-Muʾminīn, 1994.

Subḥānī, Jaʿfar, *al-Mūjiz fī uṣūl al-fiqh*. Qum: Maktabat al-Tawḥīd, 2008.

Tabātabāʾī, Hossein Modarressi, *An Introduction to Shīʿī Law: A Bibliographical Study*. London: Ithaca Press, 1984.

CHAPTER 7

Maqāṣid al-Sharīʿa Discourse in Contemporary Shīʿī Jurisprudence

Hassan Beloushi

There has been much debate in the last century about how to modernise Islamic law so as to make it appropriate for a changing society. Among the solutions that have been proposed is the theory of *maqāṣid al-sharīʿa* as a legal theory for Islamic law. In the contemporary Shīʿī context, the calling for the *maqāṣid al-sharīʿa* is happening in a particular socio-political and cultural context for the Shīʿa and within a particular epistemological construction. Accordingly, it has particular ramifications with regards to this context. The aims of this chapter are to contextualise *maqāṣid al-sharīʿa* discourse within Shīʿī legal discourse and to introduce the main trends that call for *maqāṣid* and their possible ramifications. The chapter does not aim to argue for a particular preferred trend, rather it is an exploratory study to identify the features of this phenomena within Shīʿī jurisprudential debates.

1 *Maqāṣid al-Sharīʿa* in Sunnī Legal Discourse

In general terms, the theory of *maqāṣid al-sharīʿa* refers to the idea that the *sharīʿa*, as the legal element of God's message, encompasses aims and purposes, which should be fulfilled, even indirectly, and through which God's will for humanity in this world and the hereafter will be achieved. This idea, on the face of it, is not that different from the Muslim jurists' understanding of the *sharīʿa*. It is a common understanding that the *sharīʿa* has purposes, aims and benefits (*maṣāliḥ*) for humanity. However, what makes the theory of *maqāṣid al-sharīʿa* unique, compared to other theories, is its emphasis on practical solutions to legal challenges. *Maqāṣid al-sharīʿa* was provided a mature expression in the words of an Andalusian Mālikī Sunnī scholar in the fourteenth century – Abū Isḥāq al-Shāṭibī (d. 1388) – though its roots can be seen in earlier scholars' works such as al-Ghazālī (d. 1111) and al-Juwaynī (d. 1085).[1] al-Shāṭibī argued

1 Masud has studied the roots of *maqāṣid al-sharīʿa* prior to al-Shāṭibī, see: M.K. Masud, *Islamic Legal Philosophy: A Study of Abū Isḥāq Al-Shāṭibī's Life and Thought* (Delhi: International Islamic Publishers, 1989), 149–169.

© KONINKLIJKE BRILL NV, LEIDEN, 2020 | DOI:10.1163/9789004413948_009

that the *sharīʿa* was established for the benefit of human beings and therefore all legal norms aimed to preserve three levels of benefits[2] for humans. The first level is that of necessities[3] (*ḍarūriyyāt*) which comprises the five universals of which the "lack of all or any one of them in a community or society will lead to anarchy and great loss of life, as well as to loss of salvation in the hereafter".[4] These five universal necessities are religion (*dīn*), life (*nafs*), progeny (*ʿird*), property (*māl*) and intellect (*ʿaql*). The second level of benefit pertains to 'what is needed' (*ḥājiyyāt*) which "signify those aspects of the law that are needed in order to alleviate hardship so that the law can be followed without causing distress or predicament",[5] for example, "the abridgment of ritual obligations under circumstances of hardship and illness",[6] such as praying without performing *wuḍūʾ* in case of lack of water. The third level, according to al-Shāṭibī, pertains to the improvements (*taḥsīniyyāt*) which "are not needed to such an extent that without them the law becomes inoperable or deficient, and relinquishing them is not detrimental to the *ḍarūriyyāt* or the *ḥājiyyāt*, but they certainly *improve* the general character of the Sharīʿa".[7] Examples of this are the legal issues of purifications (*ṭahārāt*) outside of performing the prayer, and considerations such as the social etiquette of eating. al-Shāṭibī, although an Ashʿarī, based his theory theologically on a Muʿtazilite view of the religion, in particular their view of the ontology of ethics, in which God's legal will is based on moral rational foundations. As Johnston puts it, "Whereas the Muʿtazilites claimed an objective existence to ethical values which God takes into account in his dealings with people and his created order (objectivism), the Ashʿarites taught that these values may be defined only in terms of what God decrees (theistic subjectivism, or ethical voluntarism)".[8] As a ramification of this attitude, Muʿtazilites would believe that these moral values, especially in their basics, can be understood independently by individuals through the intellect (*ʿaql*). However, for al-Shāṭibī, the purposes and aims of the law (*sharīʿa*) underlining each legal ruling can be understood and should be the basis for any

2 Ibrāhīm ibn Mūsā al-Shāṭibī, *al-Muwāfaqāt fī Uṣūl al-Sharīʿa* (Cairo: Dār al-fikr al-ʿarābī, n.d.), 2:6.

3 It is matter of debate how to translate these three levels of *maqāṣid al-sharīʿa* into English. Scholars have translated them differently. See: Wael B. Hallaq, *A History of Islamic Legal Theories: An Introduction to Sunni Usul Al-fiqh* (Cambridge University Press, 1999), 168. See also: Yasir S. Ibrahim, "An Examination of the Modern Discourse on Maqāṣid al-Sharīʿa", *The Journal of the Middle East and Africa* 5 (2014), 43.

4 Ibrahim, "An Examination of the Modern Discourse on Maqāṣid al-Sharīʿa", 44.

5 Hallaq, *A History of Islamic Legal Theories*, 168.

6 Ibid.

7 Ibid., 169.

8 David Johnston, "A Turn in the Epistemology and Hermeneutics of Twentieth Century Uṣūl Al-Fiqh" in *Islamic Law and Society* 11 (2004), 236.

derived legal issue. Al-Shāṭibī, in contrast to Muʿtazilites, differentiated his jurisprudential methodology by minimizing the role of an independent use of the intellect in discovering the *maqāṣid al-sharīʿah*. He begins his second volume of his *uṣūl al-fiqh* work, which is devoted to deal with his *maqāṣid* theory, by providing a theological proof of the notion of objectivist morality upon which the Sharīʿa is based.[9] Interestingly, on the other hand, he proved the main idea of the theory and based his categories methodologically on an inductive method by surveying the *sharīʿa* legal instructions rather than attempting to derive them by the intellect as Muʿtazilites believe is possible. He says, "If the induction proves this [that the *sharīʿa* is based on aims and purposes that benefit human beings], and it leads to *ʿilm* within this subject, then we are certain that it continues throughout all *sharīʿa*'s particulars".[10]

Khalid Masud, in his study on al-Shāṭibī entitled: *Islamic Legal Philosophy: A Study of Abū ʾIshāq al-Shāṭibī's Life and Thought*, argues that the rise of the theory of *maqāṣid al-sharīʿa* with al-Shāṭibī was a result of the socio-political and economic changes that happened in his society. These changes required a flexibility and adaptability from Islamic law to be compatible with the new reality at the time of al-Shāṭibī. That is to say, his "concept of *maṣlaḥa* in relation to his doctrine of *maqāṣid al-sharīʿah* was the product of the need of his time to adapt Islamic law to the new social conditions".[11] These changes were the consolidation of political power to the Sultan, which affected the role of jurists, the "new educational system, judicial structure, penetration of *Ṣūfī ṭarīqas* and spread of liberal thought all supported by the political system"[12] in addition to economic development.[13] Hallaq on the other hand argues that the rise of al-Shāṭibī's theory was "by no means embedded in a desire to create a theoretical apparatus which would provide for flexibility and adaptability in positive law".[14] These social conditions are two groups that adulterated the true law of Islam according to Hallaq's reading, namely, "the lax attitudes of the jurisconsults and, far more importantly, the excessive legal demands imposed by what seems to have been the majority of contemporary Ṣūfīs".[15]

Whatever the reasons behind the emergence of al-Shāṭibī's theory of *maqāṣid al-sharīʿa* may have been, it did not spread within Sunnī legal theory as

9 Shāṭibī, *al-Muwāfaqāt fī Uṣūl al-Sharīʿa*, 2:6–7.
10 Ibid., 8.
11 M.K. Masud, *Islamic Legal Philosophy: A Study of Abū Isḥāq al-Shāṭibī's Life and Thought*, 25. Also, see 35.
12 Ibid., 35.
13 Ibid., 36.
14 Hallaq, *A History of Islamic Legal Theories*, 163.
15 Ibid.

a distinct jurisprudential discourse until the modern era in the early twentieth century, through the efforts of Muḥammad 'Abduh (d. 1905) and especially his student 'Abdullāh Dirāz (d. 1932) who published Shāṭibī's work *al-Muwāfaqāt* with his own commentary. Since then, the *maqāṣidī* discourse has become a popular legal discourse within, not only Sunnī legal thought, but also amongst intellectualists, so-called reformists and even Islamic movements.

Having said that, the popularity of *maqāṣidī* discourse in the twentieth century is now such that the individual has a vast array of material to survey from what has been produced over the last century,[16] a survey beyond the scope of this chapter. However, its revival in the early part of the twentieth century has incited scholars to investigate the reasons behind this, especially since it is interesting that the *maqāṣidī* discourse has not been limited to the jurists, but also attracts interest from those deemed to be "liberals" or "reformists".[17] Moreover, it has become a significant discourse for, not only Muslim scholars in the east, but a notable trend of Muslim scholars who live in the West have also embraced the *maqāṣidī* discourse.[18] In other words, there are two contexts, apart from the classical context of the medieval period where the

16 The Centre of *Maqāṣid al-sharī'a* Studies has produced a bibliography of *maqāṣid al-sharī'a* (*al-Dalīl al-irshādī ilā maqāṣid al-sharī'a*) which surveys all the topics related to *maqāṣid*, and is now available online in digital format. See: http://www.al-furqan.com/maqasid accessed: 18.2.2015.

17 Hallaq has studied some of them such as Rashād Riḍā, Khallāf, al-Fāsī and al-Turābī, on one hand. On the other hand, he has studied al-'Ashmāwī, Fazlur Rahmān and Shaḥrūr. See: Hallaq, *A History of Islamic Legal Theories*, 214–53. Johnston has studied Muhammad 'Abduh, Muhammad Rashīd Riḍā, 'Abd al-Razzāq Sanhūrī, 'Abd al-Wahhāb Khallāf, Muhammad Abu Zahra, and Muhammad Hashim Kamali. See: Johnston, "A Turn in the Epistemology and Hermeneutics of Twentieth Century *Uṣūl al-Fiqh*", 233–82. Also, in another article, Johnston studied some other *maqāṣidī* thinkers such as Muhammad al-Ghazālī, Muhammad 'Amāra, Muhammad Talbi, Muhammad al-Mutawakkal, Rāshid al-Ghannūshī, Ebrahim Moosa and Khaled Abou El Fadl. See: "Maqāṣid al-Sharī'a: Epistemology and Hermeneutics of Muslim Theologies of Human Rights," *Die Welt des Islams* 47 (2007), 149–87. In his recent article, he also studied a contemporary Sunnī scholar who embraces the *maqāṣidī* approach such as al-Qaraḍāwī, see: Johnston, David L. "Yūsuf al-Qaraḍāwī's Purposive Fiqh: Promoting or Demoting the Future Role of the 'ulamā'?," in *Maqasid Al-Shari'a and Contemporary Reformist Muslim Thought: An Examination*, ed. Adis Duderija (New York: Palgrave Macmillan, 2014).

18 See for example, Ṭāriq Ramaḍān, Hashim Kamali and Ebrahim Moosa. For an analysis of Ramaḍān's work see: David Warren "Doha – The Center of Reformist Islam? Considering *Radical Reform* in the Qatar Context: Tariq Ramadan and the Research Center for Islamic Legislation and Ethics (CILE)", in *Maqasid Al-Shari'a and Contemporary Reformist Muslim Thought: An Examination, ed.* A. Duderija, (New York: Palgrave Macmillan: 2014), 73–100. For an analysis of Hashim Kamali's work, see: Adis Duderija's "Islamic Law Reform and *Maqāṣid al-Sharī'a* in the Thought of Mohammad Hashim Kamali" in ibid., 13–38.

original *maqāṣid* theory was produced, in which *maqāṣid al-sharīʿa* has become a notable discourse. The first is the eastern Muslim scholars, especially in the Arab world, and the second the Western Muslim scholars and intellectuals.

Many scholars believe that modernity, especially in the late colonial and early post-colonial period, was the main cause of the emerging *maqāṣidī* discourse amongst Muslim scholars in the early part of the twentieth century. The falling of the Caliphate as a socio-political order for Muslims and the rise of the nation-state had led to serious and fundamental changes in the Muslim community. One of these changes was the codification of the state law, which was mainly not Islamic in a sense, but had been adopted from Western countries. This was seen as a challenge for the Muslim nations, especially for the religious institution represented by the scholars, which in turn had provoked Muslim thinkers and scholars to propose an "Islamic" solution. March argues that 'this meant theorizing a form of Islam that would serve the integrating and standardizing purposes of the modern nation-state. It also meant reformulating Islamic legal concepts in line with current normative conceptions of the "modern"'.[19] In this context, an old Islamic debate had been revived amongst those seen as reformists, that is to say, the Muʿtazilī-Ashʿarī debate regarding the role of intellect in understanding God's law. Muḥammad ʿAbduh is considered the main scholar who began to revive the Muʿtazilī-like theological tradition, and it is in this context that he encouraged his students to study Shāṭibī's jurisprudential thought. Subsequently, his student ʿAbdullah Dirāz published a version of Shāṭibī's jurisprudential book *al-Muwāfaqāt* with his own commentary. This intellectual line has continued with other thinkers and scholars such as Rashīd Riḍā (d. 1935), ʿAllāl al-Fāsī (d. 1974) and al-Ṭāhir Ibn ʿĀshūr (d. 1973). Although they all shared a *maqāṣidī* discourse, *maqāṣid al-sharīʿa* theory at that time was a framework that those thinkers and scholars were employing for the purposes of their own socio-political context. Thus, not all of them have followed Shāṭibī's legal theorisation in regards to *maqāṣid* and its categories and schemes, nor did they all agree with his methodology of establishing the purposes of the *sharīʿa*. An example for this is what Hallaq has stated, arguably, that Riḍā's thought of *maqāṣid al-sharīʿa* is a new development of the classical legal theory that goes beyond even al-Shāṭibī's. This new development, Hallaq insists, by "the religious utilitarianists – Riḍā, Khallāf and others – pay no more

19 Andrew F. March, "Naturalizing Shari'a: Foundationalist Ambiguities in Modern Islamic Apologetics" *Islamic Law and Society* 22 (2015), 48.

than lip service to Islamic legal values; for their ultimate frame of reference remains confined to the concepts of interest, need and necessity".[20]

Johnston, more precisely, adds another context in which *maqāṣidī*-like discourse had emerged, in addition to the Muʿtazilī-Ashʿarī debate, which is the theological foundation of this debate, namely the absence or erosion of the central political order. Within this context, he sees the emergence and growth of *siyāsa sharʿiyya* literatures in the classical period, which were presented by al-Ghazālī through his emphasis on the role of public interest (*maṣlaha mursala*) and by Ibn Taymiyya through calling for renewing *ijtihād*, and which paved the way for the modern Muslim scholars. Johnston says: "Henceforth, reason and revelation renew their mutual cooperation, and especially in eighteenth and nineteenth century India and Egypt, when Muslims called upon an Umma in decline to shake off the straightjacket of *taqlīd*, and exercise *ijtihād* in order to face the challenges of western modernity".[21]

Amongst Muslim scholars and intellectualists in the west, the *maqāṣidī* discourse is notable, especially over the last three decades. Arguably, the most famous two are Tariq Ramadan[22] and Hashim Kamali.[23] Despite their different approaches towards *maqāṣid al-sharīʿa*, they all share a notion that the *maqāṣid* project is the most compatible approach of Islamic law with their situation in the West, that is to say, in being a minority and having a different identity within a secular non-Muslim state and community.

2 *Maqāṣid al-Sharīʿa* in the Shīʿī Context

In the contemporary Shīʿī context, the calling for *maqāṣid al-sharīʿa* is within a particular socio-political and cultural context for the Shīʿa and a particular

20 Hallaq, *A History of Islamic Legal Theories*, 254. Yasir Ibrahim argues against this understanding of Riḍā, instead holding that the better understanding is to deal with the concept of *maṣlaḥa* in Riḍā's thought as a component of the greater framework, that is *maqāṣid al-sharīʿa*. For the fuller discussion see: Yasir S. Ibrahim, "Rashīd Riḍā and Maqāṣid al-Sharīʿa," *Studia Islamica* 102/103 (2006), 157–98.

21 Johnston, "A Turn in the Epistemology and Hermeneutics of Twentieth Century Uṣūl al-Fiqh," 278. Hallaq, in his critical paper, also mentions the influence of modernity on the growth of *maqāṣidī* discourse, see: Wael B. Hallaq, "Maqāṣid and the Challenges of Modernity," *Al-Jamiʿah* 49 (2011), 1–32.

22 See for example his work: Tariq Ramadan, *Radical Reform: Islamic Ethics and Liberation* (Oxford: Oxford University Press, 2009).

23 Kamali has written extensively on *maqāṣid al-sharīʿa*, his most important work being: Mohammed Hashim Kamali, *Maqāṣid al-Sharīʿah, Ijtihad and Civilisational Renewal* (International Institute of Islamic Thought, 2012).

epistemological construction. Accordingly, there are particular ramifications for this context. It is seen as a paradox, as mentioned above, that the *maqāṣid al-sharīʿa* has emerged from scholars with an Ashʿarī background. Trends known as having *ʿAdlī* tendencies, such as Shīʿism and Muʿtazilism, who are seen as epistemologically and theologically well-prepared for such discourse, did not take a risk to establish *maqāṣid al-sharīʿa* within their legal system. This can be said especially for Shīʿīsm, which has survived not only as a theological doctrine, but also as a legal doctrine. In order to contextualise the emergence of *maqāṣid al-sharīʿa* in Shīʿī jurisprudence, it can be said that there were two synchronous factors which have contributed to the rise of *maqāṣid al-sharīʿa* within the Shīʿī discourse.

2.1 *The Fall of the Islamic Caliphate and the Rise of the Modern Shīʿī State in Iran*

The rise of the nation state after the fall of the Islamic Caliphate in the early decades of the twentieth century is seen as the beginning of the secularisation of Islamic communities especially in the Middle East region. Although some might argue that the secularisation of Islamic communities began in the late period of the Ottoman Empire, or in the era of Muḥammad ʿAlī Bāshā for the Arab world, the falling of the Islamic caliphate made the process of secularisation systematic.[24] In particular, for the Arab world and maybe partly for Iran, which are of interest here, the rise of the nation state and the systematic secularisation of the public sectors, especially education, represented a serious challenge for religious institutions. It was the moment when the question of the validity and consistency of religious discourse for the modern age insistently arose. Also, it was a moment of the manifesting of a new educated social class which had been challenging religious authority. In other words, the rise of the

---

24 Bishārah believes that the relationship between religion and secularism can only be understood with a historical reading of the secularisation of the Islamic community. For that he proposed an intellectual project to study the matter. He suggests that the starting point of this historical reading should begin with the late period of the Ottoman Empire. See ʿAzmī Bishārah, *al-Dīn wa al-ʿAlmāniyyah fī Siyāq Tārīkhī* (Qatar: Arab Centre for Research and Political Studies, 2013). Others had dealt with the secularisation not only from political perspective, but also from cultural and social perspectives. See Nazik Saba Yared, *Secularism and the Arab World* (1850–1939) (London: Saqi Books, 2002) for the role of the Christians communities in secularisation of the Arab culture. For more cultural and social focus on the development of secularization see; Bingbing Wu "Secularism and Secularization in the Arab World", *Journal of Middle Eastern and Islamic Studies* (*in Asia*) 1 (2007), 55–65. A special examination of the process of secularization in the Caliphate before and after the fall of Ottoman Caliphate is well tracked by Nurullah Ardıç, see: Nurullah Ardıç, *Islam and the Politics of Secularism* (London, Routledge, 2012).

nation state is seen as a practical application of modernity in Islamic communities, especially in the public sectors. For Shīʿī communities, especially in Iraq and Iran in the central learning cities, the challenge of modernity was slightly delayed in comparison to the Sunnī experience. For Iran, it can be dated back to the rise of the Pahlavi regime and for Iraq it was after the revolution of 1920. In any case, the secular state and the secularisation of the public sectors posed many questions before the religious discourse. Accordingly, at that time, Sunnī as well as Shīʿī religious discourse witnessed considerable calls to renew their discourses so as to be consistent with the modern age. These can be seen in the tendency to re-open the door of *ijtihād* in Sunni thought, for instance, and in calling for renewing the religious learning curricula, the need for new theology and the tendency to renew jurisprudence in Shīʿī thought.

However, the rise of the Islamic Republic of Iran in 1979 was not only a significant event for the Shīʿa, but also an important event for all Middle-Eastern Islamic nations. Islamist movements in the Middle East were especially influenced by the revolution. The Islamic Republic of Iran was seen as the first modern Islamic state since the fall of the Islamic caliphate in the early decades of the twentieth century. However, for the Shīʿī experience, the revolution was more significant. The Shīʿa had historical experiences of political participation with some regimes, both Shīʿī and Sunnī. Also, they experienced, to a significant extent, a clerical involvement in politics, especially with issues closely related to governmental affairs. The first political experience was with the Safavid empire during the seventeenth century. The second political experience was with the Constitutional Revolution of 1905 in the Qājār period. The rise of the Islamic Republic of Iran in 1979 was the first Shīʿī political experiment to be led by a Shīʿī jurist, seeking Islamic rule in a modern age. Interestingly, although the revolution was regionally in Iran, the most important Shīʿī regions and nations were involved with the revolution. Cohesion could be seen throughout Iraq, the Gulf, and Lebanon. Interaction took place not only in the nations and among ordinary people, but also in the elite classes of these nations. The participation of jurists in Shīʿī cities of religious learning would affect not only the socio-political dimensions of these societies, but also the intellectual dimension of Shīʿī thought generally. In effect, what had happened, I would argue, was that the rise of the Islamic Republic of Iran in 1979 represented a real examination of a common slogan of the Islamist movement saying 'Islam is a solution', and in particular for Shīʿī jurisprudence. After the success of the revolution, many constitutional and legal issues appeared before Shīʿī jurists such that they were forced to revise every single traditional issue and to attempt to provide an Islamic approach for the basic matters of the state. Rafsanjānī (b. 1934) said that they thought that by simply applying Islamic law, they would build a strong modern state, but the reality was shocking and more complicated.[25] Moreover, many scholars under these circumstances revised the validity of current Shīʿī jurisprudence in dealing with these types of modern problems and this led them to find a reforming or an alternative approach. For example, Sayyid al-Khumaynī (d. 1989) delivered an important speech on the effect of time and space on deriving legal issues.[26] Also, before this, Muḥammad Bāqir al-Ṣadr (d. 1980) wrote a paper on the Islamic constitution.[27] From this time onwards, Shīʿī scholars began to take the matter of renewing the legal system in general, and jurisprudence in particular, seriously. This is reflected in the literature, the conferences organised, and the important speeches delivered by influential scholars.

2.2 *The Undermining of the Aristotelian Epistemological Paradigm*

For a long time, Aristotle was seen as a symbol of a school of thought rather than as merely a great philosopher. Aristotelianism was not only seen to be a philosophical school which was confined to the topic of metaphysics, but it was also seen as a framework for many academic disciplines, including science as we know it today. For a long time Aristotelianism could be found at the centre of the curriculum of religious schools in Europe, whether Catholic or Protestant.[28] The same can roughly be said of the curricula of Islamic schools, especially of Shīʿī thought. The epistemological framework of Shīʿī thought conceives knowledge as it was inherited from the philosophical school of Iṣfahān, which in turn was inherited from the works of Naṣīr al-Dīn al-Ṭūsī, who employed Avicenna's philosophy in Shīʿī theology. This conception of knowledge is mainly based on Aristotelian epistemology which can be found in his *Posterior Analytics*, specifically in his theory of demonstrations and demonstrative science[29] in his logical work, the *Organon*.[30] This Aristotelian tradition found its way into Shīʿī thought through al-Ṭūsī's commentary of Avicenna's work *al-Ishārāt* and *al-Shifāʾ*. According to this tradition, the concept of certain knowledge (*al-ʿilm*

25 Tawfīq al-Sayf, *Ḥudūd al-Dīmuqrātiyya al-Dīniyya* (Beirut: Dār al-Sāqī, 2008), 81–82.

26 Rūḥullāh Khumaynī, *Ṣaḥīfat al-Imām*, 22 vols. (Tehran: Mu'assasat Tanẓīm wa Nashr Āthār Imām Khumaynī, 2009), 21:242.

27 Muḥammad Bāqir al-Ṣadr, *al-Islam yaqūd al-ḥayāt* (Tehran: The Ministry of Islamic Guidance, 1982), 3–19.

28 Katherine Park and Lorraine Dastone (eds.) *The Cambridge History of Science: Volume 3, Early Modern Science* (Cambridge: Cambridge University Press, 2008), 26.

29 For further reading about Aristotle's theory of demonstrations and demonstrative science, see Robin Smith, 'Aristotle's Logic', in *The Stanford Encyclopedia of Philosophy* (Spring 2012 Edition), accessed 30 April 2019, https://plato.stanford.edu/entries/aristotle-logic/.

30 ʿAbd al-Raḥmān Badawī, *Manṭiq Arusṭū* (Kuwait: Wikālat al-Kuwayt lil-Maṭbūʿāt, 1980).

al-yaqīnī) is confined to demonstrative knowledge (*al-ʿilm al-burhānī*), which can be deducted through a demonstration (*apodeixis/burhān*). For a deduction to be demonstrative, its premises have to be self-evident (*dhātī*) or based on self-evident premises, and these premises constitute the demonstrative syllogism. Otherwise, what we acquire through deduction would be less than certain knowledge, that is, it might be supposition (*ẓann*) or delusion (*wahm*). In this case, it would not be classified as a demonstrative argument. Rather, it would be categorised under what Aristotle called a dialectical argument.[31] This perception of knowledge was the central understanding in Shīʿī thought not only for theoretical reason, but also because it transferred its understanding to practical reason (*al-ʿaql al-ʿamalī*). Practical reason is understood here as moral reasoning, which plays a crucial role in deriving many theological and jurisprudential concepts and theories. According to the Shīʿī theological tradition, which was inherited from al-Ṭūsī and employed in *uṣūl al-fiqh*, the nature of the judgments of practical reason are demonstrative just as they are in theoretical reason, though the scope of each realm of reason is different. This is what is meant in *uṣūlī* works by rational evidence (*al-dalīl al-ʿaqlī*).[32] Thus, strictly speaking, the Aristotelian concept of knowledge in both theoretical and practical reasoning is that which results exclusively from self-evident (*burhānī*) premises.

Subsequently, criticising the Aristotelian framework was seen as a sign of the beginning of the modern age in general, and of science in particular. However, if criticism of Aristotelianism in science was felt to be paving the way to development, it was not seen to be doing so in religious matters. Criticising the Aristotelian framework raised many questions for religious thinking which, in some cases, led to profound theological change. Although the Christian world (and possibly the Jewish world as well) experienced this challenge early on, the Islamic world does not seem to have encountered this shift until the middle of the nineteenth century. It was not until the first quarter of the twentieth century that it becomes a serious intellectual concern, when Islamic scholars began to seek alternatives to, as well as solutions for, this challenge. Scholars started to call for a new Islamic theology that would take into account scientific and

31 ʿAmmār Abū Radgīf, *al-Usus al-ʿaqliyya: Dirāsa lil munṭalaqāt al-ʿaqliyya lil baḥth fī ʿilm al-uṣūl* (Beirut: Dār al-faqīh, 2005).

32 In modern Shīʿī *uṣūl al-fiqh* there is a new trend that sees the nature of the judgments of practical reason, not as demonstrative, but as a collective agreement. This trend is known as the trend of philosophers (*ḥukamāʾ*), and its leading figure is Muḥammad Ḥusayn al-Iṣfahānī, along with his student Muhammad Riḍā al-Muẓaffar. For more details, see ibid., 97–149.

intellectual changes when dealing with theological issues.[33] In light of theological discussions, the concerns moved to other Islamic fields, of which jurisprudence was one. This was not surprising considering the correlation between the two fields.

Although Jamāl al-Din al-Afghānī's Shīʿism is a matter of debate, some prefer to date the beginning of Shīʿī disputes over modernity to the inception of his new theology. Others argue[34] that serious discussions (possibly accompanied by implications for practice) regarding new theology amongst Shīʿī scholars actually started with the generation of al-Ṭabāṭabāʾī (d. 1981) and his students, followed by other scholars in Iraq and Lebanon.

Many topics have been discussed within the new field of theology. A heated topic of debate was the validity of legal methodology which, in effect, relates directly to the essence of jurisprudence. Needless to say, also present was the question of the validity of the Aristotelian framework, especially in its Shīʿī version for jurisprudence.[35] The debate sometimes ensued by questioning whether Islamic texts were able to be read and interpreted by using new methodologies.[36] Ultimately, I would argue that these debates, taking into account their intellectual premises, gradually exerted considerable pressure over legal and jurisprudential discussions during the second half of the twentieth century. This pressure could, to a certain extent, be deemed as a significant challenge to Shīʿī jurisprudence.

3 Tendencies of *Maqāṣid al-Sharīʿa* in Modern Shīʿī Jurisprudence

As a result of the previous explained challenges, three main tendencies have emerged in the Shīʿī legal discourse calling for *maqāṣid al-sharīʿa*. Each one of these tendencies has a different approach towards the issue. This chapter will now proceed to explore each one.

33 For a comprehensive reading of the emergence of the so-called new theology in the Islamic context and how Muslim scholars conceived of it, see ʿAbdaljabār al-Rifāʿī, *al-Ijtihād al-kalāmī: Manāhij wa ruʾā mutanāwiʿa fī al-kalām al-jadīd* (Beirut: Dār al-Hādī, n.d.).

34 Ḥaydar Ḥubballah argues that within Shīʿī discourse, al-Ṭabāṭabāʾī was the first to begin the trend of new theology. See his *ʿIlm al-kalām al-jadīd: Qirāʾah awwaliyya*. Accessed 2 July 2014, http://aafaqcenter.com/index.php/post/669.

35 Rifāʿī, *al-Ijtihād al-kalāmī*, 294.

36 Ibid., 267.

3.1 *Reforming Current Shīʿī Jurisprudence*

This tendency argues that the current jurisprudential and legal paradigm, especially in terms of its epistemological and methodological frameworks, is capable of functioning as a mechanism of deriving legal rulings. The only requirement is to improve some of its concepts and tools in addition to expanding its scope to accommodate modern issues. This means that, according to this view, the progress of Shīʿī jurisprudence happens quite normally as it responds to the challenges in each historical stage by improving its own concepts and tools. However, what is required now, given these modern challenges, is to expand the scope of the paradigm's effectiveness. This should take place through interaction with modern fields, especially those that relate to societal issues, such as the political institution, the economic system, and the judicial system. There are four principal scholars who can be associated with this tendency. They are Muḥammad Bāqir al-Ṣadr (d. 1980), Muḥammad Mahdī Shams al-Dīn (d. 2001), Muḥammad al-Shīrāzī (d. 2002), and ʿAlī Ḥubballāh (b. 1961). The reason for choosing these scholars is that, despite differences, they each share a similar approach.

Muḥammad Bāqir al-Ṣadr carefully read the history of Shīʿī *uṣūl al-fiqh* and, therefore, was aware of its developments throughout Shīʿī history.[37] Nevertheless, he believed in the capacity of the current legal paradigm, especially with Shaykh al-Anṣārī's contribution. Consequently, in terms of his *uṣūlī* research, there were a few attempts to improve the current Shīʿī *uṣūlī* thought. For example, he tried to remodel the structure of *uṣūl al-fiqh*, revise the nature of practical reason and its applications in the *uṣūlī* field, and produce a few simple and new ideas in several *uṣūlī* issues. However, his real contribution lay not only in these ideas, but also in the way that he invested *uṣūlī* tools into societal issues. This can be seen in his approach to ways of dealing with contradictory evidence where he argued that the purposes of the law (the *maqāṣid al-sharīʿa*) have to be a basis for weighing some evidence over others.[38] Moreover, it can also be seen in his calling for a social reading of the holy texts.[39] Essentially, Ṣadr attempted to invest the *uṣūlī* concepts and tools into societal issues in a way that would enable *uṣūl al-fiqh* to deal better with public as well as individual concerns.

---

37 See Muḥammad Bāqir al-Ṣadr, *al-Maʿālim al-jadīda li-ʿilm al-uṣūl* (Tehran: Maktabat al-Najāḥ, 1975).

38 Muḥammad Bāqir al-Ṣadr, *Buḥūth fī ʿilm al-uṣūl*, 7 vols. (Tehran: Muʾassasat Dār al-Maʿārif, 1997), 7:333–4.

39 Muḥammad Bāqir al-Ṣadr, *Ikhtarnā lakum* (Beirut: Dār al-Zahrāʾ, 1975), 90–9.

Muḥammad Mahdī Shams al-Dīn's approach was similar to that of al-Ṣadr but he, additionally, addressed sensitive societal issues. He did not generally have a problem with the current legal paradigm. Rather, he appreciated the depth of Shīʿī *uṣūlī* scholars but questioned the extent to which philosophical ideas had been used in a field deemed to have the social scope for them.[40] Shams al-Dīn wrote only a few short articles on *uṣūlī* issues and left no systematic work on *uṣūl al-fiqh*.[41] However, he diligently used *uṣūlī* tools when he addressed societal issues, such as the Islamic social institution, the political theory of Islamic government, and what he described as sensitive women's issues and some economic issues. Although he had a sense of *maqāṣid al-sharīʿa* in his approaches to *fiqhī* matters, which he both dealt with and called for, he did not provide a theoretical jurisprudential framework.

In contrast to Shams al-Dīn, Muḥammad al-Shīrāzī has written extensively on *uṣūl al-fiqh*. Shīrāzī's publications have followed a traditional course, both in terms of the way that they have been structured as well as the way that he has commented on the traditional textbooks of Shīʿī *uṣūl*.[42] Although Shīrāzī did not attempt to provide new jurisprudential ideas, he did expand the scope of the application of the current legal paradigm so that rulings pertaining to modern affairs could be derived. For example, he wrote Islamic laws (*fiqh*) pertaining to media, politics, globalisation, social institutions, traffic, liberty, Islamic government, the economy, the environment, and other matters. Thus, Shīrāzī, within this tendency, represents a model of a practical application, which has attempted to invest the capacity of the current paradigm as much as possible as a response to the challenges stated above.

The last example of this tendency is ʿAlī Ḥubballāh, who is a contemporary Shīʿī Lebanese scholar. Although he is more recent than the other scholars mentioned, it is reasonable to associate his *uṣūlī* works with this tendency. In his extensive volume on *uṣūl al-fiqh*, *Dirāsāt fī falsafat uṣūl al-fiqh wa al-sharīʿa wa naẓariyyat al-Maqāṣid*,[43] he discusses the issue of renewing Shīʿī jurisprudence and attempts to provide recommendations for improvement. His main criticism is not levied against any of the foundations of the current paradigm's frameworks (the epistemological, methodological, and functional

---

40 Mahmūd Qanṣū, *al-Muqaddimāt wa al-tanbīhāt fī sharḥ uṣūl al-fiqh*, 8 vols., (Beirut: Dār al-mu'arikh al-ʿarābī, 2009), 1:5–34.

41 For an overview of Shams al-Dīn's jurisprudential opinions, see Zakī al-Milād, 'Al-Shaykh Muḥammad Mahdī Shams al-Dīn wa al-naqd al-manhajī li-uṣūl al-fiqh', *al-Kalimah*, no. 74 (2012), 5–20.

42 See Muḥammad al-Shīrāzī, *al-Uṣūl*, 8 vols. (Qum: Dār al-Hudā, 1993).

43 ʿAlī Ḥubballah *Dirāsāt fī falsafat uṣūl al-fiqh wa al-sharia wa al-fiqh* (Beirut: Dār al-hādī, 2005).

frameworks). On the contrary, Ḥubballāh believes that it has the capacity to generate new tools and concepts which are able to deal with modern issues. However, this generating capacity, according to him, has not been correctly activated. Ḥubballāh, sees his main task as being the reactivation of the generating capacity of the current paradigm and the establishment of new tools based on the paradigm's foundation.[44] In his view, the two principal requirements needed to activate a real sense of *ijtihād* are: (i) reintegrating intellectually with other Islamic legal schools by having comparative studies in jurisprudence, and (ii) embracing the theory of *maqāṣid al-sharī'a* with a Shī'ī foundation.[45]

In summary, this tendency was a response to the modern challenges faced by the current paradigm. Although each of the four scholars discussed take a different approach to the challenge, they all, I would argue, believe in the generating capacity of the foundation of the legal paradigm. Some of the four scholars chose to work on *uṣūl al-fiqh* more than *fiqh* itself, and vice versa.

3.2 *Calling for an Alternative Field to Reform*

This tendency argues that the current legal and jurisprudential paradigm has been firmly established and has provided many sophisticated tools, concepts, and theories, especially in linguistic analysis, the epistemological foundation of justifying the value of legal evidence (what is known as *al-ḥujjiyya*), and the practical principle of dealing with unknown cases. According to this tendency, the process of self-improvement within current Shī'ī jurisprudence is sufficient to meet challenges. However, according to this trend, dealing with modern challenges is not the business of *uṣūl al-fiqh* for both conceptual and practical reasons. With regard to conceptual reasons it is argued that the function of *uṣūl al-fiqh* is to determine the reliability of the legal evidence which may be used to derive legal rulings. The way to make legal rulings more consistent with the modern age and to be able to achieve the purposes of the law is not the prerogative of *uṣūl al-fiqh*. With regard to the practical reasons, it is argued that the field of *uṣūl al-fiqh* – with its extensive subject matter – is already at its capacity and unable to accommodate further demands. That is to say, the scholars and students of the field of *uṣūl al-fiqh* would normally take a quite long period of time to make adjustments to jurisprudential theories and concepts, let alone applying them to theories in *fiqh*. It follows that there must be another field to deal with these issues. The process of creating another theoretical field, as the argument goes, is the natural process for all fields that have grown and expanded. Subsequently, this tendency calls for creating a new

44 Ibid., 10.
45 Ibid., 11–12.

field, and the most popular one, which has received much attention and intellectual work, is what is called 'the philosophy of *fiqh*'. Famous scholars at the forefront of such advocacy are Mahdī Mahrīzī (b. 1962),[46] Ḥaydar Ḥubballāh (b. 1973),[47] and Muḥammad Muṣṭafawī.[48]

Several points have been addressed amongst the scholars who are interested in the philosophy of *fiqh*, the most important of which is the very question of the function of the field and its scope. With regard to the nature of the field, there is somehow a common agreement amongst the scholars that the purpose of the philosophy of *fiqh* is not the derivation of legal rulings. However, this is not to say that the philosophy of *fiqh* does not indirectly affect the derivation of legal rulings. This would happen, according to their argument, by making the jurist aware of what the epistemological, ethical, and methodological assumptions of jurisprudence are. With regard to the scope of the field, the scholars advocating for the philosophy of *fiqh*, who were mentioned above, have made different suggestions. Some have suggested that the field should include more than ten subjects, whereas others have just suggested merely a few subjects. The subjects of interest here are only three in number. Firstly, *maqāṣid al-sharīʿa*: scholars have debated whether the purposes of the law are part of the field or whether they are a separate field, as seen in the approach of recent Sunnī work. Despite differing views, all agree that awareness of *maqāṣid al-sharīʿa* is important when dealing with modern issues. Secondly, the relationship between *fiqh* and time: there is a common agreement that this subject should be included in the philosophy of *fiqh*. The basic question of this topic is how the changes that take place throughout the ages would affect the mechanism of deriving legal issues.[49] Thirdly, hermeneutics: here, also, there

46 Mahdī Mahrīzī, *Madkhal ilā falsafat al-fiqh*, trans. Ḥaydar Najaf (Beirut: Dār al-Hādī, 2002).

47 Ḥaydar Ḥubballāh presented his ideas regarding the philosophy of *fiqh* in thirteen lectures. See Ḥaydar Ḥubballāh, *Falsafat al-fiqh*, accessed 22 May 2015, http://hobbollah.com/mohazerat_category/%D9%81%D9%84%D8%B3%D9%81%D8%A9-%D8%A7%D9%84%D9%81%D9%82%D9%87/.

48 Muḥammad Muṣṭafawī, *Falsafat al-fiqh: Dirāsa fī al-uṣūl al-manhājiyya lil-fiqh al-islāmī* (Beirut: Markaz al-ḥaḍāra li-tanmiyat al-fikr al-islāmī, 2000).

49 The role of time in *fiqh* has not been subject to independent discussion in the classical Shīʿī tradition, though some elements of the subject have been treated tangentially within broader jurisprudential discussions. It has been raised as a focal issue explicitly after the Iranian revolution, particularly after the famous speech of Imam Khomainī in 1989, becoming a central issue for discussion and debates amongst jurists. Many theoretical issues have been discussed in this regard; just to mention a few, Subḥānī has written *Risālah fī ta'thīr al-zamān wa al-makān ʿalā istinbāṭ al-ʿaḥkām* (Qum: Mu'asasat al-Imām al-Sādiq, 1997); ʿAlī Ḥubballah has dedicated a chapter to the issue in his *Dirāsāt fī falsafat uṣūl al-fiqh wa al-sharia wa al-fiqh* (Beirut: Dār al-hādī, 2005) pp. 394–436; al-Mudarrisi also

is a common agreement on including this subject within the field. However, the question of hermeneutics in this context is different from the one that is usually dealt with in traditional jurisprudence. The question here concerns the relationship between the reader, who here is the jurist, as a person attached with a tradition and then the text, which here is the holy text. There are other topics, which have been debated and discussed in the field, but these three are the most relevant to our interest as they reflect an alternative way of dealing with modern challenges.

3.3 *Calling for a New Paradigm*

In this tendency, the current paradigm is viewed as having reached a dead end in which it is epistemologically, methodologically, and functionally incapable of responding to modern challenges. Although previously consistent with a particular historical stage, given all these new changes, the paradigm is no longer sufficient.

According to this tendency, demonstrated arguably exclusively in the ideas of Muḥammad Taqī al-Mudarrisī (b. 1945), Shīʿī jurisprudence is characterised by three general features that make it both historically confined to a particular situation and now functionally ineffective. Firstly, the current legal paradigm was formulated in specific historical circumstances, whereby the Shīʿa were under the pressure of dictatorial and sectarian regimes. According to al-Mudarrisī, in these circumstances any group of human beings would be expected to take a defensive position. In terms of jurisprudence, this means the derivation of a mechanism that would save the necessary elements of group identity. Mudarrisī calls this 'the *fiqh* of necessity'.[50] This character manifests itself in jurisprudence in many ways; one way, for instance, is the expansion of practical principles (*al-uṣūl al-ʿamaliyya*), something that has been very noticeable in Shīʿī jurisprudence over the last two centuries. The basic idea of practical principles is that in the absence of textual evidence determining the ruling for a specific matter, the jurist should apply a practical principle to at least eliminate confusion and provide a practical instruction. This, in a sense, shows that the Shīʿī jurist is uncomfortable with moving away from textual evidence to providing moral principles taken from the purposes of the law rather than offering a merely practical instruction. Furthermore, the dominance of

---

dedicates a chapter to the issue in *al-Tashrīʿ al-Islāmī* (Tehran: 'Intisharāt Mudarrisi, 1992) and Musṭafawī in *Falsafat Al-Fiqh*, 99–120. However, the extent to which such ideas have been practised as established theory in the actual derivation of legal rulings is the subject of debate that should be discussed elsewhere.

50 Muḥammad Taqī al-Mudarrisī, *al-Tashrīʿ al-Islāmī: Manāhijuhu wa maqāṣiduhu*, (Tehran: 'Intisharāt Mudarrisi, 1992), 2:34.

a cautious mentality in the current paradigm is another manifestation of the influence of those historical circumstances, which, according to Mudarrisī, reflect a desire to conserve the minimum elements of the group's identity. Secondly, Shī'ī jurisprudence was conceptually and functionally established to deal with the legal issues of individuals. As a result, its conceptual tools and theories were not able to address collective and societal issues, whereas in modern societies any legal system would not be valid if it lacked societal as well as conceptual tools and theories in deriving legal rulings.[51] Thirdly, the current paradigm was in many parts based on, as Mudarrisī argues, a particular philosophical school that infiltrated Shīʿī theological thought early on, subsequently finding its way into jurisprudence. This philosophical school, as Mudarrisī sees it, is a Hellenistic Greek philosophy generally based on a polemic characteristic which is unproductive epistemologically, especially in the legal system.[52]

Given these criticisms, this tendency calls for a new jurisprudential paradigm which represents a break from the current paradigm and would be able to deal with modern issues. Mudarrisī proposes the *maqāṣidī* paradigm and suggests it should be based on a new epistemological foundation. This proposed paradigm should have a social sense in deriving legal issues and should be characterised by a spirit of initiative. Having said that, the breaking away that this tendency represents does not entail a sharp rupture with the tradition. Rather, there would be a level of continuity with the tradition, for Mudarrisī associates himself with, and regards himself to be a part of the traditional circle. Despite his novel departures, his continuity with the tradition can be clearly seen in both his works on the Qur'ān and in *fiqh*.[53]

4 Conclusion

This chapter attempted to explore the tendencies of *maqāṣid al-sharīʿa* within current Shīʿī jurisprudence and to contextualise them within the specific socio-political and intellectual factors informing Shīʿī thought as compared to the Sunnī context. One can say that current Shīʿī jurisprudence, in calling for *maqāṣid al-sharīʿa*, has been motivated by factors that were essentially

51 Ibid., 28–32.

52 Ibid., 1:77.

53 I have studied his works in further detail and discussed to what extent he represents a shift from the tradition. See: Hassan Beloushi, "The Theory of Maqāṣid al-Sharīʿa in Shīʿī Jurisprudence: Muḥammad Taqī al-Mudarrisī as a Model" (PhD dissertation, University of Exeter, 2014).

different from those of the Sunnī context. The emergence of *maqāṣid al-sharīʿa* in Shīʿī thought had its own concerns and it will have its own ramifications. Yet it seems that such trends will take a long time before they can be firmly established within the mainstay of Shīʿī jurisprudence. The trends towards *maqāṣid al-sharīʿa* are relatively new, and although espoused by scholars considered to be active thinkers in the religious community they are ultimately deemed second class, or more specifically, for they do not yet hold the statuses of *marjaʿiyya*. Further research on how the specific methodological contributions and hermeneutical tools of each of these emergent tendencies would do much to help assess how the emergent Shīʿī versions of *maqāṣid al-sharīʿa* would deal with the concerns that have been occupying *maqāṣidī* discourse in Islamic thought in general.

Bibliography

Abū Radgīf, ʿAmmār, *al-Usus al-ʿaqliyya: Dirāsa lil munṭalaqāt al-ʿaqliyya lil baḥth fī ʿilm al-uṣūl*. Beirut: Dār al-faqīh, 2005.

Ardıç, Nurullah, *Islam and the Politics of Secularism*. London, Routledge, 2012.

Badawī, ʿAbd al-Raḥmān, *Manṭiq Arusṭū*. Kuwait: Wikālat al-Kuwayt lil-Maṭbūʿāt, 1980.

Beloushi, Hassan, "The Theory of Maqāṣid al-Sharīʿa in Shīʿī Jurisprudence: Muḥammad Taqī al-Mudarrisī as a Model". PhD dissertation, University of Exeter, 2014.

Bishārah, ʿAzmī, *al-Dīn wa al-ʿAlmāniyyah fī Siyāq Tārīkhī*. Qatar: Arab Centre for Research and Political Studies, 2013.

Duderija, Adis, "Islamic Law Reform and *Maqāṣid al-Sharīʿa* in the Thought of Mohammad Hashim Kamali" in *Maqasid Al-Shariʿa and Contemporary Reformist Muslim Thought: An Examination*, ed. A. Duderija. New York: Palgrave Macmillan, 2014.

Hallaq, Wael B., *A History of Islamic Legal Theories: An Introduction to Sunni Usul Al-fiqh*. Cambridge University Press, 1999.

Hallaq, Wael B., "Maqāṣid and the Challenges of Modernity," *Al-Jamiʿah* 49 (2011), 1–32.

Ḥubballah, Ḥaydar, *ʿIlm al-kalām al-jadīd: Qirāʾah awwaliyya*. Accessed 2 July 2014, http://aafaqcenter.com/index.php/post/669.

Ḥubballah, Ḥaydar, *Falsafat al-fiqh*. Accessed 22 May 2015, http://hobbollah.com/mohazerat_category/%D9%81%D9%84%D8%B3%D9%81%D8%A9-%D8%A7%D9%84%D9%81%D9%82%D9%87/.

Ḥubballah, ʿAlī, *Dirāsāt fī falsafat uṣūl al-fiqh wa al-sharia wa al-fiqh*. Beirut: Dār al-hādī, 2005.

Ibrahim, Yasir S., "Rashīd Riḍā and Maqāṣid al-Sharīʿa," *Studia Islamica* 102/103 (2006), 157–98.

Ibrahim, Yasir S., "An Examination of the Modern Discourse on Maqāṣid al-Sharīʿa" *The Journal of the Middle East and Africa* 5 (2014), 39–60.

Johnston, David, "A Turn in the Epistemology and Hermeneutics of Twentieth Century Uṣūl Al-Fiqh" in *Islamic Law and Society* 11 (2004), 233–282.

Johnston, David, "Maqāṣid al-Sharī'a: Epistemology and Hermeneutics of Muslim Theologies of Human Rights," *Die Welt des Islams* 47 (2007), 149–87.

Johnston, David, "Yūsuf al-Qaraḍāwī's Purposive Fiqh: Promoting or Demoting the Future Role of the ʿulamā'?," in *Maqasid Al-Shari'a and Contemporary Reformist Muslim Thought: An Examination*, ed. Adis Duderija. New York: Palgrave Macmillan, 2014.

Kamali, Mohammed Hashim, *Maqāṣid al-Sharīåh, Ijtihad and Civilisational Renewal.* International Institute of Islamic Thought, 2012.

Khumaynī, Rūḥullāh, *Ṣaḥīfat al-Imām*, 22 vols. Tehran: Mu'assasat Tanẓīm wa Nashr Āthār Imām Khumaynī, 2009.

Mahrīzī, Mahdī, *Madkhal ilā falsafat al-fiqh*, trans. Ḥaydar Najaf. Beirut: Dār al-Hādī, 2002.

March, Andrew F., "Naturalizing Shari'a: Foundationalist Ambiguities in Modern Islamic Apologetics" *Islamic Law and Society* 22 (2015), 45–81.

Masud, M.K., *Islamic Legal Philosophy: A Study of Abū Isḥāq Al-Shāṭibī's Life and Thought.* Delhi: International Islamic Publishers, 1989.

al-Mīlād, Zakī, "Al-Shaykh Muḥammad Mahdī Shams al-Dīn wa al-naqd al-manhajī li-uṣūl al-fiqh", *al-Kalimah*, 74 (2012), 5–20.

al-Mudarrisī, Muḥammad Taqī, *al-Tashrīʿ al-Islāmī: Manāhijuhu wa maqāṣiduhu.* Tehran: 'Intisharāt Mudarrisi, 1992.

Muṣṭafawī, Muḥammad, *Falsafat al-fiqh: Dirāsa fī al-uṣūl al-manhājiyya lil-fiqh al-islāmī.* Beirut: Markaz al-ḥaḍāra li-tanmiyat al-fikr al-islāmī, 2000.

Ramadan, Tariq, *Radical Reform: Islamic Ethics and Liberation.* Oxford: Oxford University Press, 2009.

al-Rifāʿī, ʿAbdaljabār, *al-Ijtihād al-kalāmī: Manāhij wa ru'ā mutanāwiʿa fī al-kalām al-jadīd.* Beirut: Dār al-Hādī. n.d.

al-Ṣadr, Muḥammad Bāqir, *Ikhtarnā lakum.* Beirut: Dār al-Zahrā', 1975.

al-Ṣadr, Muḥammad Bāqir, *al-Islam yaqūd al-ḥayāt.* Tehran: The Ministry of Islamic Guidance, 1982.

al-Ṣadr, Muḥammad Bāqir, *al-Maʿālim al-jadīda li-ʿilm al-uṣūl.* Tehran: Maktabat al-Najāḥ, 1975.

al-Ṣadr, Muḥammad Bāqir, *Buḥūth fī ʿilm al-uṣūl*, 7 vols. Tehran: Mu'assasat Dār al-Maʿārif, 1997.

al-Sayf, Tawfīq, *Ḥudūd al-Dīmuqrātiyya al-Dīniyya.* Beirut: Dār al-Sāqī, 2008.

al-Shāṭibī, Ibrāhīm ibn Mūsā, *al-Muwāfaqāt fī Uṣūl al-Sharīʿa.* Cairo: Dār al-fikr al-ʿarābī. n.d.

al-Shīrāzī, Muḥammad, *al-Uṣūl*, 8 vols. Qum: Dār al-Hudā, 1993.

Subḥānī, *Risālah fī ta'thīr al-zamān wa al-makān 'alā istinbāṭ al-'aḥkām*. Qum: Mu'asasat al-Imām al-Sādiq, 1997.

Warren, David, "Doha – The Center of Reformist Islam? Considering *Radical Reform* in the Qatar Context: Tariq Ramadan and the Research Center for Islamic Legislation and Ethics (CILE)" in *Maqasid Al-Shari'a and Contemporary Reformist Muslim Thought: An Examination*, ed. A. Duderija. New York: Palgrave Macmillan, 2014.

Wu, Bingbing, "Secularism and Secularization in the Arab World," *Journal of Middle Eastern and Islamic Studies (in Asia)* 1 (2007), 55–65.

Yared, Nazik Saba, *Secularism and the Arab World* (1850–1939). London: Saqi Books, 2002.

Epilogue

Robert Gleave

The essays in this volume represent some of the more adventurous elements of contemporary Shīʿī legal theory, in which the theological drive for justice developed from Imāmī Shiʿism's Muʿtazilī base is fully exploited. Though not fully incorporating the *maqāṣid* paradigm, there is clearly an acceptance that rules provided by God need to have a purpose and a benefit. Without this, they cease to be worthy of both obedience and discovery. This is what Damad refers to in the first chapter as the "utility" of certain legal hermeneutic procedures. That the old Muʿtazilī moral ontology has been challenged and changed is clear for Damad, such that all *mujtahids'* rulings, both those which accord with reality and those which do not, are essentially equal. Similarly, and perhaps even more so, Bata in the second chapter, explores the authoritativeness of certainty in modern Shīʿī *uṣūl*. Bata's argument for a modified epistemology which might allow some notion of certainty to be reintroduced into legal theory represents a challenge to the paradigm under which so many of the contemporary Shīʿī *uṣūlīs* are operating. In a similar vein, perhaps, Nobahar, in chapter 3, concludes his exploration of the interpretation of the Qur'an by arguing that, in a strange way, the Akhbārī argument (against the contemporary Uṣūlīs) that the Qur'an is difficult to understand should be received positively, and should form the basis for further theorization. It is a short step from the Akhbārī position to the notion that Quranic interpretation should only be done "suitably trained scholars". Whether the spirit of the times will allow such elitism in Quranic interpretation remains to be seen. Another challenge to the dominant method of Uṣūlī legal theory is the incorporation of case law proposed by Panjwani in chapter 4. His argument is that law, as a subject of study, seems under-developed since the jurists seem obsessed with epistemology. By arguing for a more practical development of legal theory, based on the accepted theory of "the practice of rational people" as a form of legal indicator, Panjwani displays both his frustration, but also his optimism for the potentials of Shīʿī legal theory.

The trajectory of argumentation in these studies is, then, that practical implications of legal rules should override any sentimental attachment to established legal structures. If legal theory prevents the full potential of justice and fairness being realized, then Shīʿī legal theory has mechanisms for the removal of these impediments. If in practice, laws which have no precedent within the history of legal discussion, and which cannot be textually traced, prevent the

© KONINKLIJKE BRILL NV, LEIDEN, 2020 | DOI:10.1163/9789004413948_010

emergence of a truly God-centred legal regime, then they too can be reconsidered. Hamoudi highlights that Shīʿī jurists, who hold the highest status in the Shīʿī public's estimation, live with the contradictions created by the dual allegiance to political progress and the *fiqh* tradition. Similarly, Bhojani bemoans the limitation of more traditional scholarly discourses to the old paradigm, which though accepting that legal demonstration which falls short of certainty can be authoritative, continues to hold certainty as the ideal form of legal demonstration. That contemporary philosophical developments are undermining this foundationalism means, for Bhojani, that new sources of human understanding must be incorporated into the theoretical framework of legal derivation. For these new sources, certainty is more than simply unavailable; it is irrelevant to the source's authority. For readers familiar with Sunni legal theory, this discussion may appear rather overblown and over-theoretical. Many contemporary Sunni legal theorists believe they have answered these questions through the paradigm of *maqāṣid al-sharīʿa* – the notion that the law has aims which are divinely intended within the Shariʿa, and which enable individual regulations to be discarded when in conflict with these aims. The problem, for Shīʿī legal theorists with this paradigm, is that the over-ruling of the regulation for the sake of the *maqāṣid* does not, sufficiently obliterate the positive moral status of the original regulation. It is not simply the case that the new *maqāṣid*-based ruling is authoritative *despite* the residual validity of the original rule. Contemporary Shīʿī Uṣulīs appear to have reached the view that, whilst the moral qualities themselves have enduring validity, in themselves, legal rules have no permanent moral quality. These debates form the background to Beloushi's exploration of how contemporary Shīʿī legal theorists deal with the popularly persuasive rhetoric of *maqāṣid al-sharīʿa*, whilst at the same time trying to root this within the theological-juristic framework of post-Akhbārī *uṣūl al-fiqh*.

The loss of certainty – or the closing of the door to certainty (*insidād bāb al-ʿilm*) as it is often referred to in contemporary Shīʿī *uṣūl* writing – might leave the *mujtahid* with justified belief concerning the God's assessment in a particular case, but not necessarily justified *true* belief. A belief that is a derivation from the evidence, and not pure guesswork, whim or fancy is categorized as *ẓann*. Given the paucity of assessments accompanied by indubitable indicators, most assessments proposed by the *mujtahids* will be classed as *ẓann*. Fundamental to a legal system where *ẓann* is recognized as an unavoidable epistemological category is whether things which are *ẓann* have the ability to "prove" things – that is, are they the sorts of things from which valid legal assessments can be drawn. This is termed the *ḥujjiyya* ("probative force") of *ẓann*, and both establishing that *ẓann* can have this power, and whether it has this unconditionally and absolutely has been much discussed in the Shīʿī works encountered in this volume.

One modern discussion can be found in the influential work of Ayatallāh Jaʿfar Subḥānī.[1] He lists a number of proofs which have been used to argue for the absolute probative force of *ẓann*. One should be clear from the outset that by *ẓann* he means informed *ẓann*, reached after a process of reasoning and by a qualified individual (in the legal sphere, this means the *mujtahid*). The strongest argument for treating such *ẓann* as having unconditional probative force in his view involves the following reasoning:

> When a qualified scholar (a *mujtahid*) expends all his effort (*ijtihād*) to reach an opinion (*ẓann*) as to what the sources indicate to be the law, then opposing that opinion would lead to a risk of performing an incorrect action, and therefore harm (*ḍarar*) to oneself or others. Exposing oneself to this sort of risk, when there is an opinion based on a scholar's study and effort, available is rationally indefensible. Therefore following the scholar's opinion, always and unconditionally (*muṭlaqan*) the best course of action; his opinion then has absolute probative force.

Jaʿfar Subḥānī identifies a number of issues with this argument. He expresses it as a syllogism:

> Opposing the *ẓann* of the *mujtahid* leads to a risk (another *ẓann* if you like) of harm [Minor premise]
>
> Reason holds that one should always avoid a risk of harm [Major premise]

These two premises lead, logically it is thought, on to the conclusion:

> The *mujtahid*'s opinion has probative force unconditionally [Conclusion]

The scholars, Subḥānī tells us, have rejected this argument by attacking the validity of the minor and major premises. The general tendency has been for the scholars of the early period (*al-qudamāʾ*) to attack the major premise (that is, the general rule around avoiding the risk of harm), and the later scholars (*al-mutaʾakhkhirīn*) to attack the minor premise (that is, opposing the *mujtahid*'s *ẓann* leads to a risk of harm). He considers the arguments against

1 The following exposition follows the dense argumentation in Subḥānī, *al-Mabsūṭ fī uṣūl al-fiqh* (Qum: Muʾassasat al-Imām al-Ṣādiq), 2:341–344.

the major premise to be weak, and they need not detain us here. Moving on straight to the recent arguments against the minor premise, he produces the following account.

Against the minor premise, the argument revolves around a typology of the sort of harm which might come about from not treating the *mujtahid*'s *ẓann* as having probative force (that is, by rejecting the *mujtahid*'s *ẓann* as authoritative for oneself). The harm that might be caused by ignoring the *mujtahid*'s opinion could be of two types, Subḥānī says: this worldly and otherworldly. That is, by ignoring the *mujtahid*'s opinion one could be causing harm to yourself or others in this world; and/or you could be causing harm to your fate in the next world. These two types of harm require, for Subḥānī, different treatments.

For other worldly harm, Subḥānī begins with the observation that there is a relationship of necessary entailment (*mulāzama*) between the obligation to perform an action, and the punishment for nonperformance. However, there is the maxim that "to punish without giving an explanation is morally repugnant" (*qubḥ al-ʿiqāb bilā bayān*); therefore the obligation must be explained to the legal subjects. The simple case is when there is a clearly established obligation to perform an action from the divine Lawgiver; the legal subject refuses to perform that action; the legal subject can then be punished. In this sense there is a necessary connection between the obligation and the punishment.

What is the situation, though, if the explanation of the obligation is not clear? If, due to this lack of clarity, one only has an opinion as to the obligatory nature of an action, the necessary connection to punishment is broken. An opinion of a ruling (*al-ẓann bil-ḥukm*) which knows itself to be less than certain cannot, by necessary entailment, lead to punishment for non-compliance. Necessary entailment between obligation and punishment requires certainty as to the ruling, not mere opinion. Subḥānī goes further than this. There is no relationship of necessary entailment between an opinion of a ruling (*al-ẓann bil-ḥukm*) and an opinion that an individual deserves punishment for noncompliance (*al-ẓann bil-ʿuqūba*). Just because there is *ẓann* about a rule does not mean there is also *ẓann* about the punishment for that rule for noncompliance. The lack of certainty as the rule means punishment for noncompliance not only cannot follow, but also cannot be thought to be entailed. If a *mujtahid* considers the evidence, and though it is not decisive, still forms the opinion that an action is obligatory, he is aware that his conclusion is not certain but his own opinion. Once he is aware of this, he cannot then have the opinion that a legal subject will be punished for not following his (uncertain) conclusions. To do so would be to claim a level of certainty for his ruling which he has already ruled out. For Subḥānī, if there is no necessary connection between transgression and punishment (as in the case of *ẓann bil-ḥukm* and *ẓann bil-ʿūqūba*), then there is no inherent probative force for *ẓann*. If an opinion of a ruling cannot establish an opinion as to the punishment for transgressing that ruling, then in what sense can we say that the opinion of the ruling establishes anything at all? Therefore, with regard to establishing rulings and thereby establishing divine punishment as a justified outcome, *ẓann* has no probative force.

Those who hold that the *mujtahid*'s opinion has unconditional probative force argue that ignoring his opinion leads to harm. Subḥānī has established that it cannot be a harm in the next world (i.e. a divine punishment in heaven or hell), but could it be harm in this world? Because God's rulings create benefits or prevent evil, ignoring a *mujtahid*'s opinion (i.e. not treating his *ẓann* as unconditionally probative) leads to a benefit being prevented or an evil being created. Subḥānī entertains various arguments against this position, none of which he appears to find fully convincing. The most convincing, or at least the argument to which he does not provide counter arguments, is cited as "another response of al-Shaykh Anṣārī". The argument is that the harm resulting from not following the opinion of the *mujtahid* (i.e. from not treating his opinion as unconditionally probative) is not, itself, a harm based on certainty. Instead it is a harm which is assumed or presumed – or simply uncertain, itself based on an opinion (*al-ḍarar al-maẓnūn*). The Lawgiver has made a rule – which is known with certain, or is itself opinion-based – that in cases of *ẓann* one should resort to the "procedural principles" (such as the assumption of there being no legislative requirement or the presumption of continuity; *al-barāʾa wal-istiṣḥāb*). So if there really was suspected to be an uncertain, opinion-based harm resulting from ignoring the *ẓann* of the *mujtahid*, then in these cases, the procedural principles should be followed. These indicate (in particular the assumption of there being no legal requirement – *al-barāʾa*) that one should not be troubled by the suspected, opinion-based harm. Instead, these procedural principles establish that this suspected harm should be tolerated and allowed to exist as an acceptable risk, overridden by the more widely established principle of following *barāʾa* in cases of *ẓann*.

From this argumentation, it becomes clear that the authoritativeness of *ẓann* was not a dispute which was seen as solved and settled, notwithstanding the dominance of the position that *ẓann*, in and of itself, has no probative force. For the majority of scholars, Subḥānī included, *ẓann* has no probative force; certain procedures which give rise to *ẓann* were permitted to be used providing they were supported by clear indicators from indubitable sources (namely, scripture and reason). For the opponents, the situation was reversed. A position usually associated with Mīrzā Qummī holds that *ẓann* has probative force unless there is a clear indication that this *ẓann*-producing procedure is prohibited. This is what has happened with the debated procedure labelled *qiyās* (though the definition of this term is hardly consistent across the Shīʿī *uṣūlīs*). This, if you like, is the starting point for much more involved and controversial debates around how the individual legal subject knows he or she has fulfilled the law. If *ẓann* has absolute probative force, then following the *mujtahid* appears straightforward; if it is does not, then the legal subject has to be sure that the *mujtahid* is qualified to utilize those hermeneutic mechanisms which produce *ẓann* at the appropriate points and in the appropriate manner. This, to an extent, lies at the heart of the debate explored in the chapters of this volume. Both the scriptural texts and rational processes have failed to provide a certainty of the actual rulings of the Sharīʿa. Whilst accepting this uncertainty, discovering how to remain compliant with the demands of the Divine Law has proved particularly challenging – both intellectually and practically.

•••

Translation of Jaʿfar Subḥānī's Discussion of the Absolute Probative Force of *Ẓann*

[1. Title] On the absolute probative force of *ẓann*

[2. The Proofs of those who argue that *ẓann* has unconditional probative force]
There are four proofs that *ẓann* has probative force in an absolute fashion, the fourth of which is the [argument from the] closing of the door of knowledge. You should study the other three reasons, the first [one mentioned here] having priority over all the others.

[2.1 The First Proof]
The first is that an opinion as to the ruling is an opinion that harm [may come about]. (*al-ẓann bil-ḥukm ẓann bil-ḍarar*)

[2.1.1 The Syllogism]
That is, if one opposes a qualified jurist (*mujtahid*), when he forms an opinion of a ruling on the obligation or prohibition [of performing an action], one is entering into the area of "uncertain" harm (*maẓannat al-ḍarar*). This is the minor premise [of the syllogism]. That it is necessary to avoid all uncertain harm is the major premise.

Concerning the minor premise, injury can result in either punishment in the next world, or harm in this world. It has been said that an opinion that a thing is permitted or prohibited logically entails the opinion that opposing it will lead to punishment [in the next world]; or alternatively, [it leads to an] opinion that there is a harm [from it] in this world, based on the doctrine that the rulings follow on from the good and evil [effects of the actions subject to the rulings in this world].

Concerning the major premise – that is, that avoiding an uncertain harm is necessary – that is an obvious conclusion given our commitment to the ability of reason to discover the morally good and bad qualities [of actions – *qulnā bil-taḥsīn wa'l-taqbīḥ*]. So, reason declares that it is morally wrong [or bad] to carry out an action which is possibly harmful.

Say we were not to hold the view that reason can independently determine the morally good and bad qualities of actions. Even then, reason would be able to discover, independently, that one should nevertheless avoid harm – whether it is likely or even just possible. This is the reasoning here.

[3. The Rebuttals of this Proof]

In terms of a riposte [to this line of reasoning], the early [Shīʿī scholars, *al-qudamā'*] have disputed the major premise, and the more recent scholars (*al-muta'akhkhirīn*) have disputed the minor premise.

[3.1 Rebuttals of the major premise]

The first group [that is, the early scholars] sometimes argue [i] that avoiding a suspected harm is merely a recommended precaution [and not, therefore, an obligatory action at all]. At other times they argue [ii] that the obligation to repel [a suspected injury] applies to matters of this world and not the next. At yet other times, [iii] they bring up counter examples – such as the prohibition on accepting a miscreant's report, or the acceptance of conclusions reached through analogous reasoning – and yet both of those furnish you with an opinion that there might be harm.

[3.2 Rebuttals of the minor premise]

You will see that all these three ripostes are weak, and for that reason the more recent scholars have shifted from invalidating the major premise to invalidating the minor premise. [They say] an opinion that something is obligatory or forbidden does not necessarily lead to an opinion that there will be harm – whether one understands that [harm] to be a punishment in the next world, or a harm in this. Here is, for you, a clarification of the response:

[3.2.1 "Harm" meaning punishment in the next world]

If we say that the meaning of "harm" is [only] punishment in the next world, then there are two principles in operation here:

> First: there is the principle that it is morally repugnant to punish someone without an explanation [of the legal requirement – *qubḥ al-ʿiqāb bilā bayān*]
>
> Second: there is a principle that one must repel a possible harm – [the possible harm being] the otherworldly punishment.

[So they conclude that] if we accept these formulations of the two principles, then the minor premise will clearly be invalidated.

[3.2.2 Subḥānī's reasoning]
We say:

> Concerning the first [i.e. the principle that "it is morally repugnant to punish someone without an explanation"] – it is an intuitively persuasive supposition. That is, it concerns things for which no explanation (*bayān*) has actually come. Therefore, there is no necessary relationship between the opinion that the ruling [is such and such] and the opinion that [disobeying it results in] punishment. This is because reason can independently recognize that it would be morally repugnant to punish someone without a clarification (*bayān*) of [the rule] having arrived. There is only a necessary connection between a ruling which has been communicated to the legal subject (*mukallaf*) and punishment. And "communicated" here means that it is known for certain, or [that it is supported by a] definitive legal proof [for the legal subject]. The whole point [of the argument here] is that there is no [knowledge or definitive legal proof] because one doesn't know if mere opinion has probative force.

All of this involves the first principle [namely "it is morally repugnant to punish someone without an explanation"]. Regarding the second – that is, one must avoid a suspected harm (in this case, punishment [in the next world]) – this specifically applies to punishments established through a legal proof. The "possibility" of punishment, like the "opinion" that there might be a punishment, is realized here.

"Opinion" is, for example, when one knows that one of two cups contains wine. If you drink from either of them, an opinion that punishment will follow is formed.

"Possibility" though is when there is a wider range of possibilities, without them being unlimited. For example, wine is to be found in one of 10 cups.

In both instances one is obligated to avoid [drinking from any cup], since the proof in both cases is complete.

What is clear from what we have said is that an opinion about a ruling does not logically entail an opinion about punishment [for disobeying that opinion-based ruling]. This is because the probative force of *ẓann* in and of itself is not proven, and that is the underlying assumption of the argument. It is only logically entailed when the clarification has actually been communicated [to the legal subject].

[3.2.3 "Harm" being in this world]

All of the above applies to those occasions when, by "harm", one means punishment in the next world. If one means by it "punishment in this world", then two great scholars – al-Anṣārī and al-Khurasānī – have provided two counter arguments [against the argument that not following the *ẓann* of the *mujtahid* leads to a harm, and therefore *ẓann* must have probative force]:

1. Even if rulings do follow on from the good and evil [effects] found in the thing to which [the ruling] is attached, they follow from them in a generic rather than specific way. That is, it is not the case that every generic evil will bring about a specific harm; performing the [action in question] may even bring about a specific benefit, as in the prohibition on interest. Not every generic benefit has a specific benefit – in fact, there might be a specific harm in it – as in general expenditure.
2. They [the rulings] are based on the notion that rulings follow on from good and evil elements of the thing being assessed; but [this need not be the case], perhaps they follow on from good or evil elements in the rulings themselves.

With regard to the first answer here, one can say that the distinction between a generic and specific harm is unsound; and the opinion that one can find a specific benefit in a generic harm (like *ribā*) is a short-term conclusion; in truth, though, [the harm] will apply to him in a long-term way. God says, "Spend in the way of God so you do not fall, by your own hands, into perdition; and do good, for God loves those who do good." (2.195) – since after his statement here, comes the statement "so you do not fall …". This shows that if you forbid spending completely, then those who are wealthy and blessed, will face annihilation because the have-nots will rise up against the haves in a violent revolution, thereby threatening the life of those who have.[2]

2 [From this Subḥānī concludes that the distinction between a generic and specific benefit, which was the basis of the argument, is unsound, and therefore not an appropriate point from which to initiative an argument against the view that rulings follow on from the evil or good consequences of actions.]

With regard to the second answer – that is that the rulings follow the good and evil in the rulings themselves – this is also unsound. If it were [to be sound] then following them [i.e. the rulings] would not necessarily bring about achieving the basis of the matter itself. It is agreed that the view that there is an underlying foundational issue in the rulings themselves is sound in orders which act as a test, but not for real rulings.[3]

[3.2.4 Subḥānī's reasoning]

It is preferred to respond that this-worldly harms are in two categories:

1. Ones that might have a low possibility (or there is some doubt about them), but the result is serious – as in [the following example]: since there is a one in 100 chance that smoking near petrol will result in the supply catching light and exploding, reason dictates when an unlikely outcome is extremely serious, one should avoid doing this, even though the likelihood is low.
2. The second is when the likelihood is high, but the result is not serious. This is the case when drinking fizzy drinks – one forms an opinion that this may give one stomach ache; but one ignores the possibility and drinks it.

In accordance with this, one has to examine the this-worldly benefit which comes from the opinion about the rulings, and make a distinction between these two types.[4]

---

3 [Subḥānī's point here is that if God issues rulings not because they bring about good results, but because of something inherently good in the rulings themselves, then following the ruling would not necessarily bring about a good result. Rather it would simply bring about the following of the ruling, and this simple act of obedience cannot be a good in and of itself. The one exception to this, for Subḥānī, is though rulings which are issued as tests. If a legal subject obeys these rulings, then the whole point of the rulings is achieved – namely to test whether the legal subject is obedient or not. Hence, the argument that rulings might not be issued for the good they produce but for some inherent good within them is, for Subḥānī, unsound.]

4 [The implicit argument here is that if the *mujtahid*'s *ẓann* was to have no probative force in and of itself, then disobeying it represents a risk of this world-harm. In some things this would be a "low probability, serious outcome" risk; and in others it would be a "high probability, insignificant outcome" risk. In the former one takes notice of the *mujtahid*'s *ẓann*, and in the latter one does not. The result is, though, that one cannot treat the *ẓann* as being equally and unconditionally probative in all cases. This appears to be Subḥānī's own argument against the "harm" argument for the unconditional probative force of *ẓann*. If the probative force is dependent on the harm caused by not following the *mutjahid's ẓann*, then it there will be some harms which are worth the risk, and others which are not. In either case, there can be no unconditional probative force of the *ẓann*.]

[3.2.5 al-Shaykh al-Anṣārī's additional argument]
There is another reply of al-Shaykh al-Ansārī; that is: if the harm is [not certain but based] on opinion, then the ruling of the Lawgiver, be it known with certainty or even just on the basis of opinion, is that one should resort, incases of doubt, to the assumption of there being no legal assessment, or on the continuation of the ruling (*al-barāʾa wal-istiṣḥāb*). [The Lawgiver's] permission to abandon following the opinion necessarily brings about certainty, or an [alternative] opinion that this harm, which is based on opinion, can continue [without there being any infringement of rationality].[5]

[4. The Irrelevance of the Other Three Arguments for *ẓann*'s unconditional probative force]
Furthermore, those who argue for the unconditional probative force of opinion base their opinion on 4 arguments, the first of which has just been mentioned. The second and the third are not independent proofs, but rather are dependent on the fourth argument – which is the argument from the closing [of door of knowledge]. Since contemporary scholars have invalidated the argument from the closing [of the gate of knowledge], it can be disregarded; and it is necessary to spend our time on more important matters …

5 [Murtaḍā al-Anṣārī, *Farāʾid al-uṣūl*, (Qum: Majmaʿ al-Fikr al-Islāmī, 1991), 1:376 – and if this were not the case, then the permission to act on the basis of the *aṣl* in opposition to a *ẓann* will bring about a *mafsada* – and that cannot be right.…]

APPENDIX

al-Sayyid ʿAlī al-Ḥusaynī al-Sīstānī on *Uṣūl al-fiqh* in Twelver Shīʿī Thought: Its Importance and Historical Phases

Ali-Reza Bhojani

What follows is a translation of the first, and part of the second, introductory discussions in the transcribed notes of al-Sayyid ʿAlī al-Ḥusaynī al-Sīstānī's (b. 1930) advanced lectures on *uṣūl al-fiqh* published as *al-Rāfid fī ʿilm al-uṣūl*. al-Sīstānī is one of the most authoritative and influential Twelver Shīʿī jurists of the day. Although born and raised in Iran, he currently resides in Najaf, Iraq holding a seat of supreme religious authority with a global following.

The first section discusses the importance of *uṣūl al-fiqh* (referred to throughout as *ʿilm al-uṣūl*) in the Twelver Imāmī Shīʿī school by responding to an internal Imāmī critique that claimed the discipline of *uṣūl al-fiqh* is little more than a needless concoction of issues brought together as a result of Sunnī influence on Shīʿī scholars. al-Sīstānī's unequivocal rejection of this position aims to set out the independence of *uṣūl al-fiqh*, its originality, early development and importance within Shīʿī thought. The second section classifies the history of *uṣūl al-fiqh* in Imāmī thought into three phases. Each phase is characterized by distinct intellectual struggles impacting the progression of ideas within the discipline. For al-Sīstānī, the first phase was shaped by intra-Muslim debates whilst the second was shaped by intra-Shīʿī ones. The third phase, mentioned only briefly here, is the current period in which we now live. According to al-Sīstānī, the mark of this contemporary phase in Shīʿī jurisprudential thought is the need for it to develop, engage and respond to the broader economic, political and cultural challenges of the contemporary era.

The footnotes to the translation are limited to those found in the published Arabic version of the text, although they have been modified in form to fit the style of this publication and enable independent access to the sources mentioned. Dates of death for scholars have again only been included where they are present in the published Arabic text, although I have added the common era dates alongside the original Hijri ones.

© KONINKLIJKE BRILL NV, LEIDEN, 2020 | DOI:10.1163/9789004413948_011

ʿAlī al-Ḥusaynī al-Sīstānī, *al-Rāfid fī ʿilm al-uṣūl*, Transcribed by Munīr Qaṭīfī (Qum: Maktabat Āyatullāh Sīstānī, 1993), 12–18

The Discipline of Legal Theory in the Imāmī School

The two schools from among the Imāmī scholars – the traditionists (*muḥaddithīn*) and the legal theorists (*uṣūlīyīn*) – have differed with regard to the value of the discipline of legal theory, as well as to the extent of their emphasis upon it during the history of juristic (*fiqhī*) thought. We do not wish to delve too comprehensively into this discussion here, due to its irrelevance to our aim – which is to put forth our general thesis regarding the discipline of legal theory. However, as a prelude to entering into these core jurisprudential discussions, we will present some of the beneficial aspects in demonstrating the lofty status of the discipline of legal theory as well as its historical and current importance for the jurist (*faqīh*).

We begin by citing some words from al-Karakī's book, *Hidāyat al-abrār*, as transmitted by al-Qaṭīfī (one of the teachers of the author of *al-Wasāʾil*). He said,

> Know that the discipline of legal theory has been concocted from various sciences and diverse issues, some of which are true and some of which are false. The Sunnī's produced it due to the paucity of prophetic reports (*sunan*) in their possession that indicate to [Sharīʿa] precepts (*aḥkām*).[1]

He also stated;

> The Shīʿa had no authored works in legal theory for they had no need for it, due to the availability of all that they required of it being within the necessarily accepted axioms of religion (*al-ḍarūriyyāt al-dīn*) and its theories being in the principles relayed from the Imams of guidance. This was until Ibn Junayd came and examined the legal theory of the [Sunnī] Muslims, and took from them, composing books in accordance with that model – to the extent that he even acted upon analogical reasoning (*qiyās*).[2]

This statement can be broken down into three claims;

1. A denial of the independence of the discipline of legal theory, which in his view, is a concoction of diverse issues.
2. That the original composers of the discipline of legal theory were the Sunnī Muslims, and that the first Shīʿī author in the discipline was Ibn Junayd – who even acted upon analogical reasoning.

---

1 Ḥusayn ibn Shihāb al-Dīn al-Karakī, *Hidāyat al-abrār ilā ṭarīq al-ʿaimmat al-ʿaṭhār* (Baghdad: Muʾassasat Iḥyāʾ al-iḥyāʾ, 1977), 233–234.

2 Ibid.

3. That there is no need for the discipline of legal theory due to the presence of necessarily accepted axioms of religion and the theories of the discipline of legal theory being present in the relayed principles within the traditions of the Imams – upon them be peace.

The First Claim and Its Refutation

It is clear that there are many issues outlined in the discipline of legal theory that are not relevant to any other discipline, for example:

- The discussion on the conflicts between legislated evidence and the means of their reconciliation,
- The discussions pertaining to the authority of means and substantiated evidence; like the isolated hadith report, popular juristic opinion or consensus, and the discussion regarding conjecture when all forms of certain knowledge are deemed inaccessible (*ẓann al-insidādī*),
- The instances of applying linguistic principles such as in conflicts between the general and the specific, the unqualified and the qualified, and the abrogating and the abrogated.

All these discussions bear no relation to the discipline of linguistics, nor to juristic inference (*fiqh*), nor the biographical sciences (*rijāl*) nor any other subject, for they are all related to 'the authoritativeness of juristic evidence' (*ḥujjiyyat al-dalīl al-fiqhi*) which is the very criteria for a jurisprudential (*uṣūlī*) discussion, accordingly the appropriate [discipline] for them is the discipline of legal theory. The mere occurrence of some linguistic issues; such as postulation, usage, the real and the metaphorical – which are mentioned as preludes to certain jurisprudential discussions, and the mere occurrence of some theological and philosophical issues; such as the conformity between what is sought [by God] and [His] intention, and the discussion on the mental consideration of quiddity in unqualified and qualified notions – which are again mentioned as preludes or links to some jurisprudential issues, does nothing to remove the aforementioned issues from being jurisprudential, nor prevent the discipline in which they are found to be deemed an independent discipline in its own right – so long as the criterion for a jurisprudential issue is present therein, as will be demonstrated in what follows.

The Second Claim and Its Refutation

Here we mention two issues:

1. The earliest work in the discipline of legal theory of the Sunnī's is the *Risāla* of al-Shāfiʿī. In the same time period, the Shīʿa also wrote various treatises in the discipline of legal theory. Ibn Abī ʿUmayr (d. 216/831) and Yūnus ibn ʿAbd al-Raḥmān (d. 208/823) wrote on the reconciliation of conflicting traditions. They also both wrote on the topics of the general and the specific, as well as the abrogating and the abrogated, as can be seen by referring to their biographies

in the books of *rijāl*. al-Shāfiʿī was not from an earlier time than them, he was born in 150 AH, after the death of al-Ṣādiq (peace be upon him), whilst Yūnus ibn ʿAbd al-Raḥmān met al-Sādiq (peace be upon him). Shāfiʿī died in 205 AH close to the time of death of Yūnus ibn ʿAbd al-Raḥmān. Accordingly, it cannot be established that the original composers of the discipline of legal theory were the Sunnī school, rather it shows that the Shīʿa wrote on the discipline of legal theory in the very same period of its emergence amongst the Sunnīs. Subsequently came Abū Sahl al-Nawbakhtī who wrote two treatises; one of which was regarding the invalidity of analogical reasoning and the isolated hadith report, and the other a refutation of al-Shāfiʿī's *Risāla*. Thereafter, the scope of the discipline of legal theory was broadened by Ibn Junayd, al-Mufīd, al-Murtaḍā in *al-Dharīʿa* and al-Ṭūsī in *al-ʿUdda*. Accordingly, it also becomes clear to us that Ibn Junayd was not the first Shīʿī author in the discipline of legal theory.

2. Ibn Junayd is mentioned as having acted upon analogical reasoning (*qiyās*) in a number of books, however we hold the possibility that this attribution is out of place due to developments we have traced regarding the usage of the word *qiyās*. It is possible that what was intended by this word is what we now term 'consistency in spirit' (*al-muwāfaqa al-rūḥiyya*) with the Book and Sunna.

An explanation of this: The majority of the later legal theorists interpret traditions that command the checking of reports against the Book and the Sunna, such as "accept that which is consistent with the Book of Allah, and reject that which is inconsistent",[3] as an explicit consistency and inconsistency (*al-muwāfaqa wal-mukhālafa al-naṣṣiyya*). This means that the report is compared with a specific Quranic verse and if the relationship between the two is incongruous (*tabāyun*) or even only partially overlapping (*ʿumūm min wajh*), then the report is discarded. If the relationship is congruent (*tasāwī*) or of absolute generality (*ʿumūm muṭlaq*), it is accepted. However, we understand that what is intended by consistency is a consistency of spirit, i.e. that the content of the hadith is consistent with the general principles of Islam (*al-uṣūl al-Islāmiyya*), understood from the Book and the Sunna. Therefore, if the apparent meaning of a report suggests determinism, for example, then it is rejected due to the inconsistency with the belief in 'the middle stance between pre-determinism and absolute free will' as understood from the Book and the Sunna – without comparing the hadith to any specific verse per se. This notion that we have presented is what the later scholars of hadith termed 'holistic criticism' of a report (*al-naqd al-dākhilī*), i.e. comparing its content with the general principles and aims of

3 Muḥammad Bāqir al-Majlisī, *Biḥār al-anwār al-jāmiʿa li durar akhbār al-aʾimma al-aṭhār* (Beirut: Muʾassasat al-Wafāʾ, 1983), 2:235; al-Ḥurr al-ʿĀmilī, *Wasāʾil al-shīʿa ilā taḥṣīl masāʾil al-sharīʿa* (Qum: Muʾassasat Āl al-Bayt, 1992), 27:118.

Islam. In source texts this is referred to as *qiyās*, for example, "compare it (*fa qiṣ-hu*) with the Book of God".[4] Accordingly, it is possible that what was intended by Ibn Junayds's acting upon *qiyās*, was that he was from the school that was strict in its acceptance of traditions – that is those who required application of the theory of 'holistic criticism' to traditions and that there be 'consistency in spirit' with the Book and the Sunna – in contrast with the school of traditionists who believed in the certain issuance of the majority of traditions, irrespective of any consideration of them alongside the general principles of Islam. In support of what we have mentioned is that acting upon *qiyās* has been attributed to some of the greatest Imāmī scholars. For example, in the biographical work of Sayyid Baḥr al-ʿUlūm, he said, "Sayyid al-Murtaḍā has mentioned in his treatise on the isolated report that there are, amongst our reporters and transmitters of traditions, those who advocated *qiyās*, such as al-Faḍl bin Shādhān, Yūnus bin 'Abd al-Raḥmān and a group of well-known scholars".[5] In *Kashf al-qinā'*, the author states, "Ṣadūq relates, in various places, that a group of their foremost scholars employed *qiyās*, and amongst these were some of the very first rank, such as Zurāra ibn Aʿyan, Jamīl ibn Darrāj and 'Abd Allāh ibn Bukayr".[6] It cannot even be entertained that these giants would have employed juristic *qiyās* (analogical reasoning) after pointing out that what was meant by *qiyās* at the time was a strictness in accepting hadith by employing the theory of holistic criticism. This is further supported by that which al-Muḥaqqiq states in *al-Maʿārij*: "The sixth issue: Our teacher al-Mufīd said, 'The isolated report which is definitive in providing an excuse [before God] is the one associated with evidence, consideration of which leads to knowledge; sometimes this [evidence] may be juristic consensus (*ijmā'*), a testament from rationality or a judgment from *qiyās*".[7]

The Third Claim and Its Refutation

Here we present two points of consideration:

1. The presence of *Sharīʿa* principles in the traditions of the impeccable household (peace be upon them) does not render the discipline of legal theory futile

4 'Āmilī, *Wasā'il*, 27:123; Majlisī, *Biḥār*, 2:244. [Translators note: The citations of the hadith are either from variant editions or not exact quotations. The relevant part of the cited hadith in the editions consulted reads; "If two conflicting traditions come to you, then compare them (*fa qiṣhumā*) to the Book of God and to our traditions ..." See 'Āmilī, *Wasā'il*, 27:125–6 and Majlisī, *Biḥār*, 2:244–5.

5 al-Sayyid Mahdī Baḥr al-ʿUlūm, *Rijāl al-Sayyid Baḥr al-ʿUlūm* (Tehran: Maktabat al-Ṣādiq, 1984), 3:215.

6 Asad Allāh bin Ismāʿīl al-Kāẓimī, *Kashf al-qināʿ ʿan wujūh ḥujjiyyat al-ijmāʿ* (N.p.: N.p., n.d.), 83.

7 al-Muḥaqqiq al-Ḥillī, *Maʿārij al-uṣūl* (Qum: Mu'assasat Āl al-Bayt, 1982), 187.

because the understanding of principles and rulings from the hadith relies upon several jurisprudential elements. These include;

- Verification of the apparent meaning in accordance with the linguistic discussions set out in the discipline of legal theory such as the discussions regarding the imperative and the negative imperative, implications, the general and the specific, the unqualified and the qualified,
- An understanding of the major premise regarding the authoritativeness of the apparent meaning [of linguistic evidence],
- An understanding of the authoritativeness of the isolated report,
- Application of the principles of conflicting evidence, should there be a conflict with the text.

These elements are all compiled within a single discipline: the discipline of legal theory. Accordingly, the mere presence of principles and rulings in the texts attributed to the impeccable ones does not nullify need for the discipline of legal theory.

2. The presence of jurisprudential principles themselves within the texts and the reports – such as reports indicating the authoritativeness of the isolated report, the non-authoritativeness of *qiyās*, the authoritativeness of the principles of exemption (*al-barā'a*) and presumed continuity (*al-istiṣḥāb*), and the principles of conflicting evidence – do not nullify the value of the discipline of legal theory. Rather it emphasizes to us that this discipline has emerged from a pure source: the *Ahl al-Bayt* (peace be upon them), rather than it having come from any other school as some of the traditionists have claimed. The presence of jurisprudential issues in the texts, is like the presence of jurisprudential discussions within juristic discussions. An example of this is what al-Kulaynī mentioned from Faḍl bin Shādhān in *al-Kāfī* in the chapter of divorce, where he justified the invalidity of some forms of divorce due to 'prohibition necessitating corruption' (*al-nahy yaqtaḍī al-fasād*)[8] which is a jurisprudential principle. Similar is that which we see in the work of the author of *al-Hadā'iq* when he discusses the authoritativeness of *ijmā'* within his discussion of the Friday prayer.[9] All of this does nothing to undermine the importance and independence of the discipline of legal theory versus other disciplines. The criterion for considering an issue to be of legal theory is that it discusses the authoritativeness of juristic evidence, whether this be mentioned in an independent form or within the context of a book of hadith, or within the context of a book of juristic inference. By nature, every discipline

---

8 Muḥammad ibn Ya'qūb al-Kulaynī, *al-Furū' min al-Kāfī* (Tehran: Dār al-Kutub al-Islāmīyya, 1988) 6:93.

9 Yūsuf al-Baḥrānī, *al-Ḥadā'iq al-nāḍira fī aḥkām al-'itrat al-ṭāhira* (Qum: Mu'assasat al-Nashr, 1984) 9:361–2.

develops towards completion in a gradual manner rather than instantaneously, as demonstrated in the case of the discipline of logic. Shaykh al-Raʾīs [Ibn Sīnā] mentions in *al-Shifā* that Aristotle did not compose the discipline of logic, he only perfected that which had reached him of the discipline.[10] That some of the issues of the discipline of legal theory have been treated within various other disciplines, and were then brought together in a gradual manner into a single discipline referred to as the discipline of legal theory, due to them sharing a single common goal, does nothing to undermine the importance of the discipline and its independence.

The Phases of Jurisprudential (**uṣūlī**) *Thought*

The criterion for a phase, according to our conception of it, is not related to the time span of the discipline, as sometimes a period of time may pass without the attainment of any progress and renewal in the journey and development of that discipline. The only criterion for distinguishing one phase from another is the emergence of progressive theories that serve to propel the development of the journey of those ideas, and this usually only occurs as a result of intellectual competition and cultural development. Just as societies develop within the preserve of civilization, through economic and cultural competition amongst and between those societies, the development of any ideas requires a form of deep struggle between the founders of those ideas, that they may benefit from such struggle in the process of crystalising their theories and renewing their ideas. Accordingly it is upon this basis – that is the basis of intellectual struggles (*al-ṣirāʿ al-fikrī*) – that we shall delimit the phases of jurisprudential thought amongst the Imāmī Shīʿa.

The First Phase, Which Reflects the Stance of the Shīʿī Scholars in Contrast with Other Theoretical Schools as Well as Those Shīʿī Scholars Influenced by These Schools

Within the context of identifying *Sharīʿa* precepts, there were two mutually competing schools, the school of opinion (*madrasat al-raʾī*) and the school of hadith (*madrasat al-ḥadith*). As for the school of opinion, its mischief originated from some of the companions and caliphs who prevented the recording of the Sunna for specific political goals, whilst relying on their own personal opinions and ideas when it came to things related to public interest. This school continued into the second century whereby it became the general inclination of the Iraqis' following Abū Ḥanīfa who upheld the authoritativeness of analogical reasoning (*qiyās*) and juristic preference (*istiḥsān*), as well as requiring 'holistic criticism' (*naqd dākhilī*) of hadith by comparing them against

10 Shaykh al-Raʾīs Ibn Sīnā, *al-Shifā: al-Manṭiq* (Qum: Maktabat Āyatullāh Marʿashī Najafī, 2012) 2:356.

the general principles of Islam. As for the school of hadith, which emerged as a response to the continuity of the school of opinion and took form in the Hanbali and Maliki doctrinal schools (*madhāhib*) more so than any other, it was extreme in its reliance upon hadith simply as instances of a trustworthy report (*khabar thiqa*) without consideration of general principles.

Each one of these two schools influenced some Shīʿī scholars, as is attributed to Ibn Junayd with regard to his views on employing *qiyās* – if the attribution is correct – whilst that which resembles the opinions of the *Ḥashawiyya*[11] are attributed to some others. Accordingly, and from this starting point, Shīʿī scholars embarked upon a serious engagement into jurisprudential thought, with the first phase of the journey opposing the school of opinion, the school of hadith, and whoever from amongst the Imāmī scholars had been influenced by either of them. The biographical dictionaries record that some of the Banū Nawbakht, and others, wrote treatises on the in-authoritativeness of analogical reasoning and on [the issue of] conflicting hadith. al-Shaykh al-Ṭūsī in *al-Fihrist* and al-Sayyid al-Murtaḍā in *al-Intisār* mentioned the intense opposition to the method of Ibn Junayd,[12] whilst al-Shaykh al-Mufīd wrote a treatise on the invalidity of analogical reasoning, as well as a book titled 'The Knowledge Trove of Light for Refuting the Traditionists (*Maqābis al-anwār fī al-radd ʿalā ahl al-akhbār*)'.[13] Such treatises gave jurisprudential thought a breakthrough and perceivable progress, as can be seen in the *ʿUdda* of al-Shaykh al-Ṭūsī. After the passing of al-Ṭūsī, jurisprudential thought fluctuated between progress and stagnation. During the time of the Daylamites, further progress was made due to the presence of intellectual competition, however this progress stopped by the time of the Seljuks due to the existence of pressure and restrictions.

It [jurisprudential thought] was revived again after the battle of *al-Tutār* due to the greater scope for intellectual freedom. al-Muḥaqqiq, in *al-Tadhkira* and al-ʿAllāma, in *al-Muʿtabar*, displayed the extent of the depth of jurisprudential thought in comparative juristic inference (*al-fiqh al-muqāran*). This period, although short, left its mark even upon the thought of scholars of other doctrinal schools. Abu Zahra, in his book *Ibn Taymiyya*, mentions that Ibn Taymiyya was influenced by the juristic thought of the Shīʿa contemporary to him, as demonstrated in his juristic inference on some of the issues relating to divorce. After this period, jurisprudential and intra-school juristic thought returned to stagnation, and no sign of comparative juristic thought, nor points of Imāmi innovation in jurisprudential thought can be seen in the works of al-Shahīd

---

11 [Translators note: *Ḥashawiyya* is a pejorative term used here to refer to extreme traditionists]

12 Abū Jaʿfar Muḥammad ibn al-Ḥasan al-Ṭūsī, *al-Fihrist* (Qum: Mu'assasat al-Nashr, 1996), 209.

13 Ibid., 338–339; Aḥmad ibn ʿAlī al-Najāshī, *Rijāl al-Najāshī* (Qum: Mu'assasat al-Nashr, 1995), 399–402.

al-Awwal. In fact, al-Shahīd al-Thānī stated in his *Kitāb al-Qaḍā'* that it would suffice a student in logic and legal theory to study the *Mukhtasar* of Ibn Ḥājib[14] – even though this book demonstrates no Imāmī creativity.

The Second Phase, Which Marks the Intellectual Struggle between the Uṣūlī and Akhbārī Schools

After the Shīʿa became politically established in the Safawid era at the beginning of the 10th century, there emerged from within them the Akhbārī school, epitomized by Mulla Aḥmad Amīn al-Astarabādī and those influenced by him; such as the two Majlisī's, Fayḍ al-Kāshānī, Ḥurr al-ʿAmilī and Shaykh Yūsuf al-Baḥrānī. Among the factors that gave rise to the emergence of this school, per some Shīʿī scholars, was that the jurisprudential principles employed in inferring *Sharīʿa* precepts relied upon theological and philosophical ideas, which resulted in distancing the *Sharīʿa* precepts from their pure sources – the traditions of the *Ahl al-Bayt* (peace be upon them). From here began a deep intellectual struggle between the two schools, and jurisprudential thought made great progress through this struggle, taking remarkable steps forward at the hands of al-Wahīd al-Biḥbaḥānī, al-Muḥaqqiq al-Qummī, Ṣāḥib *al-Fuṣūl* and al-ʿAllāma al-Anṣārī.

The Third Phase, Which Marks the Contemporary Era

The period in which we currently live, due to economic and political factors, has led to a deep struggle between Islamic culture and other cultures at various levels. Accordingly, it is necessary for the discipline of legal theory and its form to progress to a level appropriate to the conditions of contemporary life.

---

14 Zayn al-Dīn al-ʿAmilī, *al-Rawḍat al-bahiyya fī sharḥ al-lumʿa al-Dimashqiyya* (Beirut: Dār al-ʿĀlam al-Islāmī, N.D.) 3:65.

Index